NUWAVE AIR FRYER COOKBOOK

480 AFFORDABLE, QUICK & EASY AIR FRYER RECIPES. | FRY, BAKE, GRILL & ROAST MOST WANTED FAMILY MEALS.

PAMELA KENDRICK

CONTENTS

Disclaimer Notice   xix
Introduction   xxi

SAUCES, DIPS AND DRESSINGS

1. Lemony Avocado Dressing	3
2. Creamy Cashew Mayo	4
3. Garlicky Cauliflower Alfredo Sauce	5
4. Southern Chimichurri	7
5. Lemony Coconut Yogurt Dressing	8
6. Homemade Ranch Dressing	9
7. Balsamic-Dijon Vinaigrette	10
8. Honey Mixed Berry Vinaigrette	11
9. Honey Lime Tahini Dressing	12
10. Creamy Hemp Dressing	13
11. Lemony Kale and Almond Pesto	14
12. Lemon-Dijon Vinaigrette	15
13. Lemony Tahini Sauce	16
14. Apple-Mushroom Gravy	17
15. Buffalo Sauce	18

WRAPS AND SANDWICHES

16. Creamy-Cheesy Wontons	21
17. Bulgogi Burgers with Korean Mayo	22
18. Golden Cabbage and Pork Gyoza	24
19. Fast Cheesy Chicken Sandwich	26
20. Golden Cheesy Potato Taquitos	28
21. Cheesy Chicken and Yogurt Taquitos	29
22. Tangy Chicken-Lettuce Wraps	30

23. Crispy Crabmeat Wontons	32
24. Cheesy Eggplant Hoagies	34
25. Feta Lamb Hamburgers	35
26. Fajita Meatball Wraps	37
27. Mexican Paprika Chicken Burgers	39
28. Fast Montreal Steak and Seeds Burgers	41
29. Nugget and Vegetable Taco Wraps	43
30. Golden Pea and Potato Samosas	44
31. Asian Pork Momos	47
32. Crispy Chicken Empanadas	49
33. Golden Smoky Chicken Sandwich	51
34. Sweet Potato-Black Bean Burritos	53
35. Thai Curry Pork Sliders	55
36. Tuna Steak and Lettuce Wraps	57
37. Easy Turkey Sliders with Chive Mayo	58
38. Turkey and Veggies Hamburger	60
39. Cheesy Veggies Salsa Wraps	62

BREAKFAST

40. Air-Fried All-in-One Toast	65
41. Asparagus Spears and Cheese Strata	67
42. Simple Bacon and Egg Bread Cups	69
43. Easy Bacon Eggs on the Go	71
44. Herbed Bacon Hot Dogs	72
45. Sweet Banana and Oat Bread Pudding	73
46. Maple Blueberry Cobbler	75
47. Sausage and Cauliflower Casserole	77
48. Sausage and Tater Tot Casserole	78
49. Cheesy Bacon Casserole	80
50. Cheesy Hash Brown Casserole	82
51. Apple-Chicken Patties	83
52. Chocolate, Banana, and Walnut Bread	85
53. Full Breakfast	87
54. Creamy Coconut Brown Rice Porridge	89
55. Golden Crustless Broccoli Quiche	90
56. Fast Sausage Pizza	92
57. Crispy Egg and Avocado Burrito	93
58. Cheesy Egg and Bacon Muffins	95

59. Air-Fried Potatoes with Veggies	96
60. Golden Avocado	97
61. Crispy Avocado Tempura	98
62. Lush Cheddar Biscuits	99
63. Air-Fried Kale and Potato Nuggets	101
64. Sweet Walnut Pancake	102
65. Cheesy Tomato and Basil Bruschetta	104
66. Mixed-Berry Dutch Baby	105
67. Honey Oat and Chia Porridge	107
68. Olives, Kale, and Almond Baked Eggs	108
69. Cheesy Onion Omelet	110
70. Creamy Parmesan Ranch Risotto	111
71. Parmesan Sausage and Egg Muffins	112
72. Fast Pita and Pepperoni Pizza	113
73. Classic Potatoes Lyonnaise	114
74. Simple Blueberry Muffins	116
75. Golden Sausage and Cheese Quiche	118
76. Fast Cinnamon Toasts	119
77. Scotch Eggs	120
78. Mushroom, Spinach and Leek Frittata	121
79. Cheesy Bacon and Ham Cups	123
80. Cheesy Frittata with Avocado Dressing	124
81. Bell Pepper, Carrot, and Onion Frittata	126
82. Golden Western Omelet	128

VEGETABLES

83. Air-Fried Winter Vegetables	133
84. Asian Spicy Broccoli	134
85. Easy Balsamic Brussels Sprouts	135
86. Cheesy Basmati Risotto	136
87. Honey-Caramelized Eggplant with Yogurt	137
88. Crispy Cayenne Tahini Kale	138
89. Golden Asparagus and Potato Platter	140
90. Parmesan Cabbage Wedges	142
91. Ritzy Roasted Veggie Salad	143
92. Fast Honey-Glazed Baby Carrots	145
93. Honey-Glazed Roasted Vegetable	146
94. Hearty Summer Rolls	148

95. Lush Roasted Veggies	150
96. Fast Mushroom and Pepper Pizza Squares	151
97. Cheesy Zucchini Chips	152
98. Tofu Scramble with Veggies	153
99. Garlicky Ratatouille	154
100. Rice, Eggplant, Cucumber Bowl	156
101. Balsamic Glazed Rosemary Beets	158
102. Cheesy Rosemary Roasted Squash	160
103. Easy Sesame-Maitake Mushrooms	161
104. Cheesy Russet Potato Gratin	162
105. Herbed Ratatouille	163
106. Hearty Veggies Spring Rolls	164
107. Fast Vegetable Burger	165
108. Cajun Sweet Potatoes with Tofu	167
109. Air-Fried Sweet Potatoes with Zucchini	169
110. Thai Spicy Brussels Sprouts	171
111. Roasted Tofu, Carrot and Cauliflower Rice	172
112. Golden Vegetarian Meatballs	174

VEGETABLE SIDES

113. Caramelized Brussels Sprouts	179
114. Russet Potatoes with Yogurt and Chives	180
115. Fast Buttered Broccoli with Parmesan	181
116. Green Beans with Sesame Seeds	182
117. Golden Cheesy Broccoli Gratin	183
118. Spicy Fingerling Potatoes	185
119. Air-Fried Spiced Acorn Squash	186
120. Creamy-Cheesy Corn Casserole	187
121. Crispy Chili Jicama Fries	189
122. Breaded Brussels Sprouts with Sage	190
123. Fast Rosemary Green Beans	191
124. Crispy Asparagus	192
125. Air-Fried Herbed Radishes	193
126. Golden Parmesan Asparagus Fries	194
127. Potato with Sour Cream	196
128. Simple Roasted Eggplant Slices	197
129. Creamy Potatoes and Asparagus	198
130. Rosemary-Garlic Roasted Potatoes	199

131. Fast Saltine Wax Beans	200
132. Air-Fried Sesame Taj Tofu	201
133. Roasted Cauliflower with Buffalo Sauce	202
134. Easy Spicy Cabbage	203
135. Curry Sweet Potato Fries	204
136. Sesame Tofu Bites	205
137. Herbed Zucchini Balls	207

STUFFED VEGETABLES

138. Rice and Olives Stuffed Bell Peppers	211
139. Breaded Mushrooms	213
140. Mushrooms with Horseradish Mayo	214
141. Bacon-Wrapped Jalapeño Poppers	216
142. Cheesy Pepperoni and Mushroom Pizza	217
143. Ricotta-Stuffed Potatoes	218
144. Stuffed Squash with Tomato and Pepper	219
145. Caramelized Stuffed Tomatoes with Vegetable	221

FISH AND SEAFOOD

146. Air Fryer Fish Sticks	225
147. Air-Fried Scallops	227
148. Bacon-Wrapped Scallops	229
149. Bacon-Wrapped Scallops	231
150. Baja Fish Tacos	232
151. Baked Flounder Fillets	234
152. Blackened Fish	236
153. Breaded Calamari with Lemon	237
154. Breaded Scallops	239
155. Browned Shrimp Patties	240
156. Cajun Fish Fillets	242
157. Chili Prawns	243
158. Coconut Chili Fish Curry	244
159. Confetti Salmon Burgers	246
160. Cornmeal-Crusted Trout Fingers	248
161. Crab Cakes with Bell Peppers	250
162. Crab Cakes with Lettuce and Apple Salad	252

163. Crab Cakes with Sriracha Mayonnaise	254
164. Crab Ratatouille with Eggplant and Tomatoes	256
165. Crawfish Creole Casserole	258
166. Crispy Crab and Fish Cakes	260
167. Crunchy Air Fried Cod Fillets	262
168. Easy Scallops	264
169. Easy Shrimp and Vegetable Paella	265
170. Fired Shrimp with Mayonnaise Sauce	267
171. Fish Sandwich with Tartar Sauce	269
172. Fried Catfish with Dijon Sauce	271
173. Fried Shrimp	273
174. Garlic Butter Shrimp Scampi	275
175. Garlic Shrimp with Parsley	277
176. Goat Cheese Shrimp	278
177. Herbed Scallops with Vegetables	280
178. Jalea	282
179. Lemony Shrimp	284
180. Moroccan Spiced Halibut with Chickpea Salad	285
181. New Orleans-Style Crab Cakes	287
182. Orange-Mustard Glazed Salmon	289
183. Oyster Po'Boy	291
184. Panko Crab Sticks with Mayo Sauce	293
185. Paprika Shrimp	295
186. Parmesan Fish Fillets	296
187. Parmesan-Crusted Hake with Garlic Sauce	298
188. Pecan-Crusted Tilapia	300
189. Piri-Piri King Prawns	302
190. Roasted Cod with Lemon-Garlic Potatoes	303
191. Roasted Salmon Fillets	305
192. Salmon Patties	306
193. Shrimp and Cherry Tomato Kebabs	307
194. Shrimp Dejonghe Skewers	309
195. Sole and Asparagus Bundles	311
196. Swordfish Skewers with Caponata	313
197. Tandoori-Spiced Salmon and Potatoes	315
198. Thai Shrimp Skewers with Peanut Dipping Sauce	317
199. Traditional Tuna Melt	319
200. Trout Amandine with Lemon Butter Sauce	321
201. Tuna-Stuffed Quinoa Patties	323

POULTRY

202. Air Fryer Chicken Fajitas	327
203. Almond-Crusted Chicken Nuggets	328
204. Apricot-Glazed Chicken	329
205. Barbecue Chicken	330
206. Barbecued Chicken with Creamy Coleslaw	332
207. Buttermilk Paprika Chicken	334
208. Cheesy Chicken Tacos	336
209. Chicken and Vegetable Fajitas	338
210. Chicken Burgers with Ham and Cheese	340
211. Chicken Manchurian	342
212. Chicken with Pineapple and Peach	344
213. China Spicy Turkey Thighs	346
214. Coconut Chicken Meatballs	348
215. Cranberry Curry Chicken	350
216. Crisp Chicken Wings	352
217. Crispy Chicken Cordon Bleu	353
218. Curried Orange Honey Chicken	355
219. Deep Fried Duck Leg Quarters	357
220. Duck Breasts with Marmalade Balsamic Glaze	358
221. Easy Tandoori Chicken	359
222. Garlic Soy Chicken Thighs	361
223. Glazed Duck with Cherry Sauce	363
224. Hawaiian Tropical Chicken	365
225. Herb-Buttermilk Chicken Breast	367
226. Herbed Turkey Breast with Simple Dijon Sauce	369
227. Jerk Chicken Leg Quarters	371
228. Korean Flavor Glazed Chicken Wings	373
229. Lemon Chicken and Spinach Salad	375
230. Lemon Garlic Chicken	377
231. Lettuce Chicken Tacos with Peanut Sauce	379
232. Lettuce-Wrapped Turkey and Mushroom Meatballs	381
233. Lime Chicken with Cilantro	383
234. Merguez Meatballs	385
235. Nice Goulash	387
236. Paprika Indian Fennel Chicken	388
237. Parmesan Chicken Wings	390
238. Pomegranate-Glazed Chicken with Couscous Salad	392
239. Roasted Chicken and Vegetable Salad	394

240. Roasted Chicken with Garlic	395
241. Rosemary Turkey Breast	396
242. Rosemary Turkey Scotch Eggs	398
243. Simple Air Fried Chicken Wings	400
244. Simple Chicken Nuggets	401
245. Simple Chicken Shawarma	403
246. Simple Whole Chicken Bake	405
247. Spanish Chicken and Mini Sweet Pepper Baguette	406
248. Spicy Chicken Skewers with Satay Sauce	408
249. Spicy Tandoori Chicken Drumsticks	410
250. Strawberry-Glazed Turkey	412
251. Sweet-and-Sour Chicken Nuggets	413
252. Teriyaki Chicken Thighs with Lemony Snow Peas	415
253. Tex-Mex Chicken Breasts	417
254. Thai Cornish Game Hens	418
255. Thai Curry Meatballs	420
256. Thai Game Hens with Cucumber and Chile Salad	422
257. Turkey and Cauliflower Meatloaf	424
258. Turkish Chicken Kebabs	426
259. Yakitori	428
260. Yellow Curry Chicken Thighs with Peanuts	430

MEATS

261. Air Fried Baby Back Ribs	433
262. Air Fried Beef Ribs	434
263. Air Fried Golden Wasabi Spam	435
264. Apple-Glazed Pork	436
265. Avocado Buttered Flank Steak	438
266. Bacon and Pear Stuffed Pork Chops	439
267. Bacon Wrapped Pork with Apple Gravy	441
268. Bacon-Wrapped Hot Dogs with Mayo-Ketchup Sauce	443
269. Bacon-Wrapped Sausage with Tomato Relish	445
270. BBQ Pork Steaks	447
271. Beef and Pork Sausage Meatloaf	448
272. Beef and Spinach Rolls	450
273. Beef Cheeseburger Egg Rolls	451
274. Beef Chuck Cheeseburgers	453

275. Beef Chuck with Brussels Sprouts	454
276. Beef Egg Rolls	456
277. Beef Loin with Thyme and Parsley	458
278. Carne Asada Tacos	459
279. Char Siu	461
280. Cheddar Bacon Burst with Spinach	463
281. Cheese Crusted Chops	464
282. Chicken Fried Steak	466
283. Citrus Carnitas	468
284. Classic Walliser Schnitzel	470
285. Crispy Pork Tenderloin	472
286. Crumbed Golden Filet Mignon	473
287. Greek Lamb Pita Pockets	474
288. Greek Lamb Rack	476
289. Herbed Beef	477
290. Homemade Teriyaki Pork Ribs	478
291. Italian Lamb Chops with Avocado Mayo	479
292. Kale and Beef Omelet	480
293. Kielbasa Sausage with Pierogies	481
294. Kielbasa Sausage with Pineapple and Bell Peppers	483
295. Lahmacun (Turkish Pizza)	484
296. Lamb Kofta	486
297. Lamb Loin Chops with Horseradish Cream Sauce	488
298. Lamb Rack with Pistachio	490
299. Lechon Kawali	492
300. Lemony Pork Loin Chop Schnitzel	494
301. Macadamia Nuts Crusted Pork Rack	496
302. Marinated Pork Tenderloin	498
303. Mexican Pork Chops	500
304. Peppercorn Crusted Beef Tenderloin	501
305. Pork and Tricolor Vegetables Kebabs	502
306. Pork Butt with Garlicky Coriander-Parsley Sauce	504
307. Pork Chop Stir Fry	506
308. Pork Chops with Rinds	508
309. Pork Medallions with Radicchio and Endive Salad	509
310. Pork Sausage with Cauliflower Mash	511
311. Pork Schnitzels with Sour Cream and Dill Sauce	513
312. Sausage Ratatouille	515
313. Simple Pork Meatballs with Red Chili	517
314. Smoky Paprika Pork and Vegetable Kabobs	518

315. Spicy Pork Chops with Carrots and Mushrooms — 520
316. Spicy Pork with Candy Onions — 522
317. Spinach and Beef Braciole — 524
318. Sun-dried Tomato Crusted Chops — 526
319. Super Bacon with Meat — 528
320. Tonkatsu — 529

APPETIZERS AND SNACKS

321. Air Fried Pot Stickers — 533
322. Air Fryer Chicken Wings — 535
323. Bacon-Wrapped Shrimp and Jalapeño — 537
324. Baked Ricotta — 538
325. BBQ Pork Ribs — 540
326. Beef and Mango Skewers — 542
327. Bruschetta with Basil Pesto — 544
328. Bruschetta with Tomato and Basil — 545
329. Buffalo Cauliflower with Sour Dip — 547
330. Caramelized Peaches — 548
331. Cheese and Ham Stuffed Baby Bella — 549
332. Cheesy Crab Toasts — 551
333. Cheesy Stuffed Mushrooms — 553
334. Coconut-Crusted Shrimp — 555
335. Creamy Spinach-Broccoli Dip — 557
336. Cripsy Artichoke Bites — 558
337. Crispy Apple Chips — 560
338. Crispy Cod Fingers — 561
339. Crispy Green Tomatoes with Horseradish — 562
340. Crispy Phyllo Artichoke Triangles — 564
341. Crispy Spiced Chickpeas — 566
342. Cuban Sandwiches — 568
343. Deluxe Cheese Sandwiches — 569
344. Easy Muffuletta Sliders with Olives — 570
345. Homemade BBQ Chicken Pizza — 572
346. Italian Rice Balls — 573
347. Kale Chips with Sesame — 575
348. Lemony Chicken Drumsticks — 576
349. Lemony Pear Chips — 577
350. Mozzarella Arancini — 578

351. Mushroom and Spinach Calzones	580
352. Old Bay Chicken Wings	582
353. Peppery Chicken Meatballs	584
354. Roasted Mixed Nuts	586
355. Rosemary-Garlic Shoestring Fries	587
356. Sausage and Mushroom Empanadas	588
357. Shishito Peppers with Herb Dressing	590
358. Spiced Mixed Nuts	592
359. Spiced Sweet Potato Fries	594
360. Spicy Chicken Wings	596
361. Sweet Bacon Tater Tots	598
362. Tortellini with Spicy Dipping Sauce	599
363. Turkey Bacon-Wrapped Dates	601
364. Veggie Salmon Nachos	602
365. Veggie Shrimp Toast	603

DESSERTS

366. Air Fryer Apple Fritters	607
367. Apple Wedges with Apricots	609
368. Applesauce and Chocolate Brownies	610
369. Baked Apples	612
370. Berry Crumble	613
371. Black and White Brownies	615
372. Blackberry Chocolate Cake	617
373. Bourbon Bread Pudding	619
374. Brazilian Pineapple Bake	620
375. Cardamom and Vanilla Custard	621
376. Chia Pudding	622
377. Chickpea Brownies	623
378. Chocolate and Coconut Cake	625
379. Chocolate Cake	627
380. Chocolate Croissants	629
381. Chocolate Pecan Pie	630
382. Cinnamon Almonds	632
383. Cinnamon Candied Apples	633
384. Classic Pound Cake	634
385. Coconut Pineapple Sticks	636
386. Coffee Chocolate Cake	637

387. Crispy Pineapple Rings	639
388. Easy Almond Shortbread	641
389. Easy Blackberry Cobbler	642
390. Fudge Pie	643
391. Honey-Roasted Pears	644
392. Jelly Doughnuts	645
393. Lemon Ricotta Cake	646
394. Lemony Apple Butter	647
395. Mixed Berries with Pecan Streusel Topping	648
396. Oatmeal Raisin Bars	650
397. Orange and Anise Cake	652
398. Orange Coconut Cake	654
399. Peanut Butter-Chocolate Bread Pudding	656
400. Pecan and Cherry Stuffed Apples	658
401. Pineapple Galette	659
402. Ricotta Lemon Poppy Seed Cake	661
403. Simple Apple Turnovers	663
404. Spice Cookies	664
405. Ultimate Coconut Chocolate Cake	666

HOLIDAY SPECIALS

406. Eggnog Bread	669
407. Garlicky Olive Stromboli	671
408. Golden Nuggets	673
409. Holiday Spicy Beef Roast	675
410. Jewish Blintzes	676
411. Kale Salad Sushi Rolls with Sriracha Mayonnaise	678
412. Lush Snack Mix	680
413. Milky Pecan Tart	682
414. Pão de Queijo	684
415. Pigs in a Blanket	686
416. Shrimp with Sriracha and Worcestershire Sauce	687
417. Simple Butter Cake	689
418. Supplì al Telefono (Risotto Croquettes)	691
419. Teriyaki Shrimp Skewers	694
420. Whole Chicken Roast	696

FAST AND EASY EVERYDAY FAVORITES

421. Air Fried Broccoli	701
422. Carrot and Celery Croquettes	702
423. Cheesy Potato Patties	704
424. Simple and Easy Croutons	706
425. Sweet Corn and Carrot Fritters	707
426. Bistro Potato Wedges	709
427. Spinach and Carrot Balls	711
428. Simple Pea Delight	712
429. Cheesy Sausage Balls	713
430. Bacon-Wrapped Beef Hot Dog	714
431. Beef Bratwursts	715
432. Easy Roasted Asparagus	716
433. Baked Chorizo Scotch Eggs	717
434. Rosemary and Orange Roasted Chickpeas	719
435. Pomegranate Avocado Fries	720
436. Crunchy Fried Okra	722
437. Buttery Sweet Potatoes	724
438. Corn Fritters	725
439. Bacon and Green Beans	726
440. Frico	727
441. Garlicky Baked Cherry Tomatoes	728
442. Garlicky Knots with Parsley	729
443. Garlicky Zoodles	730
444. Hearty Apple Fritters	732
445. Honey Bartlett Pears with Lemony Ricotta	734
446. Hot Wings	736
447. Golden Salmon and Carrot Croquettes	737
448. Lemony and Garlicky Asparagus	739
449. Parsnip Fries with Garlic-Yogurt Dip	740
450. Roasted Carrot Chips	742
451. Simple Air Fried Crispy Brussels Sprouts	743
452. Simple Air Fried Okra Chips	744
453. Simple Baked Green Beans	745
454. Simple Cheesy Shrimps	746
455. Spanakopita	748
456. Spicy Air Fried Old Bay Shrimp	750
457. South Carolina Shrimp and Corn Bake	751

458. Southwest Corn and Bell Pepper Roast   753
459. Sweet and Sour Peanuts   755

CASSEROLES, FRITTATAS AND QUICHES

460. Broccoli, Carrot, and Tomato Quiche   759
461. Cheesy Bacon Quiche   761
462. Chicken and Mushroom Casserole   763
463. Chicken Divan   764
464. Chorizo, Corn, and Potato Frittata   766
465. Creamy Pork Gratin   768
466. Creamy Tomato Casserole   770
467. Goat Cheese and Asparagus Frittata   771
468. Greek Frittata   773
469. Herbed Cheddar Frittata   774
470. Kale Frittata   775
471. Keto Cheese Quiche   777
472. Mediterranean Quiche   779
473. Shrimp Quiche   781
474. Shrimp Spinach Frittata   783
475. Smoked Trout and Crème Fraiche Frittata   784
476. Spinach Casserole   786
477. Sumptuous Beef and Bean Chili Casserole   787
478. Sumptuous Vegetable Frittata   789
479. Taco Beef and Chile Casserole   791

Appendix 1: Measurement Conversion Chart   793
Appendix 2: Air Fryer Cooking Timetable   795

© Copyright 2021 By Pamela Kendrick. All Rights Reserved.

This book is copyright protected. It is only for personal use. You cannot amend, distribute, sell, use, quote or paraphrase any part of the content within this book, without the consent of the author or publisher.

Under no circumstances will any blame or legal responsibility be held against the publisher, or author, for any damages, reparation, or monetary loss due to the information contained within this book, either directly or indirectly.

DISCLAIMER NOTICE

Please note the information contained within this document is for educational and entertainment purposes only. All effort has been executed to present accurate, up to date, reliable, complete information. No warranties of any kind are declared or implied. Readers acknowledge that the author is not engaged in the rendering of legal, financial, medical or professional advice. The content within this book has been derived from various sources. Please consult a licensed professional before attempting any techniques outlined in this book.

By reading this document, the reader agrees that under no circumstances is the author responsible for any losses, direct or indirect, that are incurred as a result of the use of the information contained within this document, including, but not limited to, errors, omissions, or inaccuracies.

INTRODUCTION

Imagine this: a microwave that doesn't take up half your counter, with intuitive buttons, that heats food fast and evenly... AND makes food crispy?!? If you want this then you need the Nuwave Air Fryer!

The day I got my Nuwave, my cooking experience totally changed. Before the Nuwave, my counter was filled with appliances I used seldomly. My microwave was probably the most popular, but I hated how it made my leftovers soggy and that it didn't work to reheat anything fried (my favourite!) I also found myself using my toaster oven a lot, but the problem with that was it only fit 2 slices of pizza or a few wings. Add to that my affinity for kale chips, I also had a dehydrator on my counter as well as a mini panini press... and that's not including my stovetop and oven, which I didn't bother to use a lot because I am often cooking just for myself. When I got my Nuwave, I was able to clear out all these appliances because this thing does the job of ALL of them.

The Nuwave uses super-heated air and a special air-flow design to cook anything! When I say anything, I mean ANYTHING! I've made wings, French fries, sandwiches, steaks,

Introduction

roasted vegetables and even brownies in this machine. Some nights I come home and just empty a bag of frozen broccoli on one side, and a chicken breast on the other. I go have a shower or answer some emails and come back and dinner is done! How is this possible???? I'll tell you how!

Nuwave is different from all other air fryers because it has two baskets. I can cook vegetables on one side and meat on the other, and both will come out perfectly cooked. There are plenty of pre-set buttons (just like a microwave) to make the cooking experience easier, but I went one step further and made a cookbook of my favourite recipes. This came about shortly after I got my Nuwave – I started experimenting in the kitchen and really testing this machine – could I really cook anything in it? The answer is yes!

From frozen vegetables, to the perfect steak, to popcorn, to my beloved kale chips, I've come up with 500 recipes to make in the Nuwave. I wanted to show what makes this appliance so different from my microwave, toaster oven and deep fryer. The Nuwave is a combination of all of these appliances – and the very best part is that I don't need to use messy oil when cooking with this! Think about it – if I wanted to make say, 2 lbs of chicken wings the old-fashioned way and deep-fry them... First I had wait for the oil to heat up, either in my deep fryer or a pot on the stove. This is dangerous, messy and makes the house stink for days! I would have to stand close by to make sure there was no splattering or any dangerous grease fires. Next, I'd have to blot the wings on paper towels to avoid eating all that oil. It never really helped though because they would be drenched in oil. Don't get me wrong.... This was DELICIOUS. But now, I can have delicious wings without all the time, oil and worry. Here's how I make my wings now: I empty frozen, breaded wings into the basket of my Nuwave. I press the "wings" button. I walk away, thanks for the enhanced safety features and lack of oil. When I hear the timer, I empty my perfectly crispy wings onto my dinner plate. And... done! I know it is hard to believe, and sometimes it is hard for me believe that I came up with 500 awesome recipes to make in the Nuwave... but that's how much this appliance changed my life.

Introduction

At first, I was making a lot of my favourite fried foods – wings, fries, nuggets... I couldn't believe that everything got so crispy without oil! Next, I started experimenting with other favourites that I would have made in my other appliances. This included grilled cheese sandwiches on the Panini press, kale chips in the dehydrator, pork chops in the slow cooker, chicken thighs in the oven.... and I even started experimenting with baking desserts in my Nuwave. I've come up with 500 recipes I want to share with you! These recipes have saved me time and made me healthier. I eat much less oil now and can whip up vegetables in a matter of minutes. It's also great for leftovers or keeping food warm when life gets busy. For meal prep, I also like to cook 4 chicken breasts. I just throw them into the fryer basket with some seasonings and use my favourite Chicken recipe from the book, and set the timer. 25 minutes later I've got 4 meals ready to go. I can chop one up for chicken salad, serve one with crispy roasted potatoes for dinner tomorrow. This method of cooking has again, saved me time and made me healthier!

This cookbook is great for anyone who leads a busy life and wants to be healthier... but it's also great for anyone who is sick of having so many appliances in their home that do a sub-par job. I wish I had this appliance when I was in college, desperately trying to make my leftover pizza crispy. I bought a second Nuwave for my camper this summer so I can have crispy fried food without all the fuss. Maybe my next cookbook will be about Camping with the Nuwave!

Developing these recipes was so much fun – I can't wait to show everyone how easy it is to eat healthy and how delicious air fried food can be. Happy Cooking!

SAUCES, DIPS AND DRESSINGS

1

LEMONY AVOCADO DRESSING

Prep time: 5 minutes | **Cook time:** 0 minutes | Makes 12 tablespoons

1 large avocado, pitted and peeled
½ cup water
2 tablespoons tahini
2 tablespoons freshly squeezed lemon juice
1 teaspoon dried basil
1 teaspoon white wine vinegar
1 garlic clove
¼ teaspoon pink Himalayan salt
¼ teaspoon freshly ground black pepper

1. Combine all the ingredients in a food processor and blend until smooth.

2

CREAMY CASHEW MAYO

Prep time: 5 minutes | **Cook time:** 0 minutes | Makes 18 tablespoons

1 cup cashews, soaked in hot water for at least 1 hour
¼ cup plus 3 tablespoons milk
1 tablespoon apple cider vinegar
1 tablespoon freshly squeezed lemon juice
1 tablespoon Dijon mustard
1 tablespoon aquafaba
⅛ teaspoon pink Himalayan salt

1. In a food processor, combine all the ingredients and blend until creamy and smooth.

3

GARLICKY CAULIFLOWER ALFREDO SAUCE

Prep time: 2 minutes | **Cook time:** 0 minutes | Makes 4 cups

2 tablespoons olive oil

6 garlic cloves, minced

3 cups unsweetened almond milk

1 (1-pound / 454-g) head cauliflower, cut into florets

1 teaspoon salt

¼ teaspoon freshly ground black pepper

Juice of 1 lemon

4 tablespoons nutritional yeast

1. In a medium saucepan, heat the olive oil over medium-high heat. Add the garlic and sauté for 1 minute or until fragrant. Add the almond milk, stir, and bring to a boil.

2. Gently add the cauliflower. Stir in the salt and pepper and return to a boil. Continue cooking over medium-high heat for 5 minutes or until the cauliflower is soft. Stir frequently and reduce heat if needed to prevent the liquid from boiling over.

3. Carefully transfer the cauliflower and cooking liquid to a food processor, using a slotted spoon to scoop out the larger pieces of cauliflower before pouring in the liquid. Add the lemon and nutritional yeast and blend for 1 to 2 minutes until smooth.

4. Serve immediately.

4

SOUTHERN CHIMICHURRI

Prep time: 15 minutes | **Cook time:** 0 minutes | Makes 2 cups

1 cup minced fresh parsley
½ cup minced fresh cilantro
¼ cup minced fresh mint leaves
¼ cup minced garlic (about 6 cloves)
2 tablespoons minced fresh oregano leaves
1 teaspoon fine Himalayan salt
1 cup olive oil or avocado oil
½ cup red wine vinegar
Juice of 1 lemon

1. Thoroughly mix the parsley, cilantro, mint leaves, garlic, oregano leaves, and salt in a medium bowl. Add the olive oil, vinegar, and lemon juice and whisk to combine.

2. Store in an airtight container in the refrigerator and shake before using.

3. You can serve the chimichurri over vegetables, poultry, meats, and fish. It also can be used as a marinade, dipping sauce, or condiment.

5

LEMONY COCONUT YOGURT DRESSING

Prep time: 5 minutes | **Cook time:** 0 minutes | Makes about 1 cup

8 ounces (227 g) plain coconut yogurt
2 tablespoons chopped fresh parsley
2 tablespoons freshly squeezed lemon juice
1 tablespoon snipped fresh chives
½ teaspoon salt
Pinch freshly ground black pepper

1. Stir together the coconut yogurt, parsley, lemon juice, chives, salt, and pepper in a medium bowl until completely mixed.
2. Transfer to an airtight container and refrigerate until ready to use.
3. This dressing perfectly pairs with spring mix greens, grilled chicken or even your favorite salad.

6

HOMEMADE RANCH DRESSING

Prep time: 5 minutes | **Cook time:** 0 minutes | **Serves** 8

1 cup plain Greek yogurt
¼ cup chopped fresh dill
2 tablespoons chopped fresh chives
Zest of 1 lemon
1 garlic clove, minced
½ teaspoon sea salt
⅛ teaspoon freshly cracked black pepper

1. Mix together the yogurt, dill, chives, lemon zest, garlic, sea salt, and pepper in a small bowl and whisk to combine.
2. Serve chilled.

7

BALSAMIC-DIJON VINAIGRETTE

Prep time: 5 minutes | **Cook time:** 0 minutes | Makes 12 tablespoons

- 6 tablespoons water
- 4 tablespoons Dijon mustard
- 4 tablespoons balsamic vinegar
- 1 teaspoon maple syrup
- ½ teaspoon pink Himalayan salt
- ¼ teaspoon freshly ground black pepper

1. In a bowl, whisk together all the ingredients.

8

HONEY MIXED BERRY VINAIGRETTE

Prep time: 15 minutes | **Cook time:** 0 minutes | Makes about 1½ cups

1 cup mixed berries, thawed if frozen
½ cup balsamic vinegar
⅓ cup extra-virgin olive oil
2 tablespoons freshly squeezed lemon or lime juice
1 tablespoon lemon or lime zest
1 tablespoon Dijon mustard
1 tablespoon raw honey or maple syrup
1 teaspoon salt
½ teaspoon freshly ground black pepper

1. Place all the ingredients in a blender and purée until thoroughly mixed and smooth.
2. You can serve it over a bed of greens, grilled meat, or fresh fruit salad.

9
HONEY LIME TAHINI DRESSING

Prep time: 5 minutes | **Cook time:** 0 minutes | Makes about ¾ cup

⅓ cup tahini

3 tablespoons filtered water

2 tablespoons freshly squeezed lime juice

1 tablespoon apple cider vinegar

1 teaspoon lime zest

1½ teaspoons raw honey

¼ teaspoon garlic powder

¼ teaspoon salt

1. Whisk together the tahini, water, vinegar, lime juice, lime zest, honey, salt, and garlic powder in a small bowl until well emulsified.

2. Serve immediately, or refrigerate in an airtight container for to 1 week.

10

CREAMY HEMP DRESSING

Prep time: 5 minutes | **Cook time:** 0 minutes | Makes 12 tablespoons

- ½ cup white wine vinegar
- ¼ cup tahini
- ¼ cup water
- 1 tablespoon hemp seeds
- ½ tablespoon freshly squeezed lemon juice
- 1 teaspoon garlic powder
- 1 teaspoon dried oregano
- 1 teaspoon dried basil
- 1 teaspoon red pepper flakes
- ½ teaspoon onion powder
- ½ teaspoon pink Himalayan salt
- ½ teaspoon freshly ground black pepper

1. In a bowl, combine all the ingredients and whisk until mixed well.

11

LEMONY KALE AND ALMOND PESTO

Prep time: 15 minutes | **Cook time:** 0 minutes | Makes about 1 cup

2 cups chopped kale leaves, rinsed well and stemmed
½ cup toasted almonds
2 garlic cloves
3 tablespoons extra-virgin olive oil
3 tablespoons freshly squeezed lemon juice
2 teaspoons lemon zest
1 teaspoon salt
½ teaspoon freshly ground black pepper
¼ teaspoon red pepper flakes

1. Place all the ingredients in a food processor and pulse until smoothly puréed.

2. It tastes great with the eggs, salads, soup, pasta, cracker, and sandwiches.

12

LEMON-DIJON VINAIGRETTE

Prep time: 5 minutes | **Cook time:** 0 minutes | Makes about 6 tablespoons

¼ cup extra-virgin olive oil

1 garlic clove, minced

2 tablespoons freshly squeezed lemon juice

1 teaspoon Dijon mustard

½ teaspoon raw honey

¼ teaspoon salt

¼ teaspoon dried basil

1. Place all the ingredients in a mason jar. Cover and shake vigorously until thoroughly mixed and well emulsified.
2. Serve chilled.

13

LEMONY TAHINI SAUCE

Prep time: 5 minutes | **Cook time:** 0 minutes | **Serves** 4

¾ cup water
½ cup tahini
3 garlic cloves, minced
Juice of 3 lemons
½ teaspoon pink Himalayan salt

1. In a bowl, whisk together all the ingredients until mixed well.

14

APPLE-MUSHROOM GRAVY

Prep time: 5 minutes | **Cook time:** 10 minutes | **Serves** 4

2 cups vegetable broth
½ cup finely chopped mushrooms
2 tablespoons whole wheat flour
1 tablespoon unsweetened applesauce
1 teaspoon onion powder
½ teaspoon dried thyme
¼ teaspoon dried rosemary
⅛ teaspoon pink Himalayan salt
Freshly ground black pepper, to taste

1. In a nonstick saucepan over medium-high heat, combine all the ingredients and mix well. Bring to a boil, stirring frequently, reduce the heat to low, and simmer, stirring constantly, until it thickens.

15

BUFFALO SAUCE

Prep time: 5 minutes | **Cook time:** 20 minutes | Makes 2 cups

¼ cup olive oil

4 garlic cloves, roughly chopped

1 (5-ounce / 142-g) small red onion, roughly chopped

6 red chiles, roughly chopped (about 2 ounces / 56 g in total)

1 cup water

½ cup apple cider vinegar

½ teaspoon salt

½ teaspoon freshly ground black pepper

1. In a large nonstick sauté pan, heat ¼ cup olive oil over medium-high heat. Once it's hot, add the garlic, onion, and chiles. Cook for 5 minutes, stirring occasionally, until onions are golden brown.

2. Add the water and bring to a boil. Cook for about 10 minutes or until the water has nearly evaporated.

3. Transfer the cooked onion and chile mixture to a food processor or blender and blend briefly to combine. Add the apple cider vinegar, salt, and pepper. Blend again for 30 seconds.

4. Using a mesh sieve, strain the sauce into a bowl. Use a spoon or spatula to scrape and press all the liquid from the pulp.

WRAPS AND SANDWICHES

16

CREAMY-CHEESY WONTONS

Prep time: 5 minutes | **Cook time:** 6 minutes | **Serves** 4

2 ounces (57 g) cream cheese, softened

1 tablespoon sugar

16 square wonton wrappers

Cooking spray

1. Press "Pre-Heat", set the temperature at 350°F (177°C). Spritz the air fryer basket with cooking spray.

2. In a mixing bowl, stir together the cream cheese and sugar until well mixed. Prepare a small bowl of water alongside.

3. On a clean work surface, lay the wonton wrappers. Scoop ¼ teaspoon of cream cheese in the center of each wonton wrapper. Dab the water over the wrapper edges. Fold each wonton wrapper diagonally in half over the filling to form a triangle.

4. Arrange the wontons in the air fryer basket. Spritz the wontons with cooking spray. Air fry for 6 minutes, or until golden brown and crispy. Flip once halfway through to ensure even cooking.

5. Divide the wontons among four plates. Let rest for 5 minutes before serving.

17

BULGOGI BURGERS WITH KOREAN MAYO

Prep time: 15 minutes | **Cook time:** 10 minutes | **Serves** 4

For the Burgers:
1 pound (454 g) 85% lean ground beef
2 tablespoons gochujang
¼ cup chopped scallions
2 teaspoons minced garlic
2 teaspoons minced fresh ginger
1 tablespoon soy sauce
1 tablespoon toasted sesame oil
2 teaspoons sugar
½ teaspoon kosher salt
4 hamburger buns
Cooking spray
For the Korean Mayo:
1 tablespoon gochujang
¼ cup mayonnaise
2 teaspoons sesame seeds
¼ cup chopped scallions
1 tablespoon toasted sesame oil

1. Combine the ingredients for the burgers, except for the

buns, in a large bowl. Stir to mix well, then wrap the bowl in plastic and refrigerate to marinate for at least an hour.

2.Press "Pre-Heat", set the temperature at 350°F (177°C) and spritz with cooking spray.

3.Divide the meat mixture into four portions and form into four balls. Bash the balls into patties.

4.Arrange the patties in the preheated air fryer and spritz with cooking spray. Air fry for 10 minutes or until golden brown. Flip the patties halfway through.

5.Meanwhile, combine the ingredients for the Korean mayo in a small bowl. Stir to mix well.

6.Remove the patties from the air fryer and assemble with the buns, then spread the Korean mayo over the patties to make the burgers. Serve immediately.

18

GOLDEN CABBAGE AND PORK GYOZA

Prep time: 10 minutes | **Cook time:** 10 minutes per batch | Makes 48 gyozas

1 pound (454 g) ground pork

1 small head Napa cabbage (about 1 pound / 454 g), sliced thinly and minced

½ cup minced scallions

1 teaspoon minced fresh chives

1 teaspoon soy sauce

1 teaspoon minced fresh ginger

1 tablespoon minced garlic

1 teaspoon granulated sugar

2 teaspoons kosher salt

48 to 50 wonton or dumpling wrappers

Cooking spray

1. Make the filling: Combine all the ingredients, except for the wrappers in a large bowl. Stir to mix well.

2. Unfold a wrapper on a clean work surface, then dab the edges with a little water. Scoop up 2 teaspoons of the filling mixture in the center.

3. Make the gyoza: Fold the wrapper over to filling and press

the edges to seal. Pleat the edges if desired. Repeat with remaining wrappers and fillings.

4.Press "Pre-Heat", set the temperature at 360°F (182°C) and spritz with cooking spray.

5.Arrange the gyozas in the preheated air fryer and spritz with cooking spray. Air fry for 10 minutes or until golden brown. Flip the gyozas halfway through. Work in batches to avoid overcrowding.

6.Serve immediately.

19

FAST CHEESY CHICKEN SANDWICH

Prep time: 10 minutes | **Cook time:** 5 to 7 minutes | **Serves** 1

$1/3$ cup chicken, cooked and shredded

2 Mozzarella slices

1 hamburger bun

$1/4$ cup shredded cabbage

1 teaspoon mayonnaise

2 teaspoons butter, melted

1 teaspoon olive oil

$1/2$ teaspoon balsamic vinegar

$1/4$ teaspoon smoked paprika

$1/4$ teaspoon black pepper

$1/4$ teaspoon garlic powder

Pinch of salt

1. Press "Pre-Heat", set the temperature at 370°F (188°C).

2. Brush some butter onto the outside of the hamburger bun.

3. In a bowl, coat the chicken with the garlic powder, salt, pepper, and paprika.

4. In a separate bowl, stir together the mayonnaise, olive oil, cabbage, and balsamic vinegar to make coleslaw.

5. Slice the bun in two. Start building the sandwich, starting with the chicken, followed by the Mozzarella, the coleslaw, and finally the top bun.

6. Transfer the sandwich to the air fryer and bake for 5 to 7 minutes.

7. Serve immediately.

20

GOLDEN CHEESY POTATO TAQUITOS

Prep time: 5 minutes | **Cook time:** 6 minutes per batch | Makes 12 taquitos

2 cups mashed potatoes

½ cup shredded Mexican cheese

12 corn tortillas

Cooking spray

1. Press "Pre-Heat", set the temperature at 400°F (204°C). Line the baking pan with parchment paper.

2. In a bowl, combine the potatoes and cheese until well mixed. Microwave the tortillas on high heat for 30 seconds, or until softened. Add some water to another bowl and set alongside.

3. On a clean work surface, lay the tortillas. Scoop 3 tablespoons of the potato mixture in the center of each tortilla. Roll up tightly and secure with toothpicks if necessary.

4. Arrange the filled tortillas, seam side down, in the prepared baking pan. Spritz the tortillas with cooking spray. Air fry for 6 minutes, or until crispy and golden brown, flipping once halfway through the cooking time. You may need to work in batches to avoid overcrowding.

5. Serve hot.

21

CHEESY CHICKEN AND YOGURT TAQUITOS

Prep time: 15 minutes | **Cook time:** 12 minutes | **Serves** 4

1 cup cooked chicken, shredded
¼ cup Greek yogurt
¼ cup salsa
1 cup shredded Mozzarella cheese
Salt and ground black pepper, to taste
4 flour tortillas
Cooking spray

1. Press "Pre-Heat", set the temperature at 380°F (193°C) and spritz with cooking spray.
2. Combine all the ingredients, except for the tortillas, in a large bowl. Stir to mix well.
3. Make the taquitos: Unfold the tortillas on a clean work surface, then scoop up 2 tablespoons of the chicken mixture in the middle of each tortilla. Roll the tortillas up to wrap the filling.
4. Arrange the taquitos in the preheated air fryer and spritz with cooking spray.
5. Air fry for 12 minutes or until golden brown and the cheese melts. Flip the taquitos halfway through.
6. Serve immediately.

22

TANGY CHICKEN-LETTUCE WRAPS

Prep time: 15 minutes | **Cook time:** 12 to 16 minutes | **Serves** 2 to 4

1 pound (454 g) boneless, skinless chicken thighs, trimmed
1 teaspoon vegetable oil
2 tablespoons lime juice
1 shallot, minced
1 tablespoon fish sauce, plus extra for serving
2 teaspoons packed brown sugar
1 garlic clove, minced
1/8 teaspoon red pepper flakes
1 mango, peeled, pitted, and cut into 1/4-inch pieces
1/3 cup chopped fresh mint
1/3 cup chopped fresh cilantro
1/3 cup chopped fresh Thai basil
1 head Bibb lettuce, leaves separated (8 ounces / 227 g)
1/4 cup chopped dry-roasted peanuts
2 Thai chiles, stemmed and sliced thin

1.Press "Pre-Heat", set the temperature at 400°F (204°C).
2.Pat the chicken dry with paper towels and rub with oil. Place the chicken in air fryer basket and air fry for 12 to 16 minutes, or

until the chicken registers 175°F (79°C), flipping and rotating chicken halfway through cooking.

3.Meanwhile, whisk lime juice, shallot, fish sauce, sugar, garlic, and pepper flakes together in large bowl; set aside.

4.Transfer chicken to cutting board, let cool slightly, then shred into bite-size pieces using 2 forks. Add the shredded chicken, mango, mint, cilantro, and basil to bowl with dressing and toss to coat.

5.Serve the chicken in the lettuce leaves, passing peanuts, Thai chiles, and extra fish sauce separately.

23

CRISPY CRABMEAT WONTONS

Prep time: 10 minutes | **Cook time:** 10 minutes per batch | **Serves** 6 to 8

24 wonton wrappers, thawed if frozen

Cooking spray

For the Filling:

5 ounces (142 g) lump crabmeat, drained and patted dry

4 ounces (113 g) cream cheese, at room temperature

2 scallions, sliced

1½ teaspoons toasted sesame oil

1 teaspoon Worcestershire sauce

Kosher salt and ground black pepper, to taste

1. Press "Pre-Heat", set the temperature at 350°F (177°C). Spritz the air fryer basket with cooking spray.

2. In a medium-size bowl, place all the ingredients for the filling and stir until well mixed. Prepare a small bowl of water alongside.

3. On a clean work surface, lay the wonton wrappers. Scoop 1 teaspoon of the filling in the center of each wrapper. Wet the edges with a touch of water. Fold each wonton wrapper diagonally in half over the filling to form a triangle.

4. Arrange the wontons in the air fryer basket. Spritz the wontons with cooking spray. Work in batches, 6 to 8 at a time. Air fry for 10 minutes, or until crispy and golden brown. Flip once halfway through.

5. Serve immediately.

24

CHEESY EGGPLANT HOAGIES

Prep time: 15 minutes | **Cook time:** 12 minutes | Makes 3 hoagies

6 peeled eggplant slices (about ½ inch thick and 3 inches in diameter)

¼ cup jarred pizza sauce

6 tablespoons grated Parmesan cheese

3 Italian sub rolls, split open lengthwise, warmed

Cooking spray

1. Press "Pre-Heat", set the temperature at 350°F (177°C) and spritz with cooking spray.

2. Arrange the eggplant slices in the preheated air fryer and spritz with cooking spray.

3. Air fry for 10 minutes or until lightly wilted and tender. Flip the slices halfway through.

4. Divide and spread the pizza sauce and cheese on top of the eggplant slice and air fry over 375°F (191°C) for 2 more minutes or until the cheese melts.

5. Assemble each sub roll with two slices of eggplant and serve immediately.

25

FETA LAMB HAMBURGERS

Prep time: 15 minutes | **Cook time:** 16 minutes | Makes 4 burgers

1½ pounds (680 g) ground lamb
¼ cup crumbled feta
1½ teaspoons tomato paste
1½ teaspoons minced garlic
1 teaspoon ground dried ginger
1 teaspoon ground coriander
¼ teaspoon salt
¼ teaspoon cayenne pepper
4 kaiser rolls or hamburger buns, split open lengthwise, warmed
Cooking spray

1. Press "Pre-Heat", set the temperature at 375°F (191°C) and spritz with cooking spray.
2. Combine all the ingredients, except for the buns, in a large bowl. Coarsely stir to mix well.
3. Shape the mixture into four balls, then pound the balls into four 5-inch diameter patties.

4.Arrange the patties in the preheated air fryer and spritz with cooking spray. Air fry for 16 minutes or until well browned. Flip the patties halfway through.

5.Assemble the buns with patties to make the burgers and serve immediately.

26

FAJITA MEATBALL WRAPS

Prep time: 10 minutes | **Cook time:** 10 minutes | **Serves** 4

1 pound (454 g) 85% lean ground beef
½ cup salsa, plus more for serving
¼ cup chopped onions
¼ cup diced green or red bell peppers
1 large egg, beaten
1 teaspoon fine sea salt
½ teaspoon chili powder
½ teaspoon ground cumin
1 clove garlic, minced
Cooking spray
For Serving:
8 leaves Boston lettuce
Pico de gallo or salsa
Lime slices

1. Press "Pre-Heat", set the temperature at 350°F (177°C). Spray the air fryer basket with cooking spray.
2. In a large bowl, mix together all the ingredients until well combined.
3. Shape the meat mixture into eight 1-inch balls. Place the

meatballs in the air fryer basket, leaving a little space between them. Air fry for 10 minutes, or until cooked through and no longer pink inside and the internal temperature reaches 145°F (63°C).

4.Serve each meatball on a lettuce leaf, topped with pico de gallo or salsa. Serve with lime slices.

27

MEXICAN PAPRIKA CHICKEN BURGERS

Prep time: 15 minutes | **Cook time:** 20 minutes | **Serves** 6 to 8

4 skinless and boneless chicken breasts
1 small head of cauliflower, sliced into florets
1 jalapeño pepper
3 tablespoons smoked paprika
1 tablespoon thyme
1 tablespoon oregano
1 tablespoon mustard powder
1 teaspoon cayenne pepper
1 egg
Salt and ground black pepper, to taste
2 tomatoes, sliced
2 lettuce leaves, chopped
6 to 8 brioche buns, sliced lengthwise
¾ cup taco sauce
Cooking spray

1. Press "Pre-Heat", set the temperature at 350°F (177°C) and spritz with cooking spray.
2. In a blender, add the cauliflower florets, jalapeño pepper,

paprika, thyme, oregano, mustard powder and cayenne pepper and blend until the mixture has a texture similar to breadcrumbs.

3. Transfer ¾ of the cauliflower mixture to a medium bowl and set aside. Beat the egg in a different bowl and set aside.

4. Add the chicken breasts to the blender with remaining cauliflower mixture. Sprinkle with salt and pepper. Blend until finely chopped and well mixed.

5. Remove the mixture from the blender and form into 6 to 8 patties. One by one, dredge each patty in the reserved cauliflower mixture, then into the egg. Dip them in the cauliflower mixture again for additional coating.

6. Place the coated patties into the air fryer basket and spritz with cooking spray. Air fry for 20 minutes or until golden and crispy. Flip halfway through to ensure even cooking.

7. Transfer the patties to a clean work surface and assemble with the buns, tomato slices, chopped lettuce leaves and taco sauce to make burgers. Serve and enjoy.

28

FAST MONTREAL STEAK AND SEEDS BURGERS

Prep time: 15 minutes | **Cook time:** 10 minutes | **Serves** 4

1 teaspoon cumin seeds
1 teaspoon mustard seeds
1 teaspoon coriander seeds
1 teaspoon dried minced garlic
1 teaspoon dried red pepper flakes
1 teaspoon kosher salt
2 teaspoons ground black pepper
1 pound (454 g) 85% lean ground beef
2 tablespoons Worcestershire sauce
4 hamburger buns
Mayonnaise, for serving
Cooking spray

1. Press "Pre-Heat", set the temperature at 350°F (177°C) and spritz with cooking spray.

2. Put the seeds, garlic, red pepper flakes, salt, and ground black pepper in a food processor. Pulse to coarsely ground the mixture.

3. Put the ground beef in a large bowl. Pour in the seed mixture and drizzle with Worcestershire sauce. Stir to mix well.

4.Divide the mixture into four parts and shape each part into a ball, then bash each ball into a patty.

5.Arrange the patties in the preheated air fryer and air fry for 10 minutes or until the patties are well browned. Flip the patties with tongs halfway through.

6.Assemble the buns with the patties, then drizzle the mayo over the patties to make the burgers. Serve immediately.

29

NUGGET AND VEGETABLE TACO WRAPS

Prep time: 5 minutes | **Cook time:** 15 minutes | **Serves** 4

1 tablespoon water
4 pieces commercial vegan nuggets, chopped
1 small yellow onion, diced
1 small red bell pepper, chopped
2 cobs grilled corn kernels
4 large corn tortillas
Mixed greens, for garnish

1. Press "Pre-Heat", set the temperature at 400°F (204°C).
2. Over a medium heat, sauté the nuggets in the water with the onion, corn kernels and bell pepper in a skillet, then remove from the heat.
3. Fill the tortillas with the nuggets and vegetables and fold them up. Transfer to the inside of the fryer and air fry for 15 minutes.
4. Once crispy, serve immediately, garnished with the mixed greens.

30

GOLDEN PEA AND POTATO SAMOSAS

Prep time: 30 minutes | **Cook time:** 1 hour 10 minutes | Makes 16 samosas

Dough:

4 cups all-purpose flour, plus more for flouring the work surface

¼ cup plain yogurt

½ cup cold unsalted butter, cut into cubes

2 teaspoons kosher salt

1 cup ice water

Filling:

2 tablespoons vegetable oil

1 onion, diced

1½ teaspoons coriander

1½ teaspoons cumin

1 clove garlic, minced

1 teaspoon turmeric

1 teaspoon kosher salt

½ cup peas, thawed if frozen

2 cups mashed potatoes

2 tablespoons yogurt

Cooking spray
Chutney:
1 cup mint leaves, lightly packed
2 cups cilantro leaves, lightly packed
1 green chile pepper, deseeded and minced
½ cup minced onion
Juice of 1 lime
1 teaspoon granulated sugar
1 teaspoon kosher salt
2 tablespoons vegetable oil

1. Put the flour, yogurt, butter, and salt in a food processor. Pulse to combine until grainy. Pour in the water and pulse until a smooth and firm dough forms.

2. Transfer the dough on a clean and lightly floured working surface. Knead the dough and shape it into a ball. Cut in half and flatten the halves into 2 discs. Wrap them in plastic and let sit in refrigerator until ready to use.

3. Meanwhile, make the filling: Heat the vegetable oil in a saucepan over medium heat.

4. Add the onion and sauté for 5 minutes or until lightly browned.

5. Add the coriander, cumin, garlic, turmeric, and salt and sauté for 2 minutes or until fragrant.

6. Add the peas, potatoes, and yogurt and stir to combine well. Turn off the heat and allow to cool.

7. Meanwhile, combine the ingredients for the chutney in a food processor. Pulse to mix well until glossy. Pour the chutney in a bowl and refrigerate until ready to use.

8. Make the samosas: Remove the dough discs from the refrigerator and cut each disc into 8 parts. Shape each part into a ball, then roll the ball into a 6-inch circle. Cut the circle in half and roll each half into a cone.

9. Scoop up 2 tablespoons of the filling into the cone, press the edges of the cone to seal and form into a triangle. Repeat with remaining dough and filling.

10. Press "Pre-Heat", set the temperature at 360°F (182°C) and spritz with cooking spray.

11. Arrange four samosas each batch in the preheated air fryer and spritz with cooking spray. Air fry for 15 minutes or until golden brown and crispy. Flip the samosas halfway through.

12. Serve the samosas with the chutney.

31

ASIAN PORK MOMOS

Prep time: 20 minutes | **Cook time:** 10 minutes per batch | **Serves** 4

2 tablespoons olive oil

1 pound (454 g) ground pork

1 shredded carrot

1 onion, chopped

1 teaspoon soy sauce

16 wonton wrappers

Salt and ground black pepper, to taste

1. Press "Pre-Heat", set the temperature at 320°F (160°C).

2. Heat the olive oil in a nonstick skillet over medium heat until shimmering.

3. Add the ground pork, carrot, onion, soy sauce, salt, and ground black pepper and sauté for 10 minutes or until the pork is well browned and carrots are tender.

4. Unfold the wrappers on a clean work surface, then divide the cooked pork and vegetables on the wrappers. Fold the edges around the filling to form momos. Nip the top to seal the momos.

5. Arrange the momos in the preheated air fryer and spritz

with cooking spray. Air fry for 10 minutes or until the wrappers are lightly browned. Work in batches to avoid overcrowding.

6.Serve immediately.

32

CRISPY CHICKEN EMPANADAS

Prep time: 25 minutes | **Cook time:** 24 minutes | Makes 12 empanadas

1 cup boneless, skinless rotisserie chicken breast meat, chopped finely

¼ cup salsa verde

⅔ cup shredded Cheddar cheese

1 teaspoon ground cumin

1 teaspoon ground black pepper

2 purchased refrigerated pie crusts, from a minimum 14.1-ounce box

1 large egg

2 tablespoons water

Cooking spray

1. Press "Pre-Heat", set the temperature at 350°F (177°C) and spritz with cooking spray.

2. Combine the chicken meat, salsa verde, Cheddar, cumin, and black pepper in a large bowl. Stir to mix well. Set aside.

3. Unfold the pie crusts on a clean work surface, then use a large cookie cutter to cut out 3½-inch circles as much as possible.

4. Roll the remaining crusts to a ball and flatten into a circle

which has the same thickness of the original crust. Cut out more 3½-inch circles until you have 12 circles in total.

5. Make the empanadas: Divide the chicken mixture in the middle of each circle, about 1½ tablespoons each. Dab the edges of the circle with water. Fold the circle in half over the filling to shape like a half-moon and press to seal, or you can press with a fork.

6. Whisk the egg with water in a small bowl.

7. Arrange six of the empanadas in the preheated air fryer and spritz with cooking spray. Brush with whisked egg. Air fry for 12 minutes or until golden and crispy. Flip the empanadas halfway through..

8. Serve immediately.

33

GOLDEN SMOKY CHICKEN SANDWICH

Prep time: 10 minutes | **Cook time:** 11 minutes | **Serves** 2

2 boneless, skinless chicken breasts (8 ounces / 227 g each), sliced horizontally in half and separated into 4 thinner cutlets

Kosher salt and freshly ground black pepper, to taste

½ cup all-purpose flour

3 large eggs, lightly beaten

½ cup dried bread crumbs

1 tablespoon smoked paprika

Cooking spray

½ cup marinara sauce

6 ounces (170 g) smoked Mozzarella cheese, grated

2 store-bought soft, sesame-seed hamburger or Italian buns, split

1. Press "Pre-Heat", set the temperature at 350°F (177°C).
2. Season the chicken cutlets all over with salt and pepper. Set up three shallow bowls: Place the flour in the first bowl, the eggs in the second, and stir together the bread crumbs and smoked paprika in the third. Coat the chicken pieces in the flour, then dip fully in the egg. Dredge in the paprika bread crumbs, then transfer

to a wire rack set over a baking sheet and spray both sides liberally with cooking spray.

3. Transfer 2 of the chicken cutlets to the air fryer and air fry for 6 minutes, or until beginning to brown. Spread each cutlet with 2 tablespoons of the marinara sauce and sprinkle with one-quarter of the smoked Mozzarella. Increase the temperature to 400°F (204°C) and air fry for 5 minutes more, or until the chicken is cooked through and crisp and the cheese is melted and golden brown.

4. Transfer the cutlets to a plate, stack on top of each other, and place inside a bun. Repeat with the remaining chicken cutlets, marinara, smoked Mozzarella, and bun.

5. Serve the sandwiches warm.

34

SWEET POTATO-BLACK BEAN BURRITOS

Prep time: 15 minutes | **Cook time:** 1 hour | Makes 6 burritos

- 2 sweet potatoes, peeled and cut into a small dice
- 1 tablespoon vegetable oil
- Kosher salt and ground black pepper, to taste
- 6 large flour tortillas
- 1 (16-ounce / 454-g) can refried black beans, divided
- 1½ cups baby spinach, divided
- 6 eggs, scrambled
- ¾ cup grated Cheddar cheese, divided
- ¼ cup salsa
- ¼ cup sour cream
- Cooking spray

1. Press "Pre-Heat", set the temperature at 400°F (204°C).
2. Put the sweet potatoes in a large bowl, then drizzle with vegetable oil and sprinkle with salt and black pepper. Toss to coat well.
3. Place the potatoes in the preheated air fryer and air fry for 10 minutes or until lightly browned. Shake the basket halfway through.

4. Unfold the tortillas on a clean work surface. Divide the black beans, spinach, air fried sweet potatoes, scrambled eggs, and cheese on top of the tortillas.

5. Fold the long side of the tortillas over the filling, then fold in the shorter side to wrap the filling to make the burritos.

6. Work in batches, wrap the burritos in the aluminum foil and put in the air fryer to air fry at 350°F (177°C) for 20 minutes. Flip the burritos halfway through.

7. Remove the burritos from the air fryer and put back to the air fryer. Spritz with cooking spray and air fry for 5 more minutes or until lightly browned. Repeat with remaining burritos.

8. Remove the burritos from the air fryer and spread with sour cream and salsa. Serve immediately.

35

THAI CURRY PORK SLIDERS

Prep time: 10 minutes | **Cook time:** 14 minutes | Makes 6 sliders

1 pound (454 g) ground pork
1 tablespoon Thai curry paste
1½ tablespoons fish sauce
¼ cup thinly sliced scallions, white and green parts
2 tablespoons minced peeled fresh ginger
1 tablespoon light brown sugar
1 teaspoon ground black pepper
6 slider buns, split open lengthwise, warmed
Cooking spray

1. Press "Pre-Heat", set the temperature at 375°F (191°C) and spritz with cooking spray.
2. Combine all the ingredients, except for the buns in a large bowl. Stir to mix well.
3. Divide and shape the mixture into six balls, then bash the balls into six 3-inch-diameter patties.
4. Arrange the patties in the preheated air
5. Arrange the patties in the preheated air fryer and spritz with

cooking spray. Air fry for 14 minutes or until well browned. Flip the patties halfway through.

6.Assemble the buns with patties to make the sliders and serve immediately.

36

TUNA STEAK AND LETTUCE WRAPS

Prep time: 10 minutes | **Cook time:** 4 to 7 minutes | **Serves** 4

1 pound (454 g) fresh tuna steak, cut into 1-inch cubes
1 tablespoon grated fresh ginger
2 garlic cloves, minced
½ teaspoon toasted sesame oil
4 low-sodium whole-wheat tortillas
¼ cup low-fat mayonnaise
2 cups shredded romaine lettuce
1 red bell pepper, thinly sliced

1. Press "Pre-Heat", set the temperature at 390°F (199°C).
2. In a medium bowl, mix the tuna, ginger, garlic, and sesame oil. Let it stand for 10 minutes.
3. Air fry the tuna in the air fryer basket for 4 to 7 minutes, or until lightly browned.
4. Make the wraps with the tuna, tortillas, mayonnaise, lettuce, and bell pepper.
5. Serve immediately.

37

EASY TURKEY SLIDERS WITH CHIVE MAYO

Prep time: 10 minutes | **Cook time:** 15 minutes | **Serves** 6

12 burger buns
Cooking spray
For the Turkey Sliders:
¾ pound (340 g) turkey, minced
1 tablespoon oyster sauce
¼ cup pickled jalapeno, chopped
2 tablespoons chopped scallions
1 tablespoon chopped fresh cilantro
1 to 2 cloves garlic, minced
Sea salt and ground black pepper, to taste
For the Chive Mayo:
1 tablespoon chives
1 cup mayonnaise
Zest of 1 lime
1 teaspoon salt

1.Repeat the air fryer to 365°F (185°C) and spritz with cooking spray.

2.Combine the ingredients for the turkey sliders in a large

bowl. Stir to mix well. Shape the mixture into 6 balls, then bash the balls into patties.

3.Arrange the patties in the preheated air fryer and spritz with cooking spray. Air fry for 15 minutes or until well browned. Flip the patties halfway through.

4.Meanwhile, combine the ingredients for the chive mayo in a small bowl. Stir to mix well.

5.Smear the patties with chive mayo, then assemble the patties between two buns to make the sliders. Serve immediately.

38

TURKEY AND VEGGIES HAMBURGER

Prep time: 10 minutes | **Cook time:** 20 minutes | **Serves** 4

1 cup leftover turkey, cut into bite-sized chunks
1 leek, sliced
1 Serrano pepper, deveined and chopped
2 bell peppers, deveined and chopped
2 tablespoons Tabasco sauce
½ cup sour cream
1 heaping tablespoon fresh cilantro, chopped
1 teaspoon hot paprika
¾ teaspoon kosher salt
½ teaspoon ground black pepper
4 hamburger buns
Cooking spray

1. Press "Pre-Heat", set the temperature at 385°F (196°C). Spritz a baking pan with cooking spray.

2. Mix all the ingredients, except for the buns, in a large bowl. Toss to combine well.

3. Pour the mixture in the baking pan and place in the air fryer. Bake for 20 minutes or until the turkey is well browned and the leek is tender.

4. Assemble the hamburger buns with the turkey mixture and serve immediately.

39

CHEESY VEGGIES SALSA WRAPS

Prep time: 5 minutes | **Cook time:** 7 minutes | **Serves** 4

1 cup red onion, sliced
1 zucchini, chopped
1 poblano pepper, deseeded and finely chopped
1 head lettuce
½ cup salsa
8 ounces (227 g) Mozzarella cheese

1. Press "Pre-Heat", set the temperature at 390°F (199°C).
2. Place the red onion, zucchini, and poblano pepper in the air fryer basket and air fry for 7 minutes, or until they are tender and fragrant.
3. Divide the veggie mixture among the lettuce leaves and spoon the salsa over the top. Finish off with Mozzarella cheese. Wrap the lettuce leaves around the filling.
4. Serve immediately.

BREAKFAST

40

AIR-FRIED ALL-IN-ONE TOAST

Prep time: 10 minutes | **Cook time:** 10 minutes | **Serves** 1

1 strip bacon, diced
1 slice 1-inch thick bread
1 egg
Salt and freshly ground black pepper, to taste
¼ cup grated Colby cheese

1. Press "Pre-Heat", set the temperature at 400°F (204°C).
2. Air fry the bacon for 3 minutes, shaking the basket once or twice while it cooks. Remove the bacon to a paper towel lined plate and set aside.
3. Use a sharp paring knife to score a large circle in the middle of the slice of bread, cutting halfway through, but not all the way through to the cutting board. Press down on the circle in the center of the bread slice to create an indentation.
4. Transfer the slice of bread, hole side up, to the air fryer basket. Crack the egg into the center of the bread, and season with salt and pepper.
5. Adjust the air fryer temperature to 380°F (193°C) and air fry for 5 minutes. Sprinkle the grated cheese around the edges of the bread, leaving the center of the yolk uncovered, and top with the

cooked bacon. Press the cheese and bacon into the bread lightly to help anchor it to the bread and prevent it from blowing around in the air fryer.

6.Air fry for one or two more minutes, just to melt the cheese and finish cooking the egg. Serve immediately.

41

ASPARAGUS SPEARS AND CHEESE STRATA

Prep time: 10 minutes | **Cook time:** 14 to 19 minutes | **Serves** 4

6 asparagus spears, cut into 2-inch pieces
1 tablespoon water
2 slices whole-wheat bread, cut into ½-inch cubes
4 eggs
3 tablespoons whole milk
2 tablespoons chopped flat-leaf parsley
½ cup grated Havarti or Swiss cheese
Pinch salt
Freshly ground black pepper, to taste
Cooking spray

1. Press "Pre-Heat", set the temperature at 330°F (166°C).
2. Add the asparagus spears and 1 tablespoon of water in a baking pan and transfer to the air fryer basket. Bake for 3 to 5 minutes until crisp-tender. Remove the asparagus from the pan and drain on paper towels. Spritz the pan with cooking spray.
3. Place the bread and asparagus in the pan.
4. Whisk together the eggs and milk in a medium mixing bowl

until creamy. Fold in the parsley, cheese, salt, and pepper and stir to combine. Pour this mixture into the baking pan.

5.Bake for 11 to 14 minutes or until the eggs are set and the top is lightly browned.

6.Let cool for 5 minutes before slicing and serving.

42

SIMPLE BACON AND EGG BREAD CUPS

Prep time: 10 minutes | **Cook time:** 8 to 12 minutes | **Serves** 4

4 (3-by-4-inch) crusty rolls

4 thin slices Gouda or Swiss cheese mini wedges

5 eggs

2 tablespoons heavy cream

3 strips precooked bacon, chopped

½ teaspoon dried thyme

Pinch salt

Freshly ground black pepper, to taste

1. Press "Pre-Heat", set the temperature at 330°F (166°C).

2. On a clean work surface, cut the tops off the rolls. Using your fingers, remove the insides of the rolls to make bread cups, leaving a ½-inch shell. Place a slice of cheese onto each roll bottom.

3. Whisk together the eggs and heavy cream in a medium bowl until well combined. Fold in the bacon, thyme, salt, and pepper and stir well.

4. Scrape the egg mixture into the prepared bread cups.

5. Transfer the bread cups to the basket and bake for 8 to 12 minutes, or until the eggs are cooked to your preference.
6. Serve warm.

43

EASY BACON EGGS ON THE GO

Prep time: 5 minutes | **Cook time:** 15 minutes | **Serves** 1

2 eggs

4 ounces (113 g) bacon, cooked

Salt and ground black pepper, to taste

1.Press "Pre-Heat", set the temperature at 400°F (204°C). Put liners in a regular cupcake tin.

2.Crack an egg into each of the cups and add the bacon. Season with some pepper and salt.

3.Bake in the preheated air fryer for 15 minutes, or until the eggs are set.

4.Serve warm.

44

HERBED BACON HOT DOGS

Prep time: 5 minutes | **Cook time:** 15 minutes | **Serves** 4

3 brazilian sausages, cut into 3 equal pieces

9 slices bacon

1 tablespoon Italian herbs

Salt and ground black pepper, to taste

1. Press "Pre-Heat", set the temperature at 355°F (179°C).

2. Take each slice of bacon and wrap around each piece of sausage. Sprinkle with Italian herbs, salt and pepper.

3. Air fry the sausages in the preheated air fryer for 15 minutes.

4. Serve warm.

45

SWEET BANANA AND OAT BREAD PUDDING

Prep time: 10 minutes | **Cook time:** 16 to 20 minutes | **Serves** 4

- 2 medium ripe bananas, mashed
- ½ cup low-fat milk
- 2 tablespoons maple syrup
- 2 tablespoons peanut butter
- 1 teaspoon vanilla extract
- 1 teaspoon ground cinnamon
- 2 slices whole-grain bread, cut into bite-sized cubes
- ¼ cup quick oats
- Cooking spray

1. Press "Pre-Heat", set the temperature at 350°F (177°C). Spritz a baking dish lightly with cooking spray.
2. Mix the bananas, milk, maple syrup, peanut butter, vanilla, and cinnamon in a large mixing bowl and stir until well incorporated.
3. Add the bread cubes to the banana mixture and stir until thoroughly coated. Fold in the oats and stir to combine.
4. Transfer the mixture to the baking dish. Wrap the baking dish in aluminum foil.

5.Air fry in the preheated air fryer for 10 to 12 minutes until heated through.

6.Remove the foil and cook for an additional 6 to 8 minutes, or until the pudding has set.

7.Let the pudding cool for 5 minutes before serving.

46

MAPLE BLUEBERRY COBBLER

Prep time: 5 minutes | **Cook time:** 15 minutes | **Serves** 4

¾ teaspoon baking powder
⅓ cup whole-wheat pastry flour
Dash sea salt
⅓ cup unsweetened nondairy milk
2 tablespoons maple syrup
½ teaspoon vanilla
Cooking spray
½ cup blueberries
¼ cup granola
Nondairy yogurt, for topping (optional)

1. Press "Pre-Heat", set the temperature at 347°F (175°C). Spritz a baking pan with cooking spray.
2. Mix together the baking powder, flour, and salt in a medium bowl. Add the milk, maple syrup, and vanilla and whisk to combine.
3. Scrape the mixture into the prepared pan. Scatter the blueberries and granola on top.
4. Transfer the pan to the air fryer and bake for 15 minutes, or

until the top begins to brown and a knife inserted in the center comes out clean.

5.Let the cobbler cool for 5 minutes and serve with a drizzle of nondairy yogurt.

47

SAUSAGE AND CAULIFLOWER CASSEROLE

Prep time: 5 minutes | **Cook time:** 45 minutes | **Serves** 4

1 pound (454 g) sausage, cooked and crumbled
2 cups heavy whipping cream
1 head cauliflower, chopped
1 cup grated Cheddar cheese, plus more for topping
8 eggs, beaten
Salt and ground black pepper, to taste

1. Press "Pre-Heat", set the temperature at 350°F (177°C).
2. In a large bowl, mix the sausage, heavy whipping cream, chopped cauliflower, cheese and eggs. Sprinkle with salt and ground black pepper.
3. Pour the mixture into a greased casserole dish. Bake in the preheated air fryer for 45 minutes or until firm.
4. Top with more Cheddar cheese and serve.

48

SAUSAGE AND TATER TOT CASSEROLE

Prep time: 5 minutes | **Cook time:** 17 to 19 minutes | **Serves** 4

4 eggs
1 cup milk
Salt and pepper, to taste
12 ounces (340 g) ground chicken sausage
1 pound (454 g) frozen tater tots, thawed
¾ cup grated Cheddar cheese
Cooking spray

1. Whisk together the eggs and milk in a medium bowl. Season with salt and pepper to taste and stir until mixed. Set aside.

2. Place a skillet over medium-high heat and spritz with cooking spray. Place the ground sausage in the skillet and break it into smaller pieces with a spatula or spoon. Cook for 3 to 4 minutes until the sausage starts to brown, stirring occasionally. Remove from heat and set aside.

3. Press "Pre-Heat", set the temperature at 400°F (204°C). Coat a baking pan with cooking spray.

4. Arrange the tater tots in the baking pan. Bake in the

preheated air fryer for 6 minutes. Shake the basket and stir in the egg mixture and cooked sausage. Bake for another 6 minutes.

5. Scatter the cheese on top of the tater tots. Continue to bake for 2 to 3 minutes more until the cheese is bubbly and melted.

6. Let the mixture cool for 5 minutes and serve warm.

49

CHEESY BACON CASSEROLE

Prep time: 10 minutes | **Cook time:** 14 minutes | **Serves** 4

6 slices bacon

6 eggs

Salt and pepper, to taste

Cooking spray

½ cup chopped green bell pepper

½ cup chopped onion

¾ cup shredded Cheddar cheese

1. Place the bacon in a skillet over medium-high heat and cook each side for about 4 minutes until evenly crisp. Remove from the heat to a paper towel-lined plate to drain. Crumble it into small pieces and set aside.

2. Whisk the eggs with the salt and pepper in a medium bowl.

3. Press "Pre-Heat", set the temperature at 400°F (204°C). Spritz a baking pan with cooking spray.

4. Place the whisked eggs, crumbled bacon, green bell pepper, and onion in the prepared pan. Bake in the preheated air fryer for 6 minutes.

5. Scatter the Cheddar cheese all over and bake for 2 minutes more.

6. Allow to sit for 5 minutes and serve on plates.

50

CHEESY HASH BROWN CASSEROLE

Prep time: 15 minutes | **Cook time:** 30 minutes | **Serves** 4

3½ cups frozen hash browns, thawed
1 teaspoon salt
1 teaspoon freshly ground black pepper
3 tablespoons butter, melted
1 (10.5-ounce / 298-g) can cream of chicken soup
½ cup sour cream
1 cup minced onion
½ cup shredded sharp Cheddar cheese
Cooking spray

1. Put the hash browns in a large bowl and season with salt and black pepper. Add the melted butter, cream of chicken soup, and sour cream and stir until well incorporated. Mix in the minced onion and cheese and stir well.
2. Press "Pre-Heat", set the temperature at 325°F (163°C). Spray a baking pan with cooking spray.
3. Spread the hash brown mixture evenly into the baking pan.
4. Place the pan in the air fryer basket and bake for 30 minutes until browned.
5. Cool for 5 minutes before serving.

51

APPLE-CHICKEN PATTIES

Prep time: 15 minutes | **Cook time:** 8 to 12 minutes | Makes 8 patties

1 Granny Smith apple, peeled and finely chopped
2 tablespoons apple juice
2 garlic cloves, minced
1 egg white
1/3 cup minced onion
3 tablespoons ground almonds
1/8 teaspoon freshly ground black pepper
1 pound (454 g) ground chicken breast

1. Press "Pre-Heat", set the temperature at 330°F (166°C).
2. Combine all the ingredients except the chicken in a medium mixing bowl and stir well.
3. Add the chicken breast to the apple mixture and mix with your hands until well incorporated.
4. Divide the mixture into 8 equal portions and shape into patties. Arrange the patties in the air fryer basket. You may need to work in batches depending on the size of your air fryer basket.
5. Air fry for 8 to 12 minutes, or until a meat thermometer inserted in the center of the chicken reaches at least 165°F (74°C).

6. Remove from the air fryer to a plate and repeat with the remaining patties.

7. Let the chicken cool for 5 minutes and serve warm.

52

CHOCOLATE, BANANA, AND WALNUT BREAD

Prep time: 10 minutes | **Cook time:** 30 minutes | **Serves** 4

¼ cup cocoa powder
6 tablespoons plus 2 teaspoons all-purpose flour, divided
½ teaspoon kosher salt
¼ teaspoon baking soda
1 ½ ripe bananas
1 large egg, whisked
¼ cup vegetable oil
½ cup sugar
3 tablespoons buttermilk or plain yogurt (not Greek)
½ teaspoon vanilla extract
6 tablespoons chopped white chocolate
6 tablespoons chopped walnuts

1. Press "Pre-Heat", set the temperature at 310°F (154°C).
2. Mix together the cocoa powder, 6 tablespoons of the flour, salt, and baking soda in a medium bowl.
3. Mash the bananas with a fork in another medium bowl until smooth. Fold in the egg, oil, sugar, buttermilk, and vanilla, and whisk until thoroughly combined. Add the wet mixture to the dry mixture and stir until well incorporated.

4. Combine the white chocolate, walnuts, and the remaining 2 tablespoons of flour in a third bowl and toss to coat. Add this mixture to the batter and stir until well incorporated. Pour the batter into a baking pan and smooth the top with a spatula.

5. Bake in the preheated air fryer for about 30 minutes. Check the bread for doneness: If a toothpick inserted into the center of the bread comes out clean, it's done.

6. Remove from the air fryer and allow to cool on a wire rack for 10 minutes before serving.

53

FULL BREAKFAST

Prep time: 5 minutes | **Cook time:** 25 minutes | **Serves** 2

1 cup potatoes, sliced and diced

2 cups beans in tomato sauce

2 eggs

1 tablespoon olive oil

1 sausage

Salt, to taste

1. Press "Pre-Heat", set the temperature at 390°F (199°C) and allow to warm.

2. Break the eggs onto a baking dish and sprinkle with salt.

3. Lay the beans on the dish, next to the eggs.

4. In a bowl, coat the potatoes with the olive oil. Sprinkle with salt.

5. Transfer the bowl of potato slices to the air fryer and bake for 10 minutes.

6. Swap out the bowl of potatoes for the dish containing the eggs and beans. Bake for another 10 minutes. Cover the potatoes with parchment paper.

7. Slice up the sausage and throw the slices on top of the beans and eggs. Bake for another 5 minutes.

8. Serve with the potatoes.

54

CREAMY COCONUT BROWN RICE PORRIDGE

Prep time: 5 minutes | **Cook time:** 23 minutes | **Serves** 1 or 2

½ cup cooked brown rice
1 cup canned coconut milk
¼ cup unsweetened shredded coconut
¼ cup packed dark brown sugar
4 large Medjool dates, pitted and roughly chopped
½ teaspoon kosher salt
¼ teaspoon ground cardamom
Heavy cream, for serving (optional)

1. Press "Pre-Heat", set the temperature at 375°F (191°C).
2. Place all the ingredients except the heavy cream in a baking pan and stir until blended.
3. Transfer the pan to the air fryer and bake for about 23 minutes until the porridge is thick and creamy. Stir the porridge halfway through the cooking time.
4. Remove from the air fryer and ladle the porridge into bowls.
5. Serve hot with a drizzle of the cream, if desired.

55

GOLDEN CRUSTLESS BROCCOLI QUICHE

Prep time: 5 minutes | **Cook time:** 10 minutes | **Serves** 4

1 cup broccoli florets
¾ cup chopped roasted red peppers
1¼ cups grated Fontina cheese
6 eggs
¾ cup heavy cream
½ teaspoon salt
Freshly ground black pepper, to taste
Cooking spray

1. Press "Pre-Heat", set the temperature at 325°F (163°C). Spritz a baking pan with cooking spray

2. Add the broccoli florets and roasted red peppers to the pan and scatter the grated Fontina cheese on top.

3. In a bowl, beat together the eggs and heavy cream. Sprinkle with salt and pepper. Pour the egg mixture over the top of the cheese. Wrap the pan in foil.

4. Transfer the pan to the air fryer and air fry for 8 minutes. Remove the foil and continue to cook another 2 minutes until the quiche is golden brown.

5.Rest for 5 minutes before cutting into wedges and serve warm.

56

FAST SAUSAGE PIZZA

Prep time: 10 minutes | **Cook time:** 6 minutes | **Serves** 4

2 tablespoons ketchup
1 pita bread
⅓ cup sausage
½ pound (227 g) Mozzarella cheese
1 teaspoon garlic powder
1 tablespoon olive oil

1. Press "Pre-Heat", set the temperature at 340°F (171°C).
2. Spread the ketchup over the pita bread.
3. Top with the sausage and cheese. Sprinkle with the garlic powder and olive oil.
4. Put the pizza in the air fryer basket and bake for 6 minutes.
5. Serve warm.

57

CRISPY EGG AND AVOCADO BURRITO

Prep time: 10 minutes | **Cook time:** 3 to 5 minutes | **Serves** 4

4 low-sodium whole-wheat flour tortillas
Filling:
1 hard-boiled egg, chopped
2 hard-boiled egg whites, chopped
1 ripe avocado, peeled, pitted, and chopped
1 red bell pepper, chopped
1 (1.2-ounce / 34-g) slice low-sodium, low-fat American cheese, torn into pieces
3 tablespoons low-sodium salsa, plus additional for serving (optional)
Special Equipment:
4 toothpicks (optional), soaked in water for at least 30 minutes

1. Press "Pre-Heat", set the temperature at 390°F (199°C).
2. Make the filling: Combine the egg, egg whites, avocado, red bell pepper, cheese, and salsa in a medium bowl and stir until blended.
3. Assemble the burritos: Arrange the tortillas on a clean work surface and place ¼ of the prepared filling in the middle of each

tortilla, leaving about 1½-inch on each end unfilled. Fold in the opposite sides of each tortilla and roll up. Secure with toothpicks through the center, if needed.

4. Transfer the burritos to the air fryer basket and air fry for 3 to 5 minutes, or until the burritos are crisp and golden brown.

5. Allow to cool for 5 minutes and serve with salsa, if desired.

58

CHEESY EGG AND BACON MUFFINS

Prep time: 5 minutes | **Cook time:** 15 minutes | **Serves** 1

2 eggs

Salt and ground black pepper, to taste

1 tablespoon green pesto

3 ounces (85 g) shredded Cheddar cheese

5 ounces (142 g) cooked bacon

1 scallion, chopped

1. Press "Pre-Heat", set the temperature at 350°F (177°C). Line a cupcake tin with parchment paper.

2. Beat the eggs with pepper, salt, and pesto in a bowl. Mix in the cheese.

3. Pour the eggs into the cupcake tin and top with the bacon and scallion.

4. Bake in the preheated air fryer for 15 minutes, or until the egg is set.

5. Serve immediately.

59

AIR-FRIED POTATOES WITH VEGGIES

Prep time: 10 minutes | **Cook time:** 35 minutes | **Serves** 4

1 pound (454 g) red potatoes, cut into ½-inch dices
1 large red bell pepper, cut into ½-inch dices
1 large green bell pepper, cut into ½-inch dices
1 medium onion, cut into ½-inch dices
1½ tablespoons extra-virgin olive oil
1¼ teaspoons kosher salt
¾ teaspoon sweet paprika
¾ teaspoon garlic powder
Freshly ground black pepper, to taste

1. Press "Pre-Heat", set the temperature at 350°F (177°C).
2. Mix together the potatoes, bell peppers, onion, oil, salt, paprika, garlic powder, and black pepper in a large mixing and toss to coat.
3. Transfer the potato mixture to the air fryer basket and air fry for about 35 minutes, or until the potatoes are nicely browned. Shake the basket three times during cooking.
4. Remove from the basket to a plate and serve warm.

60

GOLDEN AVOCADO

Prep time: 5 minutes | **Cook time:** 6 minutes | **Serves** 4

2 large avocados, sliced
¼ teaspoon paprika
Salt and ground black pepper, to taste
½ cup flour
2 eggs, beaten
1 cup bread crumbs

1. Press "Pre-Heat", set the temperature at 400°F (204°C).
2. Sprinkle paprika, salt and pepper on the slices of avocado.
3. Lightly coat the avocados with flour. Dredge them in the eggs, before covering with bread crumbs.
4. Transfer to the air fryer and air fry for 6 minutes.
5. Serve warm.

61

CRISPY AVOCADO TEMPURA

Prep time: 5 minutes | **Cook time:** 10 minutes | **Serves** 4

½ cup bread crumbs

½ teaspoons salt

1 Haas avocado, pitted, peeled and sliced

Liquid from 1 can white beans

1. Press "Pre-Heat", set the temperature at 350°F (177°C).

2. Mix the bread crumbs and salt in a shallow bowl until well-incorporated.

3. Dip the avocado slices in the bean liquid, then into the bread crumbs.

4. Put the avocados in the air fryer, taking care not to overlap any slices, and air fry for 10 minutes, giving the basket a good shake at the halfway point.

5. Serve immediately.

62

LUSH CHEDDAR BISCUITS

Prep time: 10 minutes | **Cook time:** 22 minutes | Makes 8 biscuits

2⅓ cups self-rising flour

2 tablespoons sugar

½ cup butter (1 stick), frozen for 15 minutes

½ cup grated Cheddar cheese, plus more to melt on top

1⅓ cups buttermilk

1 cup all-purpose flour, for shaping

1 tablespoon butter, melted

1. Line a buttered 7-inch metal cake pan with parchment paper or a silicone liner.

2. Combine the flour and sugar in a large mixing bowl. Grate the butter into the flour. Add the grated cheese and stir to coat the cheese and butter with flour. Then add the buttermilk and stir just until you can no longer see streaks of flour. The dough should be quite wet.

3. Spread the all-purpose (not self-rising) flour out on a small cookie sheet. With a spoon, scoop 8 evenly sized balls of dough into the flour, making sure they don't touch each other. With floured hands, coat each dough ball with flour and toss them

gently from hand to hand to shake off any excess flour. Put each floured dough ball into the prepared pan, right up next to the other. This will help the biscuits rise, rather than spreading out.

4. Press "Pre-Heat", set the temperature at 380°F (193°C).

5. Transfer the cake pan to the basket of the air fryer. Let the ends of the aluminum foil sling hang across the cake pan before returning the basket to the air fryer.

6. Air fry for 20 minutes. Check the biscuits twice to make sure they are not getting too brown on top. If they are, re-arrange the aluminum foil strips to cover any brown parts. After 20 minutes, check the biscuits by inserting a toothpick into the center of the biscuits. It should come out clean. If it needs a little more time, continue to air fry for two extra minutes. Brush the tops of the biscuits with some melted butter and sprinkle a little more grated cheese on top if desired. Pop the basket back into the air fryer for another 2 minutes.

7. Remove the cake pan from the air fryer. Let the biscuits cool for just a minute or two and then turn them out onto a plate and pull apart. Serve immediately.

63

AIR-FRIED KALE AND POTATO NUGGETS

Prep time: 10 minutes | **Cook time:** 18 minutes | **Serves** 4

1 teaspoon extra virgin olive oil
1 clove garlic, minced
4 cups kale, rinsed and chopped
2 cups potatoes, boiled and mashed
⅛ cup milk
Salt and ground black pepper, to taste
Cooking spray

1. Press "Pre-Heat", set the temperature at 390°F (199°C).
2. In a skillet over medium heat, sauté the garlic in the olive oil, until it turns golden brown. Sauté with the kale for an additional 3 minutes and remove from the heat.
3. Mix the mashed potatoes, kale and garlic in a bowl. Pour in the milk and sprinkle with salt and pepper.
4. Shape the mixture into nuggets and spritz with cooking spray.
5. Put in the air fryer basket and air fry for 15 minutes, flip the nuggets halfway through cooking to make sure the nuggets fry evenly.
6. Serve immediately.

64

SWEET WALNUT PANCAKE

Prep time: 10 minutes | **Cook time:** 20 minutes | **Serves** 4

3 tablespoons melted butter, divided
1 cup flour
2 tablespoons sugar
1½ teaspoons baking powder
¼ teaspoon salt
1 egg, beaten
¾ cup milk
1 teaspoon pure vanilla extract
½ cup roughly chopped walnuts
Maple syrup or fresh sliced fruit, for serving

1. Press "Pre-Heat", set the temperature at 330°F (166°C). Grease a baking pan with 1 tablespoon of melted butter.

2. Mix together the flour, sugar, baking powder, and salt in a medium bowl. Add the beaten egg, milk, the remaining 2 tablespoons of melted butter, and vanilla and stir until the batter is sticky but slightly lumpy.

3. Slowly pour the batter into the greased baking pan and scatter with the walnuts.

4.Place the pan in the air fryer basket and bake for 20 minutes until golden brown and cooked through.

5.Let the pancake rest for 5 minutes and serve topped with the maple syrup or fresh fruit, if desired.

65

CHEESY TOMATO AND BASIL BRUSCHETTA

Prep time: 5 minutes | **Cook time:** 4 minutes | **Serves** 1

½ cup tomatoes, finely chopped

3 ounces (85 g) Mozzarella cheese, grated

1 tablespoon fresh basil, chopped

1 tablespoon olive oil

1. Press "Pre-Heat", set the temperature at 350°F (177°C).

2. Put the loaf slices inside the air fryer and air fry for about 3 minutes.

3. Add the tomato, Mozzarella, basil, and olive oil on top.

4. Air fry for an additional minute before serving.

66

MIXED-BERRY DUTCH BABY

Prep time: 10 minutes | **Cook time:** 12 to 16 minutes | **Serves** 4

1 tablespoon unsalted butter, at room temperature
1 egg
2 egg whites
½ cup 2% milk
½ cup whole-wheat pastry flour
1 teaspoon pure vanilla extract
1 cup sliced fresh strawberries
½ cup fresh raspberries
½ cup fresh blueberries

1. Press "Pre-Heat", set the temperature at 330°F (166°C). Grease a baking pan with the butter.

2. Using a hand mixer, beat together the egg, egg whites, milk, pastry flour, and vanilla in a medium mixing bowl until well incorporated.

3. Pour the batter into the pan and bake in the preheated air fryer for 12 to 16 minutes, or until the pancake puffs up in the center and the edges are golden brown.

4.Allow the pancake to cool for 5 minutes and serve topped with the berries.

67

HONEY OAT AND CHIA PORRIDGE

Prep time: 10 minutes | **Cook time:** 5 minutes | **Serves** 4

2 tablespoons peanut butter
4 tablespoons honey
1 tablespoon butter, melted
4 cups milk
2 cups oats
1 cup chia seeds

1. Press "Pre-Heat", set the temperature at 390°F (199°C).
2. Put the peanut butter, honey, butter, and milk in a bowl and stir to mix. Add the oats and chia seeds and stir.
3. Transfer the mixture to a bowl and bake in the air fryer for 5 minutes. Give another stir before serving.

68

OLIVES, KALE, AND ALMOND BAKED EGGS

Prep time: 5 minutes | **Cook time:** 10 to 12 minutes | **Serves** 2

1 cup roughly chopped kale leaves, stems and center ribs removed

¼ cup grated pecorino cheese

¼ cup olive oil

1 garlic clove, peeled

3 tablespoons whole almonds

Kosher salt and freshly ground black pepper, to taste

4 large eggs

2 tablespoons heavy cream

3 tablespoons chopped pitted mixed olives

1. Place the kale, pecorino, olive oil, garlic, almonds, salt, and pepper in a small blender and blitz until well incorporated.

2. Press "Pre-Heat", set the temperature at 300°F (149°C).

3. One at a time, crack the eggs in a baking pan. Drizzle the kale pesto on top of the egg whites. Top the yolks with the cream and swirl together the yolks and the pesto.

4. Transfer the pan to the air fryer basket and bake for 10 to 12 minutes, or until the top begins to brown and the eggs are set.

Breakfast

5.Allow the eggs to cool for 5 minutes. Scatter the olives on top and serve warm.

69

CHEESY ONION OMELET

Prep time: 10 minutes | **Cook time:** 12 minutes | **Serves** 2

3 eggs
Salt and ground black pepper, to taste
½ teaspoons soy sauce
1 large onion, chopped
2 tablespoons grated Cheddar cheese
Cooking spray

1. Press "Pre-Heat", set the temperature at 355°F (179°C).
2. In a bowl, whisk together the eggs, salt, pepper, and soy sauce.
3. Spritz a small pan with cooking spray. Spread the chopped onion across the bottom of the pan, then transfer the pan to the air fryer.
4. Bake in the preheated air fryer for 6 minutes or until the onion is translucent.
5. Add the egg mixture on top of the onions to coat well. Add the cheese on top, then continue baking for another 6 minutes.
6. Allow to cool before serving.

70

CREAMY PARMESAN RANCH RISOTTO

Prep time: 10 minutes | **Cook time:** 30 minutes | **Serves** 2

1 tablespoon olive oil

1 clove garlic, minced

1 tablespoon unsalted butter

1 onion, diced

¾ cup Arborio rice

2 cups chicken stock, boiling

½ cup Parmesan cheese, grated

1. Press "Pre-Heat", set the temperature at 390°F (199°C).

2. Grease a round baking tin with olive oil and stir in the garlic, butter, and onion.

3. Transfer the tin to the air fryer and bake for 4 minutes. Add the rice and bake for 4 more minutes.

4. Turn the air fryer to 320°F (160°C) and pour in the chicken stock. Cover and bake for 22 minutes.

5. Scatter with cheese and serve.

71

PARMESAN SAUSAGE AND EGG MUFFINS

Prep time: 5 minutes | **Cook time:** 20 minutes | **Serves** 4

6 ounces (170 g) Italian sausage, sliced
6 eggs
⅛ cup heavy cream
Salt and ground black pepper, to taste
3 ounces (85 g) Parmesan cheese, grated

1. Press "Pre-Heat", set the temperature at 350°F (177°C). Grease a muffin pan.
2. Put the sliced sausage in the muffin pan.
3. Beat the eggs with the cream in a bowl and season with salt and pepper.
4. Pour half of the mixture over the sausages in the pan.
5. Sprinkle with cheese and the remaining egg mixture.
6. Bake in the preheated air fryer for 20 minutes or until set.
7. Serve immediately.

72

FAST PITA AND PEPPERONI PIZZA

Prep time: 10 minutes | **Cook time:** 6 minutes | **Serves** 1

1 teaspoon olive oil
1 tablespoon pizza sauce
1 pita bread
6 pepperoni slices
¼ cup grated Mozzarella cheese
¼ teaspoon garlic powder
¼ teaspoon dried oregano

1. Press "Pre-Heat", set the temperature at 350°F (177°C). Grease the air fryer basket with olive oil.
2. Spread the pizza sauce on top of the pita bread. Put the pepperoni slices over the sauce, followed by the Mozzarella cheese.
3. Season with garlic powder and oregano.
4. Put the pita pizza inside the air fryer and place a trivet on top.
5. Bake in the preheated air fryer for 6 minutes and serve.

73

CLASSIC POTATOES LYONNAISE

Prep time: 10 minutes | **Cook time:** 31 minutes | **Serves** 4

1 Vidalia onion, sliced

1 teaspoon butter, melted

1 teaspoon brown sugar

2 large russet potatoes (about 1 pound / 454 g in total), sliced ½-inch thick

1 tablespoon vegetable oil

Salt and freshly ground black pepper, to taste

1. Press "Pre-Heat", set the temperature at 370°F (188°C).

2. Toss the sliced onions, melted butter and brown sugar together in the air fryer basket. Air fry for 8 minutes, shaking the basket occasionally to help the onions cook evenly.

3. While the onions are cooking, bring a saucepan of salted water to a boil on the stovetop. Par-cook the potatoes in boiling water for 3 minutes. Drain the potatoes and pat them dry with a clean kitchen towel.

4. Add the potatoes to the onions in the air fryer basket and drizzle with vegetable oil. Toss to coat the potatoes with the oil and season with salt and freshly ground black pepper.

5. Increase the air fryer temperature to 400°F (204°C) and air fry for 20 minutes, tossing the vegetables a few times during the cooking time to help the potatoes brown evenly.

6. Season with salt and freshly ground black pepper and serve warm.

74

SIMPLE BLUEBERRY MUFFINS

Prep time: 10 minutes | **Cook time:** 12 minutes | Makes 8 muffins

1 1/3 cups flour
1/2 cup sugar
2 teaspoons baking powder
1/4 teaspoon salt
1/3 cup canola oil
1 egg
1/2 cup milk
2/3 cup blueberries, fresh or frozen and thawed

1. Press "Pre-Heat", set the temperature at 330°F (166°C).
2. In a medium bowl, stir together flour, sugar, baking powder, and salt.
3. In a separate bowl, combine oil, egg, and milk and mix well.
4. Add egg mixture to dry ingredients and stir just until moistened.
5. Gently stir in the blueberries.
6. Spoon batter evenly into parchment paper-lined muffin cups.

7. Put 4 muffin cups in air fryer basket and bake for 12 minutes or until tops spring back when touched lightly.
8. Repeat previous step to bake remaining muffins.
9. Serve immediately.

75

GOLDEN SAUSAGE AND CHEESE QUICHE

Prep time: 5 minutes | **Cook time:** 25 minutes | **Serves** 4

12 large eggs
1 cup heavy cream
Salt and black pepper, to taste
12 ounces (340 g) sugar-free breakfast sausage
2 cups shredded Cheddar cheese
Cooking spray

1. Press "Pre-Heat", set the temperature at 375°F (191°C). Coat a casserole dish with cooking spray.

2. Beat together the eggs, heavy cream, salt and pepper in a large bowl until creamy. Stir in the breakfast sausage and Cheddar cheese.

3. Pour the sausage mixture into the prepared casserole dish and bake for 25 minutes, or until the top of the quiche is golden brown and the eggs are set.

4. Remove from the air fryer and let sit for 5 to 10 minutes before serving.

76

FAST CINNAMON TOASTS

Prep time: 5 minutes | **Cook time:** 4 minutes | **Serves** 4

1 tablespoon salted butter
2 teaspoons ground cinnamon
4 tablespoons sugar
½ teaspoon vanilla extract
10 bread slices

1. Press "Pre-Heat", set the temperature at 380°F (193°C).
2. In a bowl, combine the butter, cinnamon, sugar, and vanilla extract. Spread onto the slices of bread.
3. Put the bread inside the air fryer and bake for 4 minutes or until golden brown.
4. Serve warm.

77

SCOTCH EGGS

Prep time: 5 minutes | **Cook time:** 25 minutes | **Serves** 4

4 large hard boiled eggs
1 (12-ounce / 340-g) package pork sausage
8 slices thick-cut bacon
Special Equipment:
4 wooden toothpicks, soaked in water for at least 30 minutes

1. Slice the sausage into four parts and place each part into a large circle.
2. Put an egg into each circle and wrap it in the sausage. Put in the refrigerator for 1 hour.
3. Press "Pre-Heat", set the temperature at 450°F (235°C).
4. Make a cross with two pieces of thick-cut bacon. Put a wrapped egg in the center, fold the bacon over top of the egg, and secure with a toothpick.
5. Air fry in the preheated air fryer for 25 minutes.
6. Serve immediately.

78

MUSHROOM, SPINACH AND LEEK FRITTATA

Prep time: 10 minutes | **Cook time:** 20 to 23 minutes | **Serves** 2

- 4 large eggs
- 4 ounces (113 g) baby bella mushrooms, chopped
- 1 cup (1 ounce / 28-g) baby spinach, chopped
- ½ cup (2 ounces / 57-g) shredded Cheddar cheese
- ⅓ cup (from 1 large) chopped leek, white part only
- ¼ cup halved grape tomatoes
- 1 tablespoon 2% milk
- ¼ teaspoon dried oregano
- ¼ teaspoon garlic powder
- ½ teaspoon kosher salt
- Freshly ground black pepper, to taste
- Cooking spray

1. Press "Pre-Heat", set the temperature at 300°F (149°C). Lightly spritz a baking dish with cooking spray.

2. Whisk the eggs in a large bowl until frothy. Add the mushrooms, baby spinach, cheese, leek, tomatoes, milk, oregano, garlic powder, salt, and pepper and stir until well blended. Pour the mixture into the prepared baking dish.

3. Put the baking dish in the air fryer basket and bake until the center is puffed up and the top is golden brown, about 20 to 23 minutes.

4. Let the frittata cool for 5 minutes before slicing to serve.

79

CHEESY BACON AND HAM CUPS

Prep time: 5 minutes | **Cook time:** 20 minutes | **Serves** 2

3 slices bacon, cooked, sliced in half
2 slices ham
1 slice tomato
2 eggs
2 teaspoons grated Parmesan cheese
Salt and ground black pepper, to taste

1. Press "Pre-Heat", set the temperature at 375°F (191°C). Line 2 greased muffin tins with 3 half-strips of bacon
2. Put one slice of ham and half slice of tomato in each muffin tin on top of the bacon
3. Crack one egg on top of the tomato in each muffin tin and sprinkle each with half a teaspoon of grated Parmesan cheese. Sprinkle with salt and ground black pepper, if desired.
4. Bake in the preheated air fryer for 20 minutes. Remove from the air fryer and let cool.
5. Serve warm.

80

CHEESY FRITTATA WITH AVOCADO DRESSING

Prep time: 10 minutes | **Cook time:** 20 minutes | **Serves** 2 or 3

½ cup cherry tomatoes, halved
Kosher salt and freshly ground black pepper, to taste
6 large eggs, lightly beaten
½ cup corn kernels, thawed if frzoen
¼ cup milk
1 tablespoon finely chopped fresh dill
½ cup shredded Monterey Jack cheese
Avocado Dressing:
1 ripe avocado, pitted and peeled
2 tablespoons fresh lime juice
¼ cup olive oil
1 scallion, finely chopped
8 fresh basil leaves, finely chopped

1.Put the tomato halves in a colander and lightly season with salt. Set aside for 10 minutes to drain well. Pour the tomatoes into a large bowl and fold in the eggs, corn, milk, and dill. Sprinkle with salt and pepper and stir until mixed.

2.Press "Pre-Heat", set the temperature at 300°F (149°C).

3. Pour the egg mixture into a baking pan. Transfer the pan to the air fryer and bake for 15 minutes.

4. Scatter the cheese on top. Increase the air fryer temperature to 315°F (157°C) and continue to cook for another 5 minutes, or until the frittata is puffy and set.

5. Meanwhile, make the avocado dressing: Mash the avocado with the lime juice in a medium bowl until smooth. Mix in the olive oil, scallion, and basil and stir until well incorporated.

6. Let the frittata cool for 5 minutes and serve alongside the avocado dressing.

81

BELL PEPPER, CARROT, AND ONION FRITTATA

Prep time: 10 minutes | **Cook time:** 8 to 12 minutes | **Serves** 4

½ cup chopped red bell pepper

⅓ cup grated carrot

⅓ cup minced onion

1 teaspoon olive oil

1 egg

6 egg whites

⅓ cup 2% milk

1 tablespoon shredded Parmesan cheese

1. Press "Pre-Heat", set the temperature at 350°F (177°C).

2. Mix together the red bell pepper, carrot, onion, and olive oil in a baking pan and stir to combine.

3. Transfer the pan to the air fryer and bake for 4 to 6 minutes until the veggies are soft. Shake the basket once during cooking.

4. Meantime, whisk together the egg, egg whites, and milk in a medium bowl until creamy.

5. When the veggies are done, pour the egg mixture over the top. Scatter with the Parmesan cheese.

6.Bake for an additional 4 to 6 minutes, or until the eggs are set and the top is golden around the edges.

7.Allow the frittata to cool for 5 minutes before slicing and serving.

82

GOLDEN WESTERN OMELET

Prep time: 5 minutes | **Cook time:** 18 to 21 minutes | **Serves** 2

¼ cup chopped bell pepper, green or red
¼ cup chopped onion
¼ cup diced ham
1 teaspoon butter
4 large eggs
2 tablespoons milk
⅛ teaspoon salt
¾ cup shredded sharp Cheddar cheese

1. Press "Pre-Heat", set the temperature at 390°F (199°C).
2. Put the bell pepper, onion, ham, and butter in a baking pan and mix well.
3. Air fry in the preheated air fryer for 1 minute. Stir and continue to cook for an additional 4 to 5 minutes until the veggies are softened.
4. Meanwhile, whisk together the eggs, milk, and salt in a bowl.
5. Pour the egg mixture over the veggie mixture. Reduce the air fryer temperature to 360°F (182°C) and bake for 13 to 15

minutes more, or until the top is lightly golden browned and the eggs are set.

6.Scatter the omelet with the shredded cheese. Bake for another 1 minute until the cheese has melted.

7.Let the omelet cool for 5 minutes before serving.

VEGETABLES

Vegan and Vegetarian

83

AIR-FRIED WINTER VEGETABLES

Prep time: 5 minutes | **Cook time:** 16 minutes | **Serves** 2

1 parsnip, sliced
1 cup sliced butternut squash
1 small red onion, cut into wedges
½ chopped celery stalk
1 tablespoon chopped fresh thyme
2 teaspoons olive oil
Salt and black pepper, to taste

1. Press "Pre-Heat", set the temperature at 380°F (193°C).
2. Toss all the ingredients in a large bowl until the vegetables are well coated.
3. Transfer the vegetables to the air fryer basket and air fry for 16 minutes, shaking the basket halfway through, or until the vegetables are golden brown and tender.
4. Remove from the basket and serve warm.

84

ASIAN SPICY BROCCOLI

Prep time: 5 minutes | **Cook time:** 10 minutes | **Serves** 2

12 ounces (340 g) broccoli florets
2 tablespoons Asian hot chili oil
1 teaspoon ground Sichuan peppercorns (or black pepper)
2 garlic cloves, finely chopped
1 (2-inch) piece fresh ginger, peeled and finely chopped
Kosher salt and freshly ground black pepper

1. Preheat the air fryer t0 375°F (191°C).
2. Toss the broccoli florets with the chili oil, Sichuan peppercorns, garlic, ginger, salt, and pepper in a mixing bowl until thoroughly coated.
3. Transfer the broccoli florets to the air fryer basket and roast for about 10 minutes, shaking the basket halfway through, or until the broccoli florets are lightly browned and tender.
4. Remove the broccoli from the basket and serve on a plate.

85

EASY BALSAMIC BRUSSELS SPROUTS

Prep time: 5 minutes | **Cook time:** 13 minutes | **Serves** 2

2 cups Brussels sprouts, halved
1 tablespoon olive oil
1 tablespoon balsamic vinegar
1 tablespoon maple syrup
¼ teaspoon sea salt

1. Press "Pre-Heat", set the temperature at 375°F (191°C).
2. Evenly coat the Brussels sprouts with the olive oil, balsamic vinegar, maple syrup, and salt.
3. Transfer to the air fryer basket and air fry for 5 minutes. Give the basket a good shake, turn the heat to 400°F (204°C) and continue to air fry for another 8 minutes.
4. Serve hot.

86

CHEESY BASMATI RISOTTO

Prep time: 10 minutes | **Cook time:** 30 minutes | **Serves** 2

1 onion, diced

1 small carrot, diced

2 cups vegetable broth, boiling

½ cup grated Cheddar cheese

1 clove garlic, minced

¾ cup long-grain basmati rice

1 tablespoon olive oil

1 tablespoon unsalted butter

1. Press "Pre-Heat", set the temperature at 390°F (199°C).

2. Grease a baking tin with oil and stir in the butter, garlic, carrot, and onion.

3. Put the tin in the air fryer and bake for 4 minutes.

4. Pour in the rice and bake for a further 4 minutes, stirring three times throughout the baking time.

5. Turn the temperature down to 320°F (160°C).

6. Add the vegetable broth and give the dish a gentle stir. Bake for 22 minutes, leaving the air fryer uncovered.

7. Pour in the cheese, stir once more and serve.

87

HONEY-CARAMELIZED EGGPLANT WITH YOGURT

Prep time: 5 minutes | **Cook time:** 15 minutes | **Serves** 2

1 medium eggplant, quartered and cut crosswise into ½-inch-thick slices

2 tablespoons vegetable oil

Kosher salt and freshly ground black pepper, to taste

½ cup plain yogurt (not Greek)

2 tablespoons harissa paste

1 garlic clove, grated

2 teaspoons honey

1. Press "Pre-Heat", set the temperature at 400°F (204°C).

2. Toss the eggplant slices with the vegetable oil, salt, and pepper in a large bowl until well coated.

3. Arrange the eggplant slices in the air fryer basket and air fry for about 15 minutes until golden brown. Shake the basket two to three times during cooking.

4. Meanwhile, make the yogurt sauce by whisking together the yogurt, harissa paste, and garlic in a small bowl.

5. Spread the yogurt sauce on a platter, and pile the eggplant slices over the top. Serve drizzled with the honey.

88

CRISPY CAYENNE TAHINI KALE

Prep time: 5 minutes | **Cook time:** 15 minutes | **Serves** 2 to 4

Dressing:
¼ cup tahini
¼ cup fresh lemon juice
2 tablespoons olive oil
1 teaspoon sesame seeds
½ teaspoon garlic powder
¼ teaspoon cayenne pepper
Kale:
4 cups packed torn kale leaves (stems and ribs removed and leaves torn into palm-size pieces)
Kosher salt and freshly ground black pepper, to taste

1. Press "Pre-Heat", set the temperature at 350°F (177°C).
2. Make the dressing: Whisk together the tahini, lemon juice, olive oil, sesame seeds, garlic powder, and cayenne pepper in a large bowl until well mixed.
3. Add the kale and massage the dressing thoroughly all over the leaves. Sprinkle the salt and pepper to season.

4.Place the kale in the air fryer basket in a single layer and air fry for about 15 minutes, or until the leaves are slightly wilted and crispy.

5.Remove from the basket and serve on a plate.

89

GOLDEN ASPARAGUS AND POTATO PLATTER

Prep time: 5 minutes | **Cook time:** 26 to 30 minutes | **Serves** 5

4 medium potatoes, cut into wedges
Cooking spray
1 bunch asparagus, trimmed
2 tablespoons olive oil
Salt and pepper, to taste
Cheese Sauce:
¼ cup crumbled cottage cheese2
¼ cup buttermilk
1 tablespoon whole-grain mustard
Salt and black pepper, to taste

1. Press "Pre-Heat", set the temperature at 400°F (204°C). Spritz the air fryer basket with cooking spray.

2. Put the potatoes in the air fryer basket and roast for 20 to 22 minutes until golden brown. Shake the basket halfway through the cooking time.

3. When ready, remove the potatoes from the basket to a platter. Cover the potatoes with foil to keep warm. Set aside.

4. Place the asparagus in the air fryer basket and drizzle with the olive oil. Sprinkle with salt and pepper.

5. Roast for 6 to 8 minutes, shaking the basket once or twice during cooking, or until the asparagus are cooked to your desired crispiness.

6. Meanwhile, make the cheese sauce by stirring together the cottage cheese, buttermilk, and mustard in a small bowl. Season as needed with salt and pepper.

7. Transfer the asparagus to the platter of potatoes and drizzle with the cheese sauce. Serve immediately.

90

PARMESAN CABBAGE WEDGES

Prep time: 5 minutes | **Cook time:** 20 minutes | **Serves** 4

4 tablespoons melted butter
1 head cabbage, cut into wedges
1 cup shredded Parmesan cheese
Salt and black pepper, to taste
½ cup shredded Mozzarella cheese

1. Press "Pre-Heat", set the temperature at 380°F (193°C).

2. Brush the melted butter over the cut sides of cabbage wedges and sprinkle both sides with the Parmesan cheese. Season with salt and pepper to taste.

3. Place the cabbage wedges in the air fryer basket and air fry for 20 minutes, flipping the cabbage halfway through, or until the cabbage wedges are lightly browned.

4. Transfer the cabbage wedges to a plate and serve with the Mozzarella cheese sprinkled on top.

91

RITZY ROASTED VEGGIE SALAD

Prep time: 5 minutes | **Cook time:** 20 minutes | **Serves** 2

1 potato, chopped
1 carrot, sliced diagonally
1 cup cherry tomatoes
½ small beetroot, sliced
¼ onion, sliced
½ teaspoon turmeric
½ teaspoon cumin
¼ teaspoon sea salt
2 tablespoons olive oil, divided
A handful of arugula
A handful of baby spinach
Juice of 1 lemon
3 tablespoons canned chickpeas, for serving
Parmesan shavings, for serving

1. Press "Pre-Heat", set the temperature at 370°F (188°C).
2. Combine the potato, carrot, cherry tomatoes, beetroot, onion, turmeric, cumin, salt, and 1 tablespoon of olive oil in a large bowl and toss until well coated.

3. Arrange the veggies in the air fryer basket and roast for 20 minutes, shaking the basket halfway through.

4. Let the veggies cool for 5 to 10 minutes in the basket.

5. Put the arugula, baby spinach, lemon juice, and remaining 1 tablespoon of olive oil in a salad bowl and stir to combine. Mix in the roasted veggies and toss well.

6. Scatter the chickpeas and Parmesan shavings on top and serve immediately.

92

FAST HONEY-GLAZED BABY CARROTS

Prep time: 5 minutes | **Cook time:** 12 minutes | **Serves** 4

1 pound (454 g) baby carrots
2 tablespoons olive oil
1 tablespoon honey
1 teaspoon dried dill
Salt and black pepper, to taste

1. Press "Pre-Heat", set the temperature at 350°F (177°C).
2. Place the carrots in a large bowl. Add the olive oil, honey, dill, salt, and pepper and toss to coat well.
3. Arrange the carrots in the air fryer basket and roast for 12 minutes until crisp-tender. Shake the basket once during cooking.
4. Serve warm.

93

HONEY-GLAZED ROASTED VEGETABLE

Prep time: 15 minutes | **Cook time:** 20 minutes | Makes 3 cups

Glaze:

2 tablespoons raw honey

2 teaspoons minced garlic

¼ teaspoon dried marjoram

¼ teaspoon dried basil

¼ teaspoon dried oregano

⅛ teaspoon dried sage

⅛ teaspoon dried rosemary

⅛ teaspoon dried thyme

½ teaspoon salt

¼ teaspoon ground black pepper

Veggies:

3 to 4 medium red potatoes, cut into 1- to 2-inch pieces

1 small zucchini, cut into 1- to 2-inch pieces

1 small carrot, sliced into ¼-inch rounds

1 (10.5-ounce / 298-g) package cherry tomatoes, halved

1 cup sliced mushrooms

3 tablespoons olive oil

Vegetables

1. Press "Pre-Heat", set the temperature at 380°F (193°C).
2. Combine the honey, garlic, marjoram, basil, oregano, sage, rosemary, thyme, salt, and pepper in a small bowl and stir to mix well. Set aside.
3. Place the red potatoes, zucchini, carrot, cherry tomatoes, and mushroom in a large bowl. Drizzle with the olive oil and toss to coat.
4. Pour the veggies into the air fryer basket and roast for 15 minutes, shaking the basket halfway through.
5. When ready, transfer the roasted veggies to the large bowl. Pour the honey mixture over the veggies, tossing to coat.
6. Spread out the veggies in a baking pan and place in the air fryer.
7. Increase the temperature to 390°F (199°C) and roast for an additional 5 minutes, or until the veggies are tender and glazed. Serve warm.

94

HEARTY SUMMER ROLLS

Prep time: 15 minutes | **Cook time:** 15 minutes | **Serves** 4

1 cup shiitake mushroom, sliced thinly
1 celery stalk, chopped
1 medium carrot, shredded
½ teaspoon finely chopped ginger
1 teaspoon sugar
1 tablespoon soy sauce
1 teaspoon nutritional yeast
8 spring roll sheets
1 teaspoon corn starch
2 tablespoons water

1. In a bowl, combine the ginger, soy sauce, nutritional yeast, carrots, celery, mushroom, and sugar.

2. Mix the cornstarch and water to create an adhesive for the spring rolls.

3. Scoop a tablespoonful of the vegetable mixture into the middle of the spring roll sheets. Brush the edges of the sheets with the cornstarch adhesive and enclose around the filling to make spring rolls.

4. Press "Pre-Heat", set the temperature at 400°F (204°C). When warm, place the rolls inside and air fry for 15 minutes or until crisp.

5. Serve hot.

95

LUSH ROASTED VEGGIES

Prep time: 15 minutes | **Cook time:** 20 minutes | **Serves** 6

1 1/3 cups small parsnips, peeled and cubed

1 1/3 cups celery

2 red onions, sliced

1 1/3 cups small butternut squash, cut in half, deseeded and cubed

1 tablespoon fresh thyme needles

1 tablespoon olive oil

Salt and ground black pepper, to taste

1. Press "Pre-Heat", set the temperature at 390°F (199°C).

2. Combine the cut vegetables with the thyme, olive oil, salt and pepper.

3. Put the vegetables in the basket and transfer the basket to the air fryer.

4. Roast for 20 minutes, stirring once throughout the roasting time, until the vegetables are nicely browned and cooked through.

5. Serve warm.

96

FAST MUSHROOM AND PEPPER PIZZA SQUARES

Prep time: 10 minutes | **Cook time:** 10 minutes | **Serves** 10

1 pizza dough, cut into squares
1 cup chopped oyster mushrooms
1 shallot, chopped
¼ red bell pepper, chopped
2 tablespoons parsley
Salt and ground black pepper, to taste

1. Press "Pre-Heat", set the temperature at 400°F (204°C).
2. In a bowl, combine the oyster mushrooms, shallot, bell pepper and parsley. Sprinkle some salt and pepper as desired.
3. Spread this mixture on top of the pizza squares.
4. Bake in the air fryer for 10 minutes.
5. Serve warm.

97

CHEESY ZUCCHINI CHIPS

Prep time: 5 minutes | **Cook time:** 14 minutes | **Serves** 4

2 egg whites
Salt and black pepper, to taste
½ cup seasoned bread crumbs
2 tablespoons grated Parmesan cheese
¼ teaspoon garlic powder
2 medium zucchini, sliced
Cooking spray

1. Press "Pre-Heat", set the temperature at 400°F (204°C). Spritz the air fryer basket with cooking spray.
2. In a bowl, beat the egg whites with salt and pepper. In a separate bowl, thoroughly combine the bread crumbs, Parmesan cheese, and garlic powder.
3. Dredge the zucchini slices in the egg white, then coat in the bread crumb mixture.
4. Arrange the zucchini slices in the air fryer basket and air fry for 14 minutes, flipping the zucchini halfway through.
5. Remove from the basket to a plate and serve.

98

TOFU SCRAMBLE WITH VEGGIES

Prep time: 15 minutes | **Cook time:** 30 minutes | **Serves** 3

2½ cups chopped red potato

2 tablespoons olive oil, divided

1 block tofu, chopped finely

2 tablespoons tamari

1 teaspoon turmeric powder

½ teaspoon onion powder

½ teaspoon garlic powder

½ cup chopped onion

4 cups broccoli florets

1. Press "Pre-Heat", set the temperature at 400°F (204°C).

2. Toss together the potatoes and 1 tablespoon of the olive oil.

3. Air fry the potatoes in a baking dish for 15 minutes, shaking once during the cooking time to ensure they fry evenly.

4. Combine the tofu, the remaining 1 tablespoon of the olive oil, turmeric, onion powder, tamari, and garlic powder together, stirring in the onions, followed by the broccoli.

5. Top the potatoes with the tofu mixture and air fry for an additional 15 minutes. Serve warm.

99

GARLICKY RATATOUILLE

Prep time: 20 minutes | **Cook time:** 25 minutes | **Serves** 4

1 sprig basil
1 sprig flat-leaf parsley
1 sprig mint
1 tablespoon coriander powder
1 teaspoon capers
½ lemon, juiced
Salt and ground black pepper, to taste
2 eggplants, sliced crosswise
2 red onions, chopped
4 cloves garlic, minced
2 red peppers, sliced crosswise
1 fennel bulb, sliced crosswise
3 large zucchinis, sliced crosswise
5 tablespoons olive oil
4 large tomatoes, chopped
2 teaspoons herbs de Provence

1.Blend the basil, parsley, coriander, mint, lemon juice and capers, with a little salt and pepper. Make sure all ingredients are well-incorporated.

2. Press "Pre-Heat", set the temperature at 400°F (204°C).

3. Coat the eggplant, onions, garlic, peppers, fennel, and zucchini with olive oil.

4. Transfer the vegetables into a baking dish and top with the tomatoes and herb purée. Sprinkle with more salt and pepper, and the herbs de Provence.

5. Air fry for 25 minutes.

6. Serve immediately.

100

RICE, EGGPLANT, CUCUMBER BOWL

Prep time: 15 minutes | **Cook time:** 10 minutes | **Serves** 4

¼ cup sliced cucumber

1 teaspoon salt

1 tablespoon sugar

7 tablespoons Japanese rice vinegar

3 medium eggplants, sliced

3 tablespoons sweet white miso paste

1 tablespoon mirin rice wine

4 cups cooked sushi rice

4 spring onions

1 tablespoon toasted sesame seeds

1.Coat the cucumber slices with the rice wine vinegar, salt, and sugar.

2.Put a dish on top of the bowl to weight it down completely.

3.In a bowl, mix the eggplants, mirin rice wine, and miso paste. Allow to marinate for half an hour.

4.Press "Pre-Heat", set the temperature at 400°F (204°C).

5.Put the eggplant slices in the air fryer and air fry for 10 minutes.

6. Fill the bottom of a serving bowl with rice and top with the eggplants and pickled cucumbers.

7. Add the spring onions and sesame seeds for garnish. Serve immediately.

101

BALSAMIC GLAZED ROSEMARY BEETS

Prep time: 5 minutes | **Cook time:** 10 minutes | **Serves** 2

Beet:
2 beets, cubed
2 tablespoons olive oil
2 springs rosemary, chopped
Salt and black pepper, to taste
Balsamic Glaze:
1/3 cup balsamic vinegar
1 tablespoon honey

1. Press "Pre-Heat", set the temperature at 400°F (204°C).
2. Combine the beets, olive oil, rosemary, salt, and pepper in a mixing bowl and toss until the beets are completely coated.
3. Place the beets in the air fryer basket and air fry for 10 minutes until the beets are crisp and browned at the edges. Shake the basket halfway through the cooking time.
4. Meanwhile, make the balsamic glaze: Place the balsamic vinegar and honey in a small saucepan and bring to a boil over medium heat. When the sauce starts to boil, reduce the heat to medium-low heat and simmer until the liquid is reduced by half.

5. When ready, remove the beets from the basket to a platter. Pour the balsamic glaze over the top and serve immediately.

102

CHEESY ROSEMARY ROASTED SQUASH

Prep time: 5 minutes | **Cook time:** 20 minutes | **Serves** 2

1 pound (454 g) butternut squash, cut into wedges
2 tablespoons olive oil
1 tablespoon dried rosemary
Salt, to salt
1 cup crumbled goat cheese
1 tablespoon maple syrup

1. Press "Pre-Heat", set the temperature at 350°F (177°C).
2. Toss the squash wedges with the olive oil, rosemary, and salt in a large bowl until well coated.
3. Transfer the squash wedges to the air fryer basket, spreading them out in as even a layer as possible.
4. Roast for 10 minutes. Flip the squash and roast for another 10 minutes until golden brown.
5. Sprinkle the goat cheese on top and serve drizzled with the maple syrup.

103

EASY SESAME-MAITAKE MUSHROOMS

Prep time: 5 minutes | **Cook time:** 15 minutes | **Serves** 2

1 tablespoon soy sauce
2 teaspoons toasted sesame oil
3 teaspoons vegetable oil, divided
1 garlic clove, minced
7 ounces (198 g) maitake (hen of the woods) mushrooms
½ teaspoon flaky sea salt
½ teaspoon sesame seeds
½ teaspoon finely chopped fresh thyme leaves

1. Press "Pre-Heat", set the temperature at 300°F (149°C).
2. Whisk together the soy sauce, sesame oil, 1 teaspoon of vegetable oil, and garlic in a small bowl.
3. Arrange the mushrooms in the air fryer basket in a single layer. Drizzle the soy sauce mixture over the mushrooms. Roast for 10 minutes.
4. Flip the mushrooms and sprinkle the sea salt, sesame seeds, and thyme leaves on top. Drizzle the remaining 2 teaspoons of vegetable oil all over. Roast for an additional 5 minutes.
5. Remove the mushrooms from the basket to a plate and serve hot.

104

CHEESY RUSSET POTATO GRATIN

Prep time: 10 minutes | **Cook time:** 35 minutes | **Serves** 6

½ cup milk
7 medium russet potatoes, peeled
Salt, to taste
1 teaspoon black pepper
½ cup heavy whipping cream
½ cup grated semi-mature cheese
½ teaspoon nutmeg

1. Press "Pre-Heat", set the temperature at 390°F (199°C).
2. Cut the potatoes into wafer-thin slices.
3. In a bowl, combine the milk and cream and sprinkle with salt, pepper, and nutmeg.
4. Use the milk mixture to coat the slices of potatoes. Put in a baking dish. Top the potatoes with the rest of the milk mixture.
5. Put the baking dish into the air fryer basket and bake for 25 minutes.
6. Pour the cheese over the potatoes.
7. Bake for an additional 10 minutes, ensuring the top is nicely browned before serving.

105

HERBED RATATOUILLE

Prep time: 15 minutes | **Cook time:** 16 minutes | **Serves** 2

2 Roma tomatoes, thinly sliced
1 zucchini, thinly sliced
2 yellow bell peppers, sliced
2 garlic cloves, minced
2 tablespoons olive oil
2 tablespoons herbes de Provence
1 tablespoon vinegar
Salt and black pepper, to taste

1. Press "Pre-Heat", set the temperature at 390°F (199°C).
2. Place the tomatoes, zucchini, bell peppers, garlic, olive oil, herbes de Provence, and vinegar in a large bowl and toss until the vegetables are evenly coated. Sprinkle with salt and pepper and toss again. Pour the vegetable mixture into a baking dish.
3. Place the baking dish in the air fryer basket and roast for 8 minutes. Stir and continue roasting for 8 minutes until tender.
4. Let the vegetable mixture stand for 5 minutes in the basket before removing and serving.

106

HEARTY VEGGIES SPRING ROLLS

Prep time: 20 minutes | **Cook time:** 10 minutes | **Serves** 6

2 potatoes, mashed
¼ cup peas
¼ cup mashed carrots
1 small cabbage, sliced
¼ cups beans
2 tablespoons sweetcorn
1 small onion, chopped
½ cup bread crumbs
1 packet spring roll sheets
½ cup cornstarch slurry

1. Press "Pre-Heat", set the temperature at 390°F (199°C).
2. Boil all the vegetables in water over a low heat. Rinse and allow to dry.
3. Unroll the spring roll sheets and spoon equal amounts of vegetable onto the center of each one. Fold into spring rolls and coat each one with the slurry and bread crumbs.
4. Air fry the rolls in the preheated air fryer for 10 minutes.
5. Serve warm.

107

FAST VEGETABLE BURGER

Prep time: 15 minutes | **Cook time:** 12 minutes | **Serves** 8

½ pound (227 g) cauliflower, steamed and diced, rinsed and drained

2 teaspoons coconut oil, melted

2 teaspoons minced garlic

¼ cup desiccated coconut

½ cup oats

3 tablespoons flour

1 tablespoon flaxseeds plus 3 tablespoons water, divided

1 teaspoon mustard powder

2 teaspoons thyme

2 teaspoons parsley

2 teaspoons chives

Salt and ground black pepper, to taste

1 cup bread crumbs

1. Press "Pre-Heat", set the temperature at 390°F (199°C).

2. Combine the cauliflower with all the ingredients, except for the bread crumbs, incorporating everything well.

3. Using the hands, shape 8 equal-sized amounts of the

mixture into burger patties. Coat the patties in bread crumbs before putting them in the air fryer basket in a single layer.

4. Air fry for 12 minutes or until crispy.
5. Serve hot.

108

CAJUN SWEET POTATOES WITH TOFU

Prep time: 15 minutes | **Cook time:** 35 minutes | **Serves** 8

- 8 sweet potatoes, scrubbed
- 2 tablespoons olive oil
- 1 large onion, chopped
- 2 green chilies, deseeded and chopped
- 8 ounces (227 g) tofu, crumbled
- 2 tablespoons Cajun seasoning
- 1 cup chopped tomatoes
- 1 can kidney beans, drained and rinsed
- Salt and ground black pepper, to taste

1. Press "Pre-Heat", set the temperature at 400°F (204°C).
2. With a knife, pierce the skin of the sweet potatoes and air fry in the air fryer for 30 minutes or until soft.
3. Remove from the air fryer, halve each potato, and set to one side.
4. Over a medium heat, fry the onions and chilies in the olive oil in a skillet for 2 minutes until fragrant.
5. Add the tofu and Cajun seasoning and air fry for a further 3 minutes before incorporating the kidney beans and tomatoes. Sprinkle some salt and pepper as desire.

6. Top each sweet potato halve with a spoonful of the tofu mixture and serve.

109

AIR-FRIED SWEET POTATOES WITH ZUCCHINI

Prep time: 20 minutes | **Cook time:** 20 minutes | **Serves** 4

2 large-sized sweet potatoes, peeled and quartered
1 medium zucchini, sliced
1 Serrano pepper, deseeded and thinly sliced
1 bell pepper, deseeded and thinly sliced
1 to 2 carrots, cut into matchsticks
¼ cup olive oil
1½ tablespoons maple syrup
½ teaspoon porcini powder
¼ teaspoon mustard powder
½ teaspoon fennel seeds
1 tablespoon garlic powder
½ teaspoon fine sea salt
¼ teaspoon ground black pepper
Tomato ketchup, for serving

1. Put the sweet potatoes, zucchini, peppers, and the carrot into the air fryer basket. Coat with a drizzling of olive oil.
2. Press "Pre-Heat", set the temperature at 350°F (177°C).
3. Air fry the vegetables for 15 minutes.

4. In the meantime, prepare the sauce by vigorously combining the other ingredients, except for the tomato ketchup, with a whisk.

5. Lightly grease a baking dish.

6. Transfer the cooked vegetables to the baking dish, pour over the sauce and coat the vegetables well.

7. Increase the temperature to 390°F (199°C) and air fry the vegetables for an additional 5 minutes.

8. Serve warm with a side of ketchup.

110

THAI SPICY BRUSSELS SPROUTS

Prep time: 5 minutes | **Cook time:** 20 minutes | **Serves** 2

¼ cup Thai sweet chili sauce

2 tablespoons black vinegar or balsamic vinegar

½ teaspoon hot sauce

2 small shallots, cut into ¼-inch-thick slices

8 ounces (227 g) Brussels sprouts, trimmed (large sprouts halved)

Kosher salt and freshly ground black pepper, to taste

2 teaspoons lightly packed fresh cilantro leaves, for garnish

1. Place the chili sauce, vinegar, and hot sauce in a large bowl and whisk to combine.

2. Add the shallots and Brussels sprouts and toss to coat. Sprinkle with the salt and pepper. Transfer the Brussels sprouts and sauce to a metal cake pan.

3. Place the metal pan in the air fryer basket and roast for about 20 minutes, or until the Brussels sprouts are crisp-tender and the sauce has reduced to a sticky glaze. Shake the basket twice during cooking.

4. Sprinkle the cilantro on top for garnish and serve warm.

111

ROASTED TOFU, CARROT AND CAULIFLOWER RICE

Prep time: 10 minutes | **Cook time:** 22 minutes | **Serves** 4

½ block tofu, crumbled
1 cup diced carrot
½ cup diced onions
2 tablespoons soy sauce
1 teaspoon turmeric
Cauliflower:
3 cups cauliflower rice
½ cup chopped broccoli
½ cup frozen peas
2 tablespoons soy sauce
1 tablespoon minced ginger
2 garlic cloves, minced
1 tablespoon rice vinegar
1½ teaspoons toasted sesame oil

1. Press "Pre-Heat", set the temperature at 370°F (188°C).
2. Mix together the tofu, carrot, onions, soy sauce, and turmeric in a baking dish and stir until well incorporated.
3. Place the baking dish in the air fryer and roast for 10 minutes.

Vegetables

4. Meanwhile, in a large bowl, combine all the ingredients for the cauliflower and toss well.

5. Remove the basket and add the cauliflower mixture to the tofu and stir to combine.

6. Return the basket to the air fryer and continue roasting for 12 minutes, or until the vegetables are cooked to your preference.

7. Cool for 5 minutes before serving.

112

GOLDEN VEGETARIAN MEATBALLS

Prep time: 15 minutes | **Cook time:** 18 minutes | **Serves** 3

½ cup grated carrots
½ cup sweet onions
2 tablespoons olive oil
1 cup rolled oats
½ cup roasted cashews
2 cups cooked chickpeas
Juice of 1 lemon
2 tablespoons soy sauce
1 tablespoon flax meal
1 teaspoon garlic powder
1 teaspoon cumin
½ teaspoon turmeric

1. Press "Pre-Heat", set the temperature at 350°F (177°C).
2. Mix together the carrots, onions, and olive oil in a baking dish and stir to combine.
3. Place the baking dish in the air fryer basket and roast for 6 minutes.
4. Meanwhile, put the oats and cashews in a food processor or blender and pulse until coarsely ground. Transfer the mixture to a

large bowl. Add the chickpeas, lemon juice, and soy sauce to the food processor and pulse until smooth. Transfer the chickpea mixture to the bowl of oat and cashew mixture.

5. Remove the carrots and onions from the basket to the bowl of chickpea mixture. Add the flax meal, garlic powder, cumin, and turmeric and stir to incorporate.

6. Scoop tablespoon-sized portions of the veggie mixture and roll them into balls with your hands. Transfer the balls to the air fryer basket in a single layer.

7. Increase the temperature to 370°F (188°C) and bake for 12 minutes until golden through. Flip the balls halfway through the cooking time.

8. Serve warm.

VEGETABLE SIDES

113

CARAMELIZED BRUSSELS SPROUTS

Prep time: 5 minutes | **Cook time:** 10 minutes | **Serves** 1

1 pound (454 g) Brussels sprouts
1 tablespoon coconut oil, melted
1 tablespoon unsalted butter, melted

1. Press "Pre-Heat", set the temperature at 400°F (204°C).
2. Prepare the Brussels sprouts by halving them, discarding any loose leaves.
3. Combine with the melted coconut oil and transfer to the air fryer.
4. Air fry for 10 minutes, giving the basket a good shake throughout the air frying time to brown them up if desired.
5. The sprouts are ready when they are partially caramelized. Remove them from the air fryer and serve with a topping of melted butter before serving.

114

RUSSET POTATOES WITH YOGURT AND CHIVES

Prep time: 5 minutes | **Cook time:** 35 minutes | **Serves** 4

4 (7-ounce / 198-g) russet potatoes, rinsed
Olive oil spray
½ teaspoon kosher salt, divided
½ cup 2% plain Greek yogurt
¼ cup minced fresh chives
Freshly ground black pepper, to taste

1. Press "Pre-Heat", set the temperature at 400°F (204°C).
2. Pat the potatoes dry and pierce them all over with a fork. Spritz the potatoes with olive oil spray. Sprinkle with ¼ teaspoon of the salt.
3. Put the potatoes in the air fryer basket and bake for 35 minutes until a knife can be inserted into the center of the potatoes easily.
4. Remove from the basket and split open the potatoes. Top with the yogurt, chives, the remaining ¼ teaspoon of salt, and finish with the black pepper. Serve immediately.

115

FAST BUTTERED BROCCOLI WITH PARMESAN

Prep time: 5 minutes | **Cook time:** 4 minutes | **Serves** 4

1 pound (454 g) broccoli florets
1 medium shallot, minced
2 tablespoons olive oil
2 tablespoons unsalted butter, melted
2 teaspoons minced garlic
¼ cup grated Parmesan cheese

1. Press "Pre-Heat", set the temperature at 360°F (182°C).
2. Combine the broccoli florets with the shallot, olive oil, butter, garlic, and Parmesan cheese in a medium bowl and toss until the broccoli florets are thoroughly coated.
3. Arrange the broccoli florets in the air fryer basket in a single layer and roast for 4 minutes until crisp-tender.
4. Serve warm.

116

GREEN BEANS WITH SESAME SEEDS

Prep time: 5 minutes | **Cook time:** 8 minutes | **Serves** 4

1 tablespoon reduced-sodium soy sauce or tamari
½ tablespoon Sriracha sauce
4 teaspoons toasted sesame oil, divided
12 ounces (340 g) trimmed green beans
½ tablespoon toasted sesame seeds

1. Press "Pre-Heat", set the temperature at 375°F (191°C).
2. Whisk together the soy sauce, Sriracha sauce, and 1 teaspoon of sesame oil in a small bowl until smooth.
3. Toss the green beans with the remaining sesame oil in a large bowl until evenly coated.
4. Place the green beans in the air fryer basket in a single layer. You may need to work in batches to avoid overcrowding.
5. Air fry for about 8 minutes until the green beans are lightly charred and tender. Shake the basket halfway through the cooking time.
6. Remove from the basket to a platter. Repeat with the remaining green beans.
7. Pour the prepared sauce over the top of green beans and toss well. Serve sprinkled with the toasted sesame seeds.

117

GOLDEN CHEESY BROCCOLI GRATIN

Prep time: 5 minutes | **Cook time:** 12 to 14 minutes | **Serves** 2

⅓ cup fat-free milk
1 tablespoon all-purpose or gluten-free flour
½ tablespoon olive oil
½ teaspoon ground sage
¼ teaspoon kosher salt
⅛ teaspoon freshly ground black pepper
2 cups roughly chopped broccoli florets
6 tablespoons shredded Cheddar cheese
2 tablespoons panko bread crumbs
1 tablespoon grated Parmesan cheese
Olive oil spray

1. Press "Pre-Heat", set the temperature at 330°F (166°C). Spritz a baking dish with olive oil spray.

2. Mix the milk, flour, olive oil, sage, salt, and pepper in a medium bowl and whisk to combine. Stir in the broccoli florets, Cheddar cheese, bread crumbs, and Parmesan cheese and toss to coat.

3. Pour the broccoli mixture into the prepared baking dish and place in the air fryer basket.

4. Bake for 12 to 14 minutes until the top is golden brown and the broccoli is tender.

5. Serve immediately.

118

SPICY FINGERLING POTATOES

Prep time: 10 minutes | **Cook time:** 16 minutes | **Serves** 4

1 pound (454 g) fingerling potatoes, rinsed and cut into wedges

1 teaspoon olive oil

1 teaspoon salt

1 teaspoon black pepper

1 teaspoon cayenne pepper

1 teaspoon nutritional yeast

½ teaspoon garlic powder

1. Press "Pre-Heat", set the temperature at 400°F (204°C).

2. Coat the potatoes with the rest of the ingredients.

3. Transfer to the air fryer basket and air fry for 16 minutes, shaking the basket at the halfway point.

4. Serve immediately.

119

AIR-FRIED SPICED ACORN SQUASH

Prep time: 5 minutes | **Cook time:** 15 minutes | **Serves** 2

1 medium acorn squash, halved crosswise and deseeded
1 teaspoon coconut oil
1 teaspoon light brown sugar
Few dashes of ground cinnamon
Few dashes of ground nutmeg

1. Press "Pre-Heat", set the temperature at 325°F (163°C).
2. On a clean work surface, rub the cut sides of the acorn squash with coconut oil. Scatter with the brown sugar, cinnamon, and nutmeg.
3. Put the squash halves in the air fryer basket, cut-side up. Air fry for 15 minutes until just tender when pierced in the center with a paring knife.
4. Rest for 5 to 10 minutes and serve warm.

120

CREAMY-CHEESY CORN CASSEROLE

Prep time: 5 minutes | **Cook time:** 15 minutes | **Serves** 4

2 cups frozen yellow corn

1 egg, beaten

3 tablespoons flour

½ cup grated Swiss or Havarti cheese

½ cup light cream

¼ cup milk

Pinch salt

Freshly ground black pepper, to taste

2 tablespoons butter, cut into cubes

Nonstick cooking spray

1. Press "Pre-Heat", set the temperature at 320°F (160°C). Spritz a baking pan with nonstick cooking spray.

2. Stir together the remaining ingredients except the butter in a medium bowl until well incorporated.

3. Transfer the mixture to the prepared baking pan and scatter with the butter cubes.

4. Place the baking pan in the air fryer basket and bake for 15 minutes, or until the top is golden brown and a toothpick inserted in the center comes out clean.

5. Let the casserole cool for 5 minutes before slicing into wedges and serving.

121

CRISPY CHILI JICAMA FRIES

Prep time: 5 minutes | **Cook time:** 20 minutes | **Serves** 1

1 small jicama, peeled
¼ teaspoon onion powder
¾ teaspoon chili powder
¼ teaspoon garlic powder
¼ teaspoon ground black pepper

1. Press "Pre-Heat", set the temperature at 350°F (177°C).
2. To make the fries, cut the jicama into matchsticks of the desired thickness.
3. In a bowl, toss them with the onion powder, chili powder, garlic powder, and black pepper to coat. Transfer the fries into the air fryer basket.
4. Air fry for 20 minutes, giving the basket an occasional shake throughout the cooking process. The fries are ready when they are hot and golden.
5. Serve immediately.

122

BREADED BRUSSELS SPROUTS WITH SAGE

Prep time: 5 minutes | **Cook time:** 15 minutes | **Serves** 4

1 pound (454 g) Brussels sprouts, halved
1 cup bread crumbs
2 tablespoons grated Grana Padano cheese
1 tablespoon paprika
2 tablespoons canola oil
1 tablespoon chopped sage

1. Press "Pre-Heat", set the temperature at 400°F (204°C). Line the air fryer basket with parchment paper.

2. In a small bowl, thoroughly mix the bread crumbs, cheese, and paprika. In a large bowl, place the Brussels sprouts and drizzle the canola oil over the top. Sprinkle with the bread crumb mixture and toss to coat.

3. Place the Brussels sprouts in the air fryer basket and roast for 15 minutes, or until the Brussels sprouts are lightly browned and crisp. Shake the basket a few times during cooking to ensure even cooking.

4. Transfer the Brussels sprouts to a plate and sprinkle the sage on top before serving.

123

FAST ROSEMARY GREEN BEANS

Prep time: 5 minutes | **Cook time:** 5 minutes | **Serves** 1

1 tablespoon butter, melted
2 tablespoons rosemary
½ teaspoon salt
3 cloves garlic, minced
¾ cup chopped green beans

1. Press "Pre-Heat", set the temperature at 390°F (199°C).
2. Combine the melted butter with the rosemary, salt, and minced garlic. Toss in the green beans, coating them well.
3. Air fry for 5 minutes.
4. Serve immediately.

124

CRISPY ASPARAGUS

Prep time: 5 minutes | **Cook time:** 10 minutes | **Serves** 4

1 pound (454 g) asparagus, woody ends trimmed
2 tablespoons olive oil
1 tablespoon balsamic vinegar
2 teaspoons minced garlic
Salt and freshly ground black pepper, to taste

1. Press "Pre-Heat", set the temperature at 400°F (204°C).
2. In a large shallow bowl, toss the asparagus with the olive oil, balsamic vinegar, garlic, salt, and pepper until thoroughly coated.
3. Arrange the asparagus in the air fryer basket and roast for 10 minutes until crispy. Flip the asparagus with tongs halfway through the cooking time.
4. Serve warm.

125

AIR-FRIED HERBED RADISHES

Prep time: 5 minutes | **Cook time:** 10 minutes | **Serves** 2

1 pound (454 g) radishes
2 tablespoons unsalted butter, melted
¼ teaspoon dried oregano
½ teaspoon dried parsley
½ teaspoon garlic powder

1. Press "Pre-Heat", set the temperature at 350°F (177°C). Prepare the radishes by cutting off their tops and bottoms and quartering them.
2. In a bowl, combine the butter, dried oregano, dried parsley, and garlic powder. Toss with the radishes to coat.
3. Transfer the radishes to the air fryer and air fry for 10 minutes, shaking the basket at the halfway point to ensure the radishes air fry evenly through. The radishes are ready when they turn brown.
4. Serve immediately.

126

GOLDEN PARMESAN ASPARAGUS FRIES

Prep time: 15 minutes | **Cook time:** 5 to 7 minutes | **Serves** 4

2 egg whites
¼ cup water
¼ cup plus 2 tablespoons grated Parmesan cheese, divided
¾ cup panko bread crumbs
¼ teaspoon salt
12 ounces (340 g) fresh asparagus spears, woody ends trimmed
Cooking spray

1. Press "Pre-Heat", set the temperature at 390°F (199°C).
2. In a shallow dish, whisk together the egg whites and water until slightly foamy. In a separate shallow dish, thoroughly combine ¼ cup of Parmesan cheese, bread crumbs, and salt.
3. Dip the asparagus in the egg white, then roll in the cheese mixture to coat well.
4. Place the asparagus in the air fryer basket in a single layer, leaving space between each spear. You may need to work in batches to avoid overcrowding.
5. Spritz the asparagus with cooking spray and air fry for 5 to 7 minutes until golden brown and crisp.

6. Repeat with the remaining asparagus spears.
7. Sprinkle with the remaining 2 tablespoons of cheese and serve hot.

127

POTATO WITH SOUR CREAM

Prep time: 5 minutes | **Cook time:** 15 minutes | **Serves** 2

2 medium potatoes
1 teaspoon butter
3 tablespoons sour cream
1 teaspoon chives
1½ tablespoons grated Parmesan cheese

1. Press "Pre-Heat", set the temperature at 350°F (177°C).
2. Pierce the potatoes with a fork and boil them in water until they are cooked.
3. Transfer to the air fryer and air fry for 15 minutes.
4. In the meantime, combine the sour cream, cheese and chives in a bowl. Cut the potatoes halfway to open them up and fill with the butter and sour cream mixture.
5. Serve immediately.

128

SIMPLE ROASTED EGGPLANT SLICES

Prep time: 5 minutes | **Cook time:** 15 minutes | **Serves** 1
 1 large eggplant, sliced
 2 tablespoons olive oil
 ¼ teaspoon salt
 ½ teaspoon garlic powder
 1. Press "Pre-Heat", set the temperature at 390°F (199°C).
 2. Apply the olive oil to the slices with a brush, coating both sides. Season each side with sprinklings of salt and garlic powder.
 3. Put the slices in the air fryer and roast for 15 minutes.
 4. Serve immediately.

129

CREAMY POTATOES AND ASPARAGUS

Prep time: 5 minutes | **Cook time:** 23 minutes | **Serves** 4

4 medium potatoes

1 bunch asparagus

1/3 cup cottage cheese

1/3 cup low-fat crème fraiche

1 tablespoon wholegrain mustard

Salt and pepper, to taste

Cooking spray

1. Press "Pre-Heat", set the temperature at 390°F (199°C). Spritz the air fryer basket with cooking spray.

2. Place the potatoes in the basket. Air fry the potatoes for 20 minutes.

3. Boil the asparagus in salted water for 3 minutes.

4. Remove the potatoes and mash them with rest of ingredients. Sprinkle with salt and pepper.

5. Serve immediately.

130

ROSEMARY-GARLIC ROASTED POTATOES

Prep time: 5 minutes | **Cook time:** 20 to 22 minutes | **Serves** 4

1½ pounds (680 g) small red potatoes, cut into 1-inch cubes

2 tablespoons olive oil

2 tablespoons minced fresh rosemary

1 tablespoon minced garlic

1 teaspoon salt, plus additional as needed

½ teaspoon freshly ground black pepper, plus additional as needed

1. Press "Pre-Heat", set the temperature at 400°F (204°C).

2. Toss the potato cubes with the olive oil, rosemary, garlic, salt, and pepper in a large bowl until thoroughly coated.

3. Arrange the potato cubes in the air fryer basket in a single layer. Roast for 20 to 22 minutes until the potatoes are tender. Shake the basket a few times during cooking for even cooking.

4. Remove from the basket to a plate. Taste and add additional salt and pepper as needed.

131

FAST SALTINE WAX BEANS

Prep time: 10 minutes | **Cook time:** 7 minutes | **Serves** 4

½ cup flour
1 teaspoon smoky chipotle powder
½ teaspoon ground black pepper
1 teaspoon sea salt flakes
2 eggs, beaten
½ cup crushed saltines
10 ounces (283 g) wax beans
Cooking spray

1. Press "Pre-Heat", set the temperature at 360°F (182°C).
2. Combine the flour, chipotle powder, black pepper, and salt in a bowl. Put the eggs in a second bowl. Put the crushed saltines in a third bowl.
3. Wash the beans with cold water and discard any tough strings.
4. Coat the beans with the flour mixture, before dipping them into the beaten egg. Cover them with the crushed saltines.
5. Spritz the beans with cooking spray.
6. Air fry for 4 minutes. Give the air fryer basket a good shake and continue to air fry for 3 minutes. Serve hot.

132

AIR-FRIED SESAME TAJ TOFU

Prep time: 5 minutes | **Cook time:** 25 minutes | **Serves** 4

1 block firm tofu, pressed and cut into 1-inch thick cubes

2 tablespoons soy sauce

2 teaspoons toasted sesame seeds

1 teaspoon rice vinegar

1 tablespoon cornstarch

1. Press "Pre-Heat", set the temperature at 400°F (204°C).

2. Add the tofu, soy sauce, sesame seeds, and rice vinegar in a bowl together and mix well to coat the tofu cubes. Then cover the tofu in cornstarch and put it in the air fryer basket.

3. Air fry for 25 minutes, giving the basket a shake at five-minute intervals to ensure the tofu cooks evenly.

4. Serve immediately.

133

ROASTED CAULIFLOWER WITH BUFFALO SAUCE

Prep time: 5 minutes | **Cook time:** 5 minutes | **Serves** 1

½ packet dry ranch seasoning

2 tablespoons salted butter, melted

1 cup cauliflower florets

¼ cup buffalo sauce

1. Press "Pre-Heat", set the temperature at 400°F (204°C).

2. In a bowl, combine the dry ranch seasoning and butter. Toss with the cauliflower florets to coat and transfer them to the air fryer.

3. Roast for 5 minutes, shaking the basket occasionally to ensure the florets roast evenly.

4. Remove the cauliflower from the air fryer, pour the buffalo sauce over it, and serve.

134

EASY SPICY CABBAGE

Prep time: 5 minutes | **Cook time:** 7 minutes | **Serves** 4

1 head cabbage, sliced into 1-inch-thick ribbons
1 tablespoon olive oil
1 teaspoon garlic powder
1 teaspoon red pepper flakes
1 teaspoon salt
1 teaspoon freshly ground black pepper

1. Press "Pre-Heat", set the temperature at 350°F (177°C).
2. Toss the cabbage with the olive oil, garlic powder, red pepper flakes, salt, and pepper in a large mixing bowl until well coated.
3. Arrange the cabbage in the air fryer basket and roast for 7 minutes until crisp. Flip the cabbage with tongs halfway through the cooking time.
4. Remove from the basket to a plate and serve warm.

135

CURRY SWEET POTATO FRIES

Prep time: 5 minutes | **Cook time:** 25 minutes | **Serves** 4

2 pounds (907 g) sweet potatoes, rinsed, sliced into matchsticks
1 teaspoon curry powder
2 tablespoons olive oil
Salt, to taste

1. Press "Pre-Heat", set the temperature at 390°F (199°C).
2. Drizzle the oil in the baking pan, place the fries inside and bake for 25 minutes.
3. Sprinkle with the curry powder and salt before serving.

136

SESAME TOFU BITES

Prep time: 15 minutes | **Cook time:** 30 minutes | **Serves** 4

1 packaged firm tofu, cubed and pressed to remove excess water

1 tablespoon soy sauce

1 tablespoon ketchup

1 tablespoon maple syrup

½ teaspoon vinegar

1 teaspoon liquid smoke

1 teaspoon hot sauce

2 tablespoons sesame seeds

1 teaspoon garlic powder

Salt and ground black pepper, to taste

Cooking spray

1. Press "Pre-Heat", set the temperature at 375°F (191°C).

2. Spritz a baking dish with cooking spray.

3. Combine all the ingredients to coat the tofu completely and allow the marinade to absorb for half an hour.

4. Transfer the tofu to the baking dish, then air fry for 15 minutes. Flip the tofu over and air fry for another 15 minutes on the other side.

5. Serve immediately.

137

HERBED ZUCCHINI BALLS

Prep time: 5 minutes | **Cook time:** 10 minutes | **Serves** 4

4 zucchinis
1 egg
½ cup grated Parmesan cheese
1 tablespoon Italian herbs
1 cup grated coconut

1. Thinly grate the zucchinis and dry with a cheesecloth, ensuring to remove all the moisture.
2. In a bowl, combine the zucchinis with the egg, Parmesan, Italian herbs, and grated coconut, mixing well to incorporate everything. Using the hands, mold the mixture into balls.
3. Press "Pre-Heat", set the temperature at 400°F (204°C).
4. Lay the zucchini balls in the air fryer basket and air fry for 10 minutes.
5. Serve hot.

STUFFED VEGETABLES

138

RICE AND OLIVES STUFFED BELL PEPPERS

Prep time: 5 minutes | **Cook time:** 16 to 17 minutes | **Serves** 4

- 4 red bell peppers, tops sliced off
- 2 cups cooked rice
- 1 cup crumbled feta cheese
- 1 onion, chopped
- ¼ cup sliced kalamata olives
- ¾ cup tomato sauce
- 1 tablespoon Greek seasoning
- Salt and black pepper, to taste
- 2 tablespoons chopped fresh dill, for serving

1. Press "Pre-Heat", set the temperature at 360°F (182°C).
2. Microwave the red bell peppers for 1 to 2 minutes until tender.
3. When ready, transfer the red bell peppers to a plate to cool.
4. Mix together the cooked rice, feta cheese, onion, kalamata olives, tomato sauce, Greek seasoning, salt, and pepper in a medium bowl and stir until well combined.
5. Divide the rice mixture among the red bell peppers and transfer to a greased baking dish.

6. Put the baking dish in the air fryer and bake for 15 minutes, or until the rice is heated through and the vegetables are soft.

7. Remove from the basket and serve with the dill sprinkled on top.

139

BREADED MUSHROOMS

Prep time: 10 minutes | **Cook time:** 10 minutes | **Serves** 4

6 small mushrooms
1 tablespoon bread crumbs
1 tablespoon olive oil
1 ounce (28 g) onion, peeled and diced
1 teaspoon parsley
1 teaspoon garlic purée
Salt and ground black pepper, to taste

1. Press "Pre-Heat", set the temperature at 350°F (177°C).
2. Combine the bread crumbs, oil, onion, parsley, salt, pepper and garlic in a bowl. Cut out the mushrooms' stalks and stuff each cap with the crumb mixture.
3. Air fry in the air fryer for 10 minutes.
4. Serve hot.

140

MUSHROOMS WITH HORSERADISH MAYO

Prep time: 15 minutes | **Cook time:** 10 minutes | **Serves** 5

½ cup bread crumbs
2 cloves garlic, pressed
2 tablespoons chopped fresh coriander
⅓ teaspoon kosher salt
½ teaspoon crushed red pepper flakes
1½ tablespoons olive oil
20 medium mushrooms, stems removed
½ cup grated Gorgonzola cheese
¼ cup low-fat mayonnaise
1 teaspoon prepared horseradish, well-drained
1 tablespoon finely chopped fresh parsley

1. Press "Pre-Heat", set the temperature at 380°F (193°C).

2. Combine the bread crumbs together with the garlic, coriander, salt, red pepper, and olive oil.

3. Take equal-sized amounts of the bread crumb mixture and use them to stuff the mushroom caps. Add the grated Gorgonzola on top of each.

4. Put the mushrooms in a baking pan and transfer to the air fryer.

5. Air fry for 10 minutes, ensuring the stuffing is warm throughout.

6. In the meantime, prepare the horseradish mayo. Mix the mayonnaise, horseradish and parsley.

7. When the mushrooms are ready, serve with the mayo.

141

BACON-WRAPPED JALAPEÑO POPPERS

Prep time: 5 minutes | **Cook time:** 33 minutes | **Serves** 4

8 medium jalapeño peppers
5 ounces (142 g) cream cheese
¼ cup grated Mozzarella cheese
½ teaspoon Italian seasoning mix
8 slices bacon

1. Press "Pre-Heat", set the temperature at 400°F (204°C).
2. Cut the jalapeños in half.
3. Use a spoon to scrape out the insides of the peppers.
4. In a bowl, add together the cream cheese, Mozzarella cheese and Italian seasoning.
5. Pack the cream cheese mixture into the jalapeño halves and place the other halves on top.
6. Wrap each pepper in 1 slice of bacon, starting from the bottom and working up.
7. Bake for 33 minutes.
8. Serve!

142

CHEESY PEPPERONI AND MUSHROOM PIZZA

Prep time: 5 minutes | **Cook time:** 18 minutes | **Serves** 4

4 large portobello mushrooms, stems removed
4 teaspoons olive oil
1 cup marinara sauce
1 cup shredded Mozzarella cheese
10 slices sugar-free pepperoni

1. Press "Pre-Heat", set the temperature at 375°F (191°C).
2. Brush each mushroom cap with the olive oil, one teaspoon for each cap.
3. Put on a baking sheet and bake, stem-side down, for 8 minutes.
4. Take out of the air fryer and divide the marinara sauce, Mozzarella cheese and pepperoni evenly among the caps.
5. Air fry for another 10 minutes until browned.
6. Serve hot.

143

RICOTTA-STUFFED POTATOES

Prep time: 15 minutes | **Cook time:** 15 minutes | **Serves** 4

4 potatoes
2 tablespoons olive oil
½ cup Ricotta cheese, at room temperature
2 tablespoons chopped scallions
1 tablespoon roughly chopped fresh parsley
1 tablespoon minced coriander
2 ounces (57 g) Cheddar cheese, preferably freshly grated
1 teaspoon celery seeds
½ teaspoon salt
½ teaspoon garlic pepper

1. Press "Pre-Heat", set the temperature at 350°F (177°C).
2. Pierce the skin of the potatoes with a knife.
3. Air fry in the air fryer basket for 13 minutes. If they are not cooked through by this time, leave for 2 to 3 minutes longer.
4. In the meantime, make the stuffing by combining all the other ingredients.
5. Cut halfway into the cooked potatoes to open them.
6. Spoon equal amounts of the stuffing into each potato and serve hot.

144

STUFFED SQUASH WITH TOMATO AND PEPPER

Prep time: 5 minutes | **Cook time:** 30 minutes | **Serves** 4

1 pound (454 g) butternut squash, ends trimmed
2 teaspoons olive oil, divided
6 grape tomatoes, halved
1 poblano pepper, cut into strips
Salt and black pepper, to taste
¼ cup grated Mozzarella cheese

1. Press "Pre-Heat", set the temperature at 350°F (177°C).
2. Using a large knife, cut the squash in half lengthwise on a flat work surface. This recipe just needs half of the squash. Scoop out the flesh to make room for the stuffing. Coat the squash half with 1 teaspoon of olive oil.
3. Put the squash half in the air fryer basket and roast for 15 minutes.
4. Meanwhile, thoroughly combine the tomatoes, poblano pepper, remaining 1 teaspoon of olive oil, salt, and pepper in a bowl.
5. Remove the basket and spoon the tomato mixture into the squash. Return to the air fryer and roast for 12 minutes until the tomatoes are soft.

6.Scatter the Mozzarella cheese on top and continue cooking for about 3 minutes, or until the cheese is melted.

7.Cool for 5 minutes before serving.

145

CARAMELIZED STUFFED TOMATOES WITH VEGETABLE

Prep time: 10 minutes | **Cook time:** 16 to 20 minutes | **Serves** 4

4 medium beefsteak tomatoes, rinsed

½ cup grated carrot

1 medium onion, chopped

1 garlic clove, minced

2 teaspoons olive oil

2 cups fresh baby spinach

¼ cup crumbled low-sodium feta cheese

½ teaspoon dried basil

1. Press "Pre-Heat", set the temperature at 350°F (177°C).

2. On your cutting board, cut a thin slice off the top of each tomato. Scoop out a ¼- to ½-inch-thick tomato pulp and place the tomatoes upside down on paper towels to drain. Set aside.

3. Stir together the carrot, onion, garlic, and olive oil in a baking pan. Place in the air fryer basket and bake for 4 to 6 minutes, or until the carrot is crisp-tender.

4. Remove the pan from the basket and stir in the spinach, feta cheese, and basil.

5. Spoon ¼ of the vegetable mixture into each tomato and transfer the stuffed tomatoes to the basket.

6. Bake for 12 to 14 minutes until the filling is hot and the tomatoes are lightly caramelized.

7. Let the tomatoes cool for 5 minutes and serve.

FISH AND SEAFOOD

146

AIR FRYER FISH STICKS

Prep time: 10 minutes | **Cook time:** 10 to 12 minutes | **Serves** 4

Salt and pepper, to taste

1½ pounds (680g) skinless haddock fillets, ¾ inch thick, sliced into 4-inch strips

2 cups panko bread crumbs

1 tablespoon vegetable oil

¼ cup all-purpose flour

¼ cup mayonnaise

2 large eggs

1 tablespoon Old Bay seasoning

Vegetable oil spray

1. Dissolve ¼ cup salt in 2 quarts cold water in a large container. Add the haddock, cover, and let sit for 15 minutes.

2. Toss the panko with the oil in a bowl until evenly coated. Microwave, stirring frequently, until light golden brown, 2 to 4 minutes; transfer to a shallow dish. Whisk the flour, mayonnaise, eggs, Old Bay, ⅛ teaspoon salt, and ⅛ teaspoon pepper together in a second shallow dish.

3. Set a wire rack in a rimmed baking sheet and spray with

vegetable oil spray. Remove the haddock from the brine and thoroughly pat dry with paper towels. Working with 1 piece at a time, dredge the haddock in the egg mixture, letting excess drip off, then coat with the panko mixture, pressing gently to adhere. Transfer the fish sticks to the prepared rack and freeze until firm, about 1 hour.

4.Press "Pre-Heat", set the temperature at 400°F (204°C). Lightly spray the air fryer basket with vegetable oil spray. Arrange up to 5 fish sticks in the prepared basket, spaced evenly apart. Air fry until fish sticks are golden and register 140°F (60°C), 10 to 12 minutes, flipping and rotating fish sticks halfway through cooking.

5.Serve warm.

147

AIR-FRIED SCALLOPS

Prep time: 10 minutes | **Cook time:** 12 minutes | **Serves** 2

⅓ cup shallots, chopped
1½ tablespoons olive oil
1½ tablespoons coconut aminos
1 tablespoon Mediterranean seasoning mix
½ tablespoon balsamic vinegar
½ teaspoon ginger, grated
1 clove garlic, chopped
1 pound (454 g) scallops, cleaned
Cooking spray
Belgian endive, for garnish

1. Place all the ingredients except the scallops and Belgian endive in a small skillet over medium heat and stir to combine. Let this mixture simmer for about 2 minutes.
2. Remove the mixture from the skillet to a large bowl and set aside to cool.
3. Add the scallops, coating them all over, then transfer to the refrigerator to marinate for at least 2 hours.
4. Press "Pre-Heat", set the temperature at 345°F (174°C).

5. Arrange the scallops in the air fryer basket in a single layer and spray with cooking spray.

6. Air fry for 10 minutes, flipping the scallops halfway through, or until the scallops are tender and opaque.

7. Serve garnished with the Belgian endive.

148

BACON-WRAPPED SCALLOPS

Prep time: 10 minutes | **Cook time:** 12 minutes | **Serves** 4

12 slices bacon

24 large sea scallops, tendons removed

1 teaspoon plus 2 tablespoons extra-virgin olive oil, divided

Salt and pepper, to taste

6 (6-inch) wooden skewers

1 tablespoon cider vinegar

1 teaspoon Dijon mustard

5 ounces (142 g) baby spinach

1 fennel bulb, stalks discarded, bulb halved, cored, and sliced thin

5 ounces (142 g) raspberries

1. Press "Pre-Heat", set the temperature at 350°F (177°C).

2. Line large plate with 4 layers of paper towels and arrange 6 slices bacon over towels in a single layer. Top with 4 more layers of paper towels and remaining 6 slices bacon. Cover with 2 layers of paper towels, place a second large plate on top, and press gently to flatten. Microwave until fat begins to render but bacon is still pliable, about 5 minutes.

3. Pat scallops dry with paper towels and toss with 1 teaspoon

oil, ⅛ teaspoon salt, and ⅛ teaspoon pepper in a bowl until evenly coated. Arrange 2 scallops side to side, flat side down, on the cutting board. Starting at narrow end, wrap 1 slice bacon tightly around sides of scallop bundle. (Bacon should overlap slightly; trim excess as needed.) Thread scallop bundle onto skewer through bacon. Repeat with remaining scallops and bacon, threading 2 bundles onto each skewer.

4. Arrange 3 skewers in air fryer basket, parallel to each other and spaced evenly apart. Arrange remaining 3 skewers on top, perpendicular to the bottom layer. Bake until bacon is crisp and scallops are firm and centers are opaque, 12 to 16 minutes, flipping and rotating skewers halfway through cooking.

5. Meanwhile, whisk remaining 2 tablespoons oil, vinegar, mustard, ⅛ teaspoon salt, and ⅛ teaspoon pepper in large serving bowl until combined. Add spinach, fennel, and raspberries and gently toss to coat. Serve skewers with salad.

149

BACON-WRAPPED SCALLOPS

Prep time: 5 minutes | **Cook time:** 10 minutes | **Serves** 4

8 slices bacon, cut in half

16 sea scallops, patted dry

Cooking spray

Salt and freshly ground black pepper, to taste

16 toothpicks, soaked in water for at least 30 minutes

1. Press "Pre-Heat", set the temperature at 370°F (188°C).

2. On a clean work surface, wrap half of a slice of bacon around each scallop and secure with a toothpick.

3. Lay the bacon-wrapped scallops in the air fryer basket in a single layer. You may need to work in batches to avoid overcrowding.

4. Spritz the scallops with cooking spray and sprinkle the salt and pepper to season.

5. Air fry for 10 minutes, flipping the scallops halfway through, or until the bacon is cooked through and the scallops are firm.

6. Remove the scallops from the basket to a plate and repeat with the remaining scallops. Serve warm.

150

BAJA FISH TACOS

Prep time: 15 minutes | **Cook time:** 10 minutes | **Serves** 4

Fried Fish:
1 pound (454 g) tilapia fillets (or other mild white fish)
½ cup all-purpose flour
1 teaspoon garlic powder
1 teaspoon kosher salt
¼ teaspoon cayenne pepper
½ cup mayonnaise
3 tablespoons milk
1¾ cups panko bread crumbs
Vegetable oil, for spraying

Tacos:
8 corn tortillas
¼ head red or green cabbage, shredded
1 ripe avocado, halved and each half cut into 4 slices
12 ounces (340 g) pico de gallo or other fresh salsa
Dollop of Mexican crema
1 lime, cut into wedges

1. To make the fish, cut the fish fillets into strips 3 to 4 inches long and 1 inch wide. Combine the flour, garlic powder, salt, and

cayenne pepper on a plate and whisk to combine. In a shallow bowl, whisk the mayonnaise and milk together. Place the panko on a separate plate. Dredge the fish strips in the seasoned flour, shaking off any excess. Dip the strips in the mayonnaise mixture, coating them completely, then dredge in the panko, shaking off any excess. Place the fish strips on a plate or rack.

2.Press "Pre-Heat", set the temperature at 400°F (204°C). Working in batches, spray half the fish strips with oil and arrange them in the air fryer basket, taking care not to crowd them. Air fry for 4 minutes, then flip and air fry for another 3 to 4 minutes until the outside is brown and crisp and the inside is opaque and flakes easily with a fork. Repeat with the remaining strips.

3.Heat the tortillas in the microwave or on the stovetop. To assemble the tacos, place 2 fish strips inside each tortilla. Top with shredded cabbage, a slice of avocado, pico de gallo, and a dollop of crema. Serve with a lime wedge on the side.

151

BAKED FLOUNDER FILLETS

Prep time: 8 minutes | **Cook time:** 12 minutes | **Serves** 2

2 flounder fillets, patted dry
1 egg
½ teaspoon Worcestershire sauce
¼ cup almond flour
¼ cup coconut flour
½ teaspoon coarse sea salt
½ teaspoon lemon pepper
¼ teaspoon chili powder
Cooking spray

1. Press "Pre-Heat", set the temperature at 390°F (199°C). Spritz the air fryer basket with cooking spray.

2. In a shallow bowl, beat together the egg with Worcestershire sauce until well incorporated.

3. In another bowl, thoroughly combine the almond flour, coconut flour, sea salt, lemon pepper, and chili powder.

4. Dredge the fillets in the egg mixture, shaking off any excess, then roll in the flour mixture to coat well.

5. Place the fillets in the air fryer basket and bake for 7

minutes. Flip the fillets and spray with cooking spray. Continue cooking for 5 minutes, or until the fish is flaky.

6. Serve warm.

152

BLACKENED FISH

Prep time: 15 minutes | **Cook time:** 8 minutes | **Serves** 4

1 large egg, beaten

Blackened seasoning, as needed

2 tablespoons light brown sugar

4 (4-ounce / 113- g) tilapia fillets

Cooking spray

1. In a shallow bowl, place the beaten egg. In a second shallow bowl, stir together the Blackened seasoning and the brown sugar.

2. One at a time, dip the fish fillets in the egg, then the brown sugar mixture, coating thoroughly.

3. Press "Pre-Heat", set the temperature at 300°F (149°C). Line the air fryer basket with parchment paper.

4. Place the coated fish on the parchment and spritz with oil.

5. Bake for 4 minutes. Flip the fish, spritz it with oil, and bake for 4 to 6 minutes more until the fish is white inside and flakes easily with a fork.

6. Serve immediately.

153

BREADED CALAMARI WITH LEMON

Prep time: 5 minutes | **Cook time:** 12 minutes | **Serves** 4

2 large eggs
2 garlic cloves, minced
½ cup cornstarch
1 cup bread crumbs
1 pound (454 g) calamari rings
Cooking spray
1 lemon, sliced

1. In a small bowl, whisk the eggs with minced garlic. Place the cornstarch and bread crumbs into separate shallow dishes.

2. Dredge the calamari rings in the cornstarch, then dip in the egg mixture, shaking off any excess, finally roll them in the bread crumbs to coat well. Let the calamari rings sit for 10 minutes in the refrigerator.

3. Press "Pre-Heat", set the temperature at 390°F (199°C). Spritz the air fryer basket with cooking spray.

4. Put the calamari rings in the basket and air fry for 12 minutes until cooked through. Shake the basket halfway through the cooking time.

5. Serve the calamari rings with the lemon slices sprinkled on top.

154

BREADED SCALLOPS

Prep time: 5 minutes | **Cook time:** 6 to 8 minutes | **Serves** 4

1 egg
3 tablespoons flour
1 cup bread crumbs
1 pound (454 g) fresh scallops
2 tablespoons olive oil
Salt and black pepper, to taste

1. Press "Pre-Heat", set the temperature at 360°F (182°C).
2. In a bowl, lightly beat the egg. Place the flour and bread crumbs into separate shallow dishes.
3. Dredge the scallops in the flour and shake off any excess. Dip the flour-coated scallops in the beaten egg and roll in the bread crumbs.
4. Brush the scallops generously with olive oil and season with salt and pepper, to taste.
5. Arrange the scallops in the air fryer basket and air fry for 6 to 8 minutes, or until the scallops are firm and reach an internal temperature of just 145°F (63°C) on a meat thermometer. Shake the basket halfway through the cooking time.
6. Let the scallops cool for 5 minutes and serve.

155

BROWNED SHRIMP PATTIES

Prep time: 15 minutes | **Cook time:** 10 to 12 minutes | **Serves** 4

½ pound (227 g) raw shrimp, shelled, deveined, and chopped finely

2 cups cooked sushi rice

¼ cup chopped red bell pepper

¼ cup chopped celery

¼ cup chopped green onion

2 teaspoons Worcestershire sauce

½ teaspoon salt

½ teaspoon garlic powder

½ teaspoon Old Bay seasoning

½ cup plain bread crumbs

Cooking spray

1. Press "Pre-Heat", set the temperature at 390°F (199°C).

2. Put all the ingredients except the bread crumbs and oil in a large bowl and stir to incorporate.

3. Scoop out the shrimp mixture and shape into 8 equal-sized patties with your hands, no more than ½-inch thick. Roll the

patties in the bread crumbs on a plate and spray both sides with cooking spray.

4. Place the patties in the air fryer basket. You may need to work in batches to avoid overcrowding.

5. Air fry for 10 to 12 minutes, flipping the patties halfway through, or until the outside is crispy brown.

6. Divide the patties among four plates and serve warm.

156

CAJUN FISH FILLETS

Prep time: 15 minutes | **Cook time:** 6 minutes | **Serves** 4

¾ cup all-purpose flour
¼ cup yellow cornmeal
1 large egg, beaten
¼ cup Cajun seasoning
4 (4-ounce / 113-g) catfish fillets
Cooking spray

1. In a shallow bowl, whisk the flour and cornmeal until blended. Place the egg in a second shallow bowl and the Cajun seasoning in a third shallow bowl.
2. One at a time, dip the catfish fillets in the breading, the egg, and the Cajun seasoning, coating thoroughly.
3. Press "Pre-Heat", set the temperature at 300°F (149°C). Line the air fryer basket with parchment paper.
4. Place the coated fish on the parchment and spritz with oil.
5. Bake for 3 minutes. Flip the fish, spritz it with oil, and bake for 3 to 5 minutes more until the fish flakes easily with a fork and reaches an internal temperature of 145°F (63°C). Serve warm.

157

CHILI PRAWNS

Prep time: 10 minutes | **Cook time:** 8 minutes | **Serves** 2

8 prawns, cleaned
Salt and black pepper, to taste
½ teaspoon ground cayenne pepper
½ teaspoon garlic powder
½ teaspoon ground cumin
½ teaspoon red chili flakes
Cooking spray

1. Press "Pre-Heat", set the temperature at 340°F (171°C). Spritz the air fryer basket with cooking spray.

2. Toss the remaining ingredients in a large bowl until the prawns are well coated.

3. Spread the coated prawns evenly in the basket and spray them with cooking spray.

4. Air fry for 8 minutes, flipping the prawns halfway through, or until the prawns are pink.

5. Remove the prawns from the basket to a plate.

158

COCONUT CHILI FISH CURRY

Prep time: 10 minutes | **Cook time:** 20 to 22 minutes | **Serves** 4

2 tablespoons sunflower oil, divided
1 pound (454 g) fish, chopped
1 ripe tomato, pureéd
2 red chilies, chopped
1 shallot, minced
1 garlic clove, minced
1 cup coconut milk
1 tablespoon coriander powder
1 teaspoon red curry paste
½ teaspoon fenugreek seeds
Salt and white pepper, to taste

1. Press "Pre-Heat", set the temperature at 380°F (193°C). Coat the air fryer basket with 1 tablespoon of sunflower oil.

2. Place the fish in the basket and air fry for 10 minutes. Flip the fish halfway through the cooking time.

3. When done, transfer the cooked fish to a baking pan greased with the remaining 1 tablespoon of sunflower oil. Stir in the remaining ingredients and return to the air fryer.

4. Reduce the temperature to 350°F (177°C) and air fry for another 10 to 12 minutes until heated through.

5. Cool for 5 to 8 minutes before serving.

159

CONFETTI SALMON BURGERS

Prep time: 10 minutes | **Cook time:** 12 minutes | **Serves** 4

14 ounces (397 g) cooked fresh or canned salmon, flaked with a fork

¼ cup minced scallion, white and light green parts only

¼ cup minced red bell pepper

¼ cup minced celery

2 small lemons

1 teaspoon crab boil seasoning such as Old Bay

½ teaspoon kosher salt

½ teaspoon black pepper

1 egg, beaten

½ cup fresh bread crumbs

Vegetable oil, for spraying

1. In a large bowl, combine the salmon, vegetables, the zest and juice of 1 of the lemons, crab boil seasoning, salt, and pepper. Add the egg and bread crumbs and stir to combine. Form the mixture into 4 patties weighing approximately 5 ounces (142 g) each. Chill until firm, about 15 minutes.

2. Press "Pre-Heat", set the temperature at 400°F (204°C).

3. Spray the salmon patties with oil on all sides and spray the air fryer basket to prevent sticking. Air fry for 12 minutes, flipping halfway through, until the burgers are browned and cooked through. Cut the remaining lemon into 4 wedges and serve with the burgers.

160

CORNMEAL-CRUSTED TROUT FINGERS

Prep time: 15 minutes | **Cook time:** 6 minutes | **Serves** 2

½ cup yellow cornmeal, medium or finely ground (not coarse)
⅓ cup all-purpose flour
1½ teaspoons baking powder
1 teaspoon kosher salt, plus more as needed
½ teaspoon freshly ground black pepper, plus more as needed
⅛ teaspoon cayenne pepper
¾ pound (340 g) skinless trout fillets, cut into strips 1 inch wide and 3 inches long
3 large eggs, lightly beaten
Cooking spray
½ cup mayonnaise
2 tablespoons capers, rinsed and finely chopped
1 tablespoon fresh tarragon
1 teaspoon fresh lemon juice, plus lemon wedges, for serving

1. Press "Pre-Heat", set the temperature at 400°F (204°C).

2. In a large bowl, whisk together the cornmeal, flour, baking powder, salt, black pepper, and cayenne. Dip the trout strips in the egg, then toss them in the cornmeal mixture until fully coated.

Fish and Seafood

Transfer the trout to a rack set over a baking sheet and liberally spray all over with cooking spray.

3. Transfer half the fish to the air fryer and air fry until the fish is cooked through and golden brown, about 6 minutes. Transfer the fish sticks to a plate and repeat with the remaining fish.

4. Meanwhile, in a bowl, whisk together the mayonnaise, capers, tarragon, and lemon juice. Season the tartar sauce with salt and black pepper.

5. Serve the trout fingers hot along with the tartar sauce and lemon wedges.

161

CRAB CAKES WITH BELL PEPPERS

Prep time: 5 minutes | **Cook time:** 10 minutes | **Serves** 4

8 ounces (227 g) jumbo lump crab meat
1 egg, beaten
Juice of ½ lemon
⅓ cup bread crumbs
¼ cup diced green bell pepper
¼ cup diced red bell pepper
¼ cup mayonnaise
1 tablespoon Old Bay seasoning
1 teaspoon flour
Cooking spray

1. Press "Pre-Heat", set the temperature at 375°F (190°C).
2. Make the crab cakes: Place all the ingredients except the flour and oil in a large bowl and stir until well incorporated.
3. Divide the crab mixture into four equal portions and shape each portion into a patty with your hands. Top each patty with a sprinkle of ¼ teaspoon of flour.
4. Arrange the crab cakes in the air fryer basket and spritz them with cooking spray.

5. Air fry for 10 minutes, flipping the crab cakes halfway through, or until they are cooked through.

6. Divide the crab cakes among four plates and serve.

162

CRAB CAKES WITH LETTUCE AND APPLE SALAD

Prep time: 10 minutes | **Cook time:** 13 minutes | **Serves** 2

8 ounces (227 g) lump crab meat, picked over for shells
2 tablespoons panko bread crumbs
1 scallion, minced
1 large egg
1 tablespoon mayonnaise
1½ teaspoons Dijon mustard
Pinch of cayenne pepper
2 shallots, sliced thin
1 tablespoon extra-virgin olive oil, divided
1 teaspoon lemon juice, plus lemon wedges for serving
⅛ teaspoon salt
Pinch of pepper
½ (3-ounce / 85-g) small head Bibb lettuce, torn into bite-size pieces
½ apple, cored and sliced thin

1. Press "Pre-Heat", set the temperature at 400°F (204°C).
2. Line large plate with triple layer of paper towels. Transfer crab meat to prepared plate and pat dry with additional paper towels. Combine panko, scallion, egg, mayonnaise, mustard, and

cayenne in a bowl. Using a rubber spatula, gently fold in crab meat until combined; discard paper towels. Divide crab mixture into 4 tightly packed balls, then flatten each into 1-inch-thick cake (cakes will be delicate). Transfer cakes to plate and refrigerate until firm, about 10 minutes.

3. Toss shallots with ½ teaspoon oil in separate bowl; transfer to air fryer basket. Air fry until shallots are browned, 5 to 7 minutes, tossing once halfway through cooking. Return shallots to now-empty bowl and set aside.

4. Arrange crab cakes in air fryer basket, spaced evenly apart. Return basket to air fryer and air fry until crab cakes are light golden brown on both sides, 8 to 10 minutes, flipping and rotating cakes halfway through cooking.

5. Meanwhile, whisk remaining 2½ teaspoons oil, lemon juice, salt, and pepper together in large bowl. Add lettuce, apple, and shallots and toss to coat. Serve crab cakes with salad, passing lemon wedges separately.

163

CRAB CAKES WITH SRIRACHA MAYONNAISE

Prep time: 15 minutes | **Cook time:** 10 minutes | **Serves** 4

Sriracha Mayonnais e :
1 cup mayonnaise
1 tablespoon sriracha
1½ teaspoons freshly squeezed lemon juice

Crab Cake s :
1 teaspoon extra-virgin olive oil
¼ cup finely diced red bell pepper
¼ cup diced onion
¼ cup diced celery
1 pound (454 g) lump crab meat
1 teaspoon Old Bay seasoning
1 egg
1½ teaspoons freshly squeezed lemon juice
1¾ cups panko bread crumbs, divided
Vegetable oil, for spraying

1. Mix the mayonnaise, sriracha, and lemon juice in a small bowl. Place ⅔ cup of the mixture in a separate bowl to form the base of the crab cakes. Cover the remaining sriracha mayonnaise

and refrigerate. (This will become dipping sauce for the crab cakes once they are cooked.)

2. Heat the olive oil in a heavy-bottomed, medium skillet over medium-high heat. Add the bell pepper, onion, and celery and sauté for 3 minutes. Transfer the vegetables to the bowl with the reserved ⅔ cup of sriracha mayonnaise. Mix in the crab, Old Bay seasoning, egg, and lemon juice. Add 1 cup of the panko. Form the crab mixture into 8 cakes. Dredge the cakes in the remaining ¾ cup of panko, turning to coat. Place on a baking sheet. Cover and refrigerate for at least 1 hour and up to 8 hours.

3. Press "Pre-Heat", set the temperature at 375°F (191°C). Spray the air fryer basket with oil. Working in batches as needed so as not to overcrowd the basket, place the chilled crab cakes in a single layer in the basket. Spray the crab cakes with oil. Bake until golden brown, 8 to 10 minutes, carefully turning halfway through cooking. Remove to a platter and keep warm. Repeat with the remaining crab cakes as needed. Serve the crab cakes immediately with sriracha mayonnaise dipping sauce.

164

CRAB RATATOUILLE WITH EGGPLANT AND TOMATOES

Prep time: 15 minutes | **Cook time:** 11 to 14 minutes | **Serves** 4

1½ cups peeled and cubed eggplant
2 large tomatoes, chopped
1 red bell pepper, chopped
1 onion, chopped
1 tablespoon olive oil
½ teaspoon dried basil
½ teaspoon dried thyme
Pinch salt
Freshly ground black pepper, to taste
1½ cups cooked crab meat

1. Press "Pre-Heat", set the temperature at 400°F (204°C).
2. In a metal bowl, stir together the eggplant, tomatoes, bell pepper, onion, olive oil, basil and thyme. Season with salt and pepper.
3. Place the bowl in the preheated air fryer and roast for 9 minutes.
4. Remove the bowl from the air fryer. Add the crab meat and

stir well and roast for another 2 to 5 minutes, or until the vegetables are softened and the ratatouille is bubbling.

5. Serve warm.

165

CRAWFISH CREOLE CASSEROLE

Prep time: 20 minutes | **Cook time:** 25 minutes | **Serves** 4

1½ cups crawfish meat
½ cup chopped celery
½ cup chopped onion
½ cup chopped green bell pepper
2 large eggs, beaten
1 cup half-and-half
1 tablespoon butter, melted
1 tablespoon cornstarch
1 teaspoon Creole seasoning
¾ teaspoon salt
½ teaspoon freshly ground black pepper
1 cup shredded Cheddar cheese
Cooking spray

1. In a medium bowl, stir together the crawfish, celery, onion, and green pepper.

2. In another medium bowl, whisk the eggs, half-and-half, butter, cornstarch, Creole seasoning, salt, and pepper until blended. Stir the egg mixture into the crawfish mixture. Add the cheese and stir to combine.

Fish and Seafood

3. Press "Pre-Heat", set the temperature at 300°F (149°C). Spritz a baking pan with oil.

4. Transfer the crawfish mixture to the prepared pan and place it in the air fryer basket.

5. Bake for 25 minutes, stirring every 10 minutes, until a knife inserted into the center comes out clean.

6. Serve immediately.

166

CRISPY CRAB AND FISH CAKES

Prep time: 20 minutes | **Cook time:** 10 to 12 minutes | **Serves** 4

8 ounces (227 g) imitation crab meat

4 ounces (113 g) leftover cooked fish (such as cod, pollock, or haddock)

2 tablespoons minced celery

2 tablespoons minced green onion

2 tablespoons light mayonnaise

1 tablespoon plus 2 teaspoons Worcestershire sauce

¾ cup crushed saltine cracker crumbs

2 teaspoons dried parsley flakes

1 teaspoon prepared yellow mustard

½ teaspoon garlic powder

½ teaspoon dried dill weed, crushed

½ teaspoon Old Bay seasoning

½ cup panko bread crumbs

Cooking spray

1.Press "Pre-Heat", set the temperature at 390°F (199°C).

2.Pulse the crab meat and fish in a food processor until finely chopped.

Fish and Seafood

3. Transfer the meat mixture to a large bowl, along with the celery, green onion, mayo, Worcestershire sauce, cracker crumbs, parsley flakes, mustard, garlic powder, dill weed, and Old Bay seasoning. Stir to mix well.

4. Scoop out the meat mixture and form into 8 equal-sized patties with your hands.

5. Place the panko bread crumbs on a plate. Roll the patties in the bread crumbs until they are evenly coated on both sides. Spritz the patties with cooking spray.

6. Put the patties in the air fryer basket and bake for 10 to 12 minutes, flipping them halfway through, or until they are golden brown and cooked through.

7. Divide the patties among four plates and serve.

167

CRUNCHY AIR FRIED COD FILLETS

Prep time: 10 minutes | **Cook time:** 12 minutes | **Serves** 2

- 1/3 cup panko bread crumbs
- 1 teaspoon vegetable oil
- 1 small shallot, minced
- 1 small garlic clove, minced
- 1/2 teaspoon minced fresh thyme
- Salt and pepper, to taste
- 1 tablespoon minced fresh parsley
- 1 tablespoon mayonnaise
- 1 large egg yolk
- 1/4 teaspoon grated lemon zest, plus lemon wedges for serving
- 2 (8-ounce / 227-g) skinless cod fillets, 1 1/4 inches thick
- Vegetable oil spray

1. Press "Pre-Heat", set the temperature at 300°F (149°C).
2. Make foil sling for air fryer basket by folding 1 long sheet of aluminum foil so it is 4 inches wide. Lay sheet of foil widthwise across basket, pressing foil into and up sides of basket. Fold excess foil as needed so that edges of foil are flush with top of basket. Lightly spray the foil and basket with vegetable oil spray.
3. Toss the panko with the oil in a bowl until evenly coated.

Stir in the shallot, garlic, thyme, ¼ teaspoon salt, and ⅛ teaspoon pepper. Microwave, stirring frequently, until the panko is light golden brown, about 2 minutes. Transfer to a shallow dish and let cool slightly; stir in the parsley. Whisk the mayonnaise, egg yolk, lemon zest, and ⅛ teaspoon pepper together in another bowl.

4.Pat the cod dry with paper towels and season with salt and pepper. Arrange the fillets, skinned-side down, on plate and brush tops evenly with mayonnaise mixture. (Tuck thinner tail ends of fillets under themselves as needed to create uniform pieces.) Working with 1 fillet at a time, dredge the coated side in panko mixture, pressing gently to adhere. Arrange the fillets, crumb-side up, on sling in the prepared basket, spaced evenly apart.

5.Bake for 12 to 16 minutes, using a sling to rotate fillets halfway through cooking. Using a sling, carefully remove cod from air fryer. Serve with the lemon wedges.

168

EASY SCALLOPS

Prep time: 5 minutes | **Cook time:** 4 minutes | **Serves** 2

12 medium sea scallops, rinsed and patted dry
1 teaspoon fine sea salt
¾ teaspoon ground black pepper, plus more for garnish
Fresh thyme leaves, for garnish (optional)
Avocado oil spray

1. Press "Pre-Heat", set the temperature at 390°F (199°C). Coat the air fryer basket with avocado oil spray.
2. Place the scallops in a medium bowl and spritz with avocado oil spray. Sprinkle the salt and pepper to season.
3. Transfer the seasoned scallops to the air fryer basket, spacing them apart. You may need to work in batches to avoid overcrowding.
4. Air fry for 4 minutes, flipping the scallops halfway through, or until the scallops are firm and reach an internal temperature of just 145°F (63°C) on a meat thermometer.
5. Remove from the basket and repeat with the remaining scallops.
6. Sprinkle the pepper and thyme leaves on top for garnish, if desired. Serve immediately.

169

EASY SHRIMP AND VEGETABLE PAELLA

Prep time: 5 minutes | **Cook time:** 14 to 17 minutes | **Serves** 4

1 (10-ounce / 284-g) package frozen cooked rice, thawed
1 (6-ounce / 170-g) jar artichoke hearts, drained and chopped
¼ cup vegetable broth
½ teaspoon dried thyme
½ teaspoon turmeric
1 cup frozen cooked small shrimp
½ cup frozen baby peas
1 tomato, diced

1. Press "Pre-Heat", set the temperature at 340°F (171°C).
2. Mix together the cooked rice, chopped artichoke hearts, vegetable broth, thyme, and turmeric in a baking pan and stir to combine.
3. Put the baking pan in the preheated air fryer and bake for about 9 minutes, or until the rice is heated through.
4. Remove the pan from the air fryer and fold in the shrimp, baby peas, and diced tomato and mix well.
5. Return to the air fryer and continue cooking for 5 to 8 minutes, or until the shrimp are done and the paella is bubbling.

6.Cool for 5 minutes before serving.

170

FIRED SHRIMP WITH MAYONNAISE SAUCE

Prep time: 5 minutes | **Cook time:** 7 minutes | **Serves** 4

Shrimp
12 jumbo shrimp
½ teaspoon garlic salt
¼ teaspoon freshly cracked mixed peppercorns
Sauce:
4 tablespoons mayonnaise
1 teaspoon grated lemon rind
1 teaspoon Dijon mustard
1 teaspoon chipotle powder
½ teaspoon cumin powder

1. Press "Pre-Heat", set the temperature at 395°F (202°C).

2. In a medium bowl, season the shrimp with garlic salt and cracked mixed peppercorns.

3. Place the shrimp in the air fryer basket and air fry for 5 minutes. Flip the shrimp and cook for another 2 minutes until they are pink and no longer opaque.

4. Meanwhile, stir together all the ingredients for the sauce in a small bowl until well mixed.

5. Remove the shrimp from the basket and serve alongside the sauce.

171

FISH SANDWICH WITH TARTAR SAUCE

Prep time: 10 minutes | **Cook time:** 17 minutes | **Serves** 2

Tartar Sauce:
½ cup mayonnaise
2 tablespoons dried minced onion
1 dill pickle spear, finely chopped
2 teaspoons pickle juice
¼ teaspoon salt
⅛ teaspoon ground black pepper
Fish:
2 tablespoons all-purpose flour
1 egg, lightly beaten
1 cup panko
2 teaspoons lemon pepper
2 tilapia fillets
Cooking spray
2 hoagie rolls

1. Press "Pre-Heat", set the temperature at 400°F (204°C).
2. In a small bowl, combine the mayonnaise, dried minced onion, pickle, pickle juice, salt, and pepper.

3. Whisk to combine and chill in the refrigerator while you make the fish.

4. Place a parchment liner in the air fryer basket.

5. Scoop the flour out onto a plate; set aside.

6. Put the beaten egg in a medium shallow bowl.

7. On another plate, mix to combine the panko and lemon pepper.

8. Dredge the tilapia fillets in the flour, then dip in the egg, and then press into the panko mixture.

9. Place the prepared fillets on the liner in the air fryer in a single layer.

10. Spray lightly with cooking spray and air fry for 8 minutes. Carefully flip the fillets, spray with more cooking spray, and air fry for an additional 9 minutes, until golden and crispy.

11. Place each cooked fillet in a hoagie roll, top with a little bit of tartar sauce, and serve.

172

FRIED CATFISH WITH DIJON SAUCE

Prep time: 20 minutes | **Cook time:** 7 minutes | **Serves** 4

4 tablespoons butter, melted
2 teaspoons Worcestershire sauce, divided
1 teaspoon lemon pepper
1 cup panko bread crumbs
4 (4-ounce / 113-g) catfish fillets
Cooking spray
½ cup sour cream
1 tablespoon Dijon mustard

1. In a shallow bowl, stir together the melted butter, 1 teaspoon of Worcestershire sauce, and the lemon pepper. Place the bread crumbs in another shallow bowl.

2. One at a time, dip both sides of the fillets in the butter mixture, then the bread crumbs, coating thoroughly.

3. Press "Pre-Heat", set the temperature at 300°F (149°C). Line the air fryer basket with parchment paper.

4. Place the coated fish on the parchment and spritz with oil.

5. Bake for 4 minutes. Flip the fish, spritz it with oil, and bake for 3 to 6 minutes more, depending on the thickness of the fillets, until the fish flakes easily with a fork.

6. In a small bowl, stir together the sour cream, Dijon, and remaining 1 teaspoon of Worcestershire sauce. This sauce can be made 1 day in advance and refrigerated before serving. Serve with the fried fish.

173

FRIED SHRIMP

Prep time: 15 minutes | **Cook time:** 5 minutes | **Serves** 4

½ cup self-rising flour

1 teaspoon paprika

1 teaspoon salt

½ teaspoon freshly ground black pepper

1 large egg, beaten

1 cup finely crushed panko bread crumbs

20 frozen large shrimp (about 1-pound / 907-g), peeled and deveined

Cooking spray

1. In a shallow bowl, whisk the flour, paprika, salt, and pepper until blended. Add the beaten egg to a second shallow bowl and the bread crumbs to a third.

2. One at a time, dip the shrimp into the flour, the egg, and the bread crumbs, coating thoroughly.

3. Press "Pre-Heat", set the temperature at 400°F (204°C). Line the air fryer basket with parchment paper.

4. Place the shrimp on the parchment and spritz with oil.

5. Air fry for 2 minutes. Shake the basket, spritz the shrimp

with oil, and air fry for 3 minutes more until lightly browned and crispy. Serve hot.

174

GARLIC BUTTER SHRIMP SCAMPI

Prep time: 5 minutes | **Cook time:** 8 minutes | **Serves** 4

Sauce:
¼ cup unsalted butter
2 tablespoons fish stock or chicken broth
2 cloves garlic, minced
2 tablespoons chopped fresh basil leaves
1 tablespoon lemon juice
1 tablespoon chopped fresh parsley, plus more for garnish
1 teaspoon red pepper flakes

Shrimp:
1 pound (454 g) large shrimp, peeled and deveined, tails removed
Fresh basil sprigs, for garnish

1. Press "Pre-Heat", set the temperature at 350°F (177°C).
2. Put all the ingredients for the sauce in a baking pan and stir to incorporate.
3. Transfer the baking pan to the air fryer and air fry for 3 minutes, or until the sauce is heated through.
4. Once done, add the shrimp to the baking pan, flipping to coat in the sauce.

5.Return to the air fryer and cook for another 5 minutes, or until the shrimp are pink and opaque. Stir the shrimp twice during cooking.

6.Serve garnished with the parsley and basil sprigs.

175

GARLIC SHRIMP WITH PARSLEY

Prep time: 10 minutes | **Cook time:** 5 minutes | **Serves** 4

18 shrimp, shelled and deveined
2 garlic cloves, peeled and minced
2 tablespoons extra-virgin olive oil
2 tablespoons freshly squeezed lemon juice
½ cup fresh parsley, coarsely chopped
1 teaspoon onion powder
1 teaspoon lemon-pepper seasoning
½ teaspoon hot paprika
½ teaspoon salt
¼ teaspoon cumin powder

1. Toss all the ingredients in a mixing bowl until the shrimp are well coated.
2. Cover and allow to marinate in the refrigerator for 30 minutes.
3. Press "Pre-Heat", set the temperature at 400°F (204°C).
4. Arrange the shrimp in the air fryer basket and air fry for 5 minutes, or until the shrimp are pink on the outside and opaque in the center.
5. Remove from the basket and serve warm.

176

GOAT CHEESE SHRIMP

Prep time: 15 minutes | **Cook time:** 7 to 8 minutes | **Serves** 2

1 pound (454 g) shrimp, deveined
1½ tablespoons olive oil
1½ tablespoons balsamic vinegar
1 tablespoon coconut aminos
½ tablespoon fresh parsley, roughly chopped
Sea salt flakes, to taste
1 teaspoon Dijon mustard
½ teaspoon smoked cayenne pepper
½ teaspoon garlic powder
Salt and ground black peppercorns, to taste
1 cup shredded goat cheese

1. Press "Pre-Heat", set the temperature at 385°F (196°C).
2. Except for the cheese, stir together all the ingredients in a large bowl until the shrimp are evenly coated.
3. Arrange the shrimp in the air fryer basket and air fry for 7 to 8 minutes, shaking the basket halfway through, or until the shrimp are pink and cooked through.

4. Serve the shrimp with the shredded goat cheese sprinkled on top.

177

HERBED SCALLOPS WITH VEGETABLES

Prep time: 15 minutes | **Cook time:** 8 to 11 minutes | **Serves** 4

- 1 cup frozen peas
- 1 cup green beans
- 1 cup frozen chopped broccoli
- 2 teaspoons olive oil
- ½ teaspoon dried oregano
- ½ teaspoon dried basil
- 12 ounces (340 g) sea scallops, rinsed and patted dry

1. Press "Pre-Heat", set the temperature at 400°F (204°C).

2. Put the peas, green beans, and broccoli in a large bowl. Drizzle with the olive oil and toss to coat well. Transfer the vegetables to the air fryer basket and air fry for 4 to 6 minutes, or until they are fork-tender.

3. Remove the vegetables from the basket to a serving bowl. Scatter with the oregano and basil and set aside.

4. Place the scallops in the air fryer basket and air fry for 4 to 5 minutes, or until the scallops are firm and just opaque in the center.

5. Transfer the cooked scallops to the bowl of vegetables and toss well. Serve warm.

178

JALEA

Prep time: 20 minutes | **Cook time:** 10 minutes | **Serves** 4

Salsa Crioll a :
½ red onion, thinly sliced
2 tomatoes, diced
1 serrano or jalapeño pepper, deseeded and diced
1 clove garlic, minced
¼ cup chopped fresh cilantro
Pinch of kosher salt
3 limes

Fried Seafoo d :
1 pound (454 g) firm, white-fleshed fish such as cod (add an extra ½-pound /227-g fish if not using shrimp)
20 large or jumbo shrimp, shelled and deveined
¼ cup all-purpose flour
¼ cup cornstarch
1 teaspoon garlic powder
1 teaspoon kosher salt
¼ teaspoon cayenne pepper
2 cups panko bread crumbs
2 eggs, beaten with 2 tablespoons water

Vegetable oil, for spraying

Mayonnaise or tartar sauce, for serving (optional)

1. To make the Salsa Criolla, combine the red onion, tomatoes, pepper, garlic, cilantro, and salt in a medium bowl. Add the juice and zest of 2 of the limes. Refrigerate the salad while you make the fish.

2. To make the seafood, cut the fish fillets into strips approximately 2 inches long and 1 inch wide. Place the flour, cornstarch, garlic powder, salt, and cayenne pepper on a plate and whisk to combine. Place the panko on a separate plate. Dredge the fish strips in the seasoned flour mixture, shaking off any excess. Dip the strips in the egg mixture, coating them completely, then dredge in the panko, shaking off any excess. Place the fish strips on a plate or rack. Repeat with the shrimp, if using.

3. Spray the air fryer basket with oil, and Press "Pre-Heat", set the temperature at 400°F (204°C). Working in 2 or 3 batches, arrange the fish and shrimp in a single layer in the basket, taking care not to crowd the basket. Spray with oil. Air fry for 5 minutes, then flip and air fry for another 4 to 5 minutes until the outside is brown and crisp and the inside of the fish is opaque and flakes easily with a fork. Repeat with the remaining seafood.

4. Place the fried seafood on a platter. Use a slotted spoon to remove the salsa criolla from the bowl, leaving behind any liquid that has accumulated. Place the salsa criolla on top of the fried seafood. Serve immediately with the remaining lime, cut into wedges, and mayonnaise or tartar sauce as desired.

179

LEMONY SHRIMP

Prep time: 10 minutes | **Cook time:** 7 to 8 minutes | **Serves** 4

1 pound (454 g) shrimp, deveined
4 tablespoons olive oil
1½ tablespoons lemon juice
1½ tablespoons fresh parsley, roughly chopped
2 cloves garlic, finely minced
1 teaspoon crushed red pepper flakes, or more to taste
Garlic pepper, to taste
Sea salt flakes, to taste

1. Press "Pre-Heat", set the temperature at 385°F (196°C).
2. Toss all the ingredients in a large bowl until the shrimp are coated on all sides.
3. Arrange the shrimp in the air fryer basket and air fry for 7 to 8 minutes, or until the shrimp are pink and cooked through.
4. Serve warm.

180

MOROCCAN SPICED HALIBUT WITH CHICKPEA SALAD

Prep time: 15 minutes | **Cook time:** 12 minutes | **Serves** 2

¾ teaspoon ground coriander
½ teaspoon ground cumin
¼ teaspoon ground ginger
⅛ teaspoon ground cinnamon
Salt and pepper, to taste
2 (8-ounce / 227-g) skinless halibut fillets, 1¼ inches thick
4 teaspoons extra-virgin olive oil, divided, plus extra for drizzling
1 (15-ounce / 425-g) can chickpeas, rinsed
1 tablespoon lemon juice, plus lemon wedges for serving
1 teaspoon harissa
½ teaspoon honey
2 carrots, peeled and shredded
2 tablespoons chopped fresh mint, divided
Vegetable oil spray

1. Press "Pre-Heat", set the temperature at 300°F (149°C).
2. Make foil sling for air fryer basket by folding 1 long sheet of aluminum foil so it is 4 inches wide. Lay sheet of foil widthwise across basket, pressing foil into and up sides of basket. Fold excess

foil as needed so that edges of foil are flush with top of basket. Lightly spray foil and basket with vegetable oil spray.

3. Combine coriander, cumin, ginger, cinnamon, ⅛ teaspoon salt, and ⅛ teaspoon pepper in a small bowl. Pat halibut dry with paper towels, rub with 1 teaspoon oil, and sprinkle all over with spice mixture. Arrange fillets skinned side down on sling in prepared basket, spaced evenly apart. Bake until halibut flakes apart when gently prodded with a paring knife and registers 140°F (60°C), 12 to 16 minutes, using the sling to rotate fillets halfway through cooking.

4. Meanwhile, microwave chickpeas in medium bowl until heated through, about 2 minutes. Stir in remaining 1 tablespoon oil, lemon juice, harissa, honey, ⅛ teaspoon salt, and ⅛ teaspoon pepper. Add carrots and 1 tablespoon mint and toss to combine. Season with salt and pepper, to taste.

5. Using sling, carefully remove halibut from air fryer and transfer to individual plates. Sprinkle with remaining 1 tablespoon mint and drizzle with extra oil to taste. Serve with salad and lemon wedges.

181

NEW ORLEANS-STYLE CRAB CAKES

Prep time: 10 minutes | **Cook time:** 8 to 10 minutes | **Serves** 4

1¼ cups bread crumbs

2 teaspoons Creole Seasoning

1 teaspoon dry mustard

1 teaspoon salt

1 teaspoon freshly ground black pepper

1½ cups crab meat

2 large eggs, beaten

1 teaspoon butter, melted

⅓ cup minced onion

Cooking spray

Pecan Tartar Sauce, for serving

1. Press "Pre-Heat", set the temperature at 350°F (177°C). Line the air fryer basket with parchment paper.

2. In a medium bowl, whisk the bread crumbs, Creole Seasoning, dry mustard, salt, and pepper until blended. Add the crab meat, eggs, butter, and onion. Stir until blended. Shape the crab mixture into 8 patties.

3. Place the crab cakes on the parchment and spritz with oil.

4. Air fry for 4 minutes. Flip the cakes, spritz them with oil, and air fry for 4 to 6 minutes more until the outsides are firm and a fork inserted into the center comes out clean. Serve with the Pecan Tartar Sauce.

182

ORANGE-MUSTARD GLAZED SALMON

Prep time: 10 minutes | **Cook time:** 10 minutes | **Serves** 2

1 tablespoon orange marmalade

¼ teaspoon grated orange zest plus 1 tablespoon juice

2 teaspoons whole-grain mustard

2 (8-ounce / 227 -g) skin-on salmon fillets, 1½ inches thick

Salt and pepper, to taste

Vegetable oil spray

1. Press "Pre-Heat", set the temperature at 400°F (204°C).

2. Make foil sling for air fryer basket by folding 1 long sheet of aluminum foil so it is 4 inches wide. Lay sheet of foil widthwise across basket, pressing foil into and up sides of basket. Fold excess foil as needed so that edges of foil are flush with top of basket. Lightly spray foil and basket with vegetable oil spray.

3. Combine marmalade, orange zest and juice, and mustard in bowl. Pat salmon dry with paper towels and season with salt and pepper. Brush tops and sides of fillets evenly with glaze. Arrange fillets skin side down on sling in prepared basket, spaced evenly apart. Air fry salmon until center is still translucent when checked with the tip of a paring knife and registers 125°F (52°C) (for

medium-rare), 10 to 14 minutes, using sling to rotate fillets halfway through cooking.

4. Using the sling, carefully remove salmon from air fryer. Slide fish spatula along underside of fillets and transfer to individual serving plates, leaving skin behind. Serve.

183

OYSTER PO'BOY

Prep time: 20 minutes | **Cook time:** 5 minutes | **Serves** 4

¾ cup all-purpose flour
¼ cup yellow cornmeal
1 tablespoon Cajun seasoning
1 teaspoon salt
2 large eggs, beaten
1 teaspoon hot sauce
1 pound (454 g) pre-shucked oysters
1 (12-inch) French baguette, quartered and sliced horizontally
Tartar Sauce, as needed
2 cups shredded lettuce, divided
2 tomatoes, cut into slices
Cooking spray

1. In a shallow bowl, whisk the flour, cornmeal, Cajun seasoning, and salt until blended. In a second shallow bowl, whisk together the eggs and hot sauce.

2. One at a time, dip the oysters in the cornmeal mixture, the eggs, and again in the cornmeal, coating thoroughly.

3. Press "Pre-Heat", set the temperature at 400°F (204°C). Line the air fryer basket with parchment paper.

4. Place the oysters on the parchment and spritz with oil.

5. Air fry for 2 minutes. Shake the basket, spritz the oysters with oil, and air fry for 3 minutes more until lightly browned and crispy.

6. Spread each sandwich half with Tartar Sauce. Assemble the po'boys by layering each sandwich with fried oysters, $\frac{1}{2}$ cup shredded lettuce, and 2 tomato slices.

7. Serve immediately.

184

PANKO CRAB STICKS WITH MAYO SAUCE

Prep time: 5 minutes | **Cook time:** 12 minutes | **Serves** 4

Crab Sticks:
2 eggs
1 cup flour
1/3 cup panko bread crumbs
1 tablespoon old bay seasoning
1 pound (454 g) crab sticks
Cooking spray
Mayo Sauce:
1/2 cup mayonnaise
1 lime, juiced
2 garlic cloves, minced

1. Preheat air fryer to 390°F (199°C).
2. In a bowl, beat the eggs. In a shallow bowl, place the flour. In another shallow bowl, thoroughly combine the panko bread crumbs and old bay seasoning.
3. Dredge the crab sticks in the flour, shaking off any excess, then in the beaten eggs, finally press them in the bread crumb mixture to coat well.

4. Arrange the crab sticks in the air fryer basket and spray with cooking spray.

5. Air fry for 12 minutes until golden brown. Flip the crab sticks halfway through the cooking time.

6. Meanwhile, make the sauce by whisking together the mayo, lime juice, and garlic in a small bowl.

7. Serve the crab sticks with the mayo sauce on the side.

185

PAPRIKA SHRIMP

Prep time: 5 minutes | **Cook time:** 10 minutes | **Serves** 4

1 pound (454 g) tiger shrimp
2 tablespoons olive oil
½ tablespoon old bay seasoning
¼ tablespoon smoked paprika
¼ teaspoon cayenne pepper
A pinch of sea salt

1. Preheat air fryer to 380°F (193°C).
2. Toss all the ingredients in a large bowl until the shrimp are evenly coated.
3. Arrange the shrimp in the air fryer basket and air fry for 10 minutes, shaking the basket halfway through, or until the shrimp are pink and cooked through.
4. Serve hot.

186

PARMESAN FISH FILLETS

Prep time: 8 minutes | **Cook time:** 17 minutes | **Serves** 4

1/3 cup grated Parmesan cheese
1/2 teaspoon fennel seed
1/2 teaspoon tarragon
1/3 teaspoon mixed peppercorns
2 eggs, beaten
4 (4-ounce / 113-g) fish fillets, halved
2 tablespoons dry white wine
1 teaspoon seasoned salt

1. Press "Pre-Heat", set the temperature at 345°F (174°C).
2. Place the grated Parmesan cheese, fennel seed, tarragon, and mixed peppercorns in a food processor and pulse for about 20 seconds until well combined. Transfer the cheese mixture to a shallow dish.
3. Place the beaten eggs in another shallow dish.
4. Drizzle the dry white wine over the top of fish fillets. Dredge each fillet in the beaten eggs on both sides, shaking off any excess, then roll them in the cheese mixture until fully coated. Season with the salt.

5. Arrange the fillets in the air fryer basket and air fry for about 17 minutes, or until the fish is cooked through and no longer translucent. Flip the fillets once halfway through the cooking time.

6. Cool for 5 minutes before serving.

187

PARMESAN-CRUSTED HAKE WITH GARLIC SAUCE

Prep time: 5 minutes | **Cook time:** 10 minutes | **Serves** 3

Fish:
6 tablespoons mayonnaise
1 tablespoon fresh lime juice
1 teaspoon Dijon mustard
1 cup grated Parmesan cheese
Salt, to taste
¼ teaspoon ground black pepper, or more to taste
3 hake fillets, patted dry
Nonstick cooking spray
Garlic Sauce:
¼ cup plain Greek yogurt
2 tablespoons olive oil
2 cloves garlic, minced
½ teaspoon minced tarragon leaves

1. Press "Pre-Heat", set the temperature at 395°F (202°C).
2. Mix the mayo, lime juice, and mustard in a shallow bowl and whisk to combine. In another shallow bowl, stir together the grated Parmesan cheese, salt, and pepper.

3. Dredge each fillet in the mayo mixture, then roll them in the cheese mixture until they are evenly coated on both sides.

4. Spray the air fryer basket with nonstick cooking spray. Arrange the fillets in the basket and air fry for 10 minutes, or until the fish flakes easily with a fork. Flip the fillets halfway through the cooking time.

5. Meanwhile, in a small bowl, whisk all the ingredients for the sauce until well incorporated.

6. Serve the fish warm alongside the sauce.

188

PECAN-CRUSTED TILAPIA

Prep time: 10minutes | **Cook time:** 10 minutes | **Serves** 4

1¼ cups pecans
¾ cup panko bread crumbs
½ cup all-purpose flour
2 tablespoons Cajun seasoning
2 eggs, beaten with 2 tablespoons water
4 (6-ounce/ 170-g) tilapia fillets
Vegetable oil, for spraying
Lemon wedges, for serving

1. Grind the pecans in the food processor until they resemble coarse meal. Combine the ground pecans with the panko on a plate. On a second plate, combine the flour and Cajun seasoning. Dry the tilapia fillets using paper towels and dredge them in the flour mixture, shaking off any excess. Dip the fillets in the egg mixture and then dredge them in the pecan and panko mixture, pressing the coating onto the fillets. Place the breaded fillets on a plate or rack.

2. Press "Pre-Heat", set the temperature at 375°F (191°C). Spray both sides of the breaded fillets with oil. Carefully transfer 2

of the fillets to the air fryer basket and air fry for 9 to 10 minutes, flipping once halfway through, until the flesh is opaque and flaky. Repeat with the remaining fillets.

3. Serve immediately with lemon wedges.

189

PIRI-PIRI KING PRAWNS

Prep time: 10 minutes | **Cook time:** 8 minutes | **Serves** 2

12 king prawns, rinsed
1 tablespoon coconut oil
Salt and ground black pepper, to taste
1 teaspoon onion powder
1 teaspoon garlic paste
1 teaspoon curry powder
½ teaspoon piri piri powder
½ teaspoon cumin powder

1. Press "Pre-Heat", set the temperature at 360°F (182°C).
2. Combine all the ingredients in a large bowl and toss until the prawns are completely coated.
3. Place the prawns in the air fryer basket and air fry for 8 minutes, shaking the basket halfway through, or until the prawns turn pink.

Serve hot.

190

ROASTED COD WITH LEMON-GARLIC POTATOES

Prep time: 10 minutes | **Cook time:** 28 minutes | **Serves** 2

3 tablespoons unsalted butter, softened, divided

2 garlic cloves, minced

1 lemon, grated to yield 2 teaspoons zest and sliced ¼ inch thick

Salt and pepper, to taste

1 large russet potato (12 ounce / 340-g), unpeeled, sliced ¼ inch thick

1 tablespoon minced fresh parsley, chives, or tarragon

2 (8-ounce / 227-g) skinless cod fillets, 1¼ inches thick

Vegetable oil spray

1. Press "Pre-Heat", set the temperature at 400°F (204°C).

2. Make foil sling for air fryer basket by folding 1 long sheet of aluminum foil so it is 4 inches wide. Lay sheet of foil widthwise across basket, pressing foil into and up sides of basket. Fold excess foil as needed so that edges of foil are flush with top of basket. Lightly spray the foil and basket with vegetable oil spray.

3. Microwave 1 tablespoon butter, garlic, 1 teaspoon lemon zest, ¼ teaspoon salt, and ⅛ teaspoon pepper in a medium bowl, stirring once, until the butter is melted and the mixture is fragrant,

about 30 seconds. Add the potato slices and toss to coat. Shingle the potato slices on sling in prepared basket to create 2 even layers. Air fry until potato slices are spotty brown and just tender, 16 to 18 minutes, using a sling to rotate potatoes halfway through cooking.

4. Combine the remaining 2 tablespoons butter, remaining 1 teaspoon lemon zest, and parsley in a small bowl. Pat the cod dry with paper towels and season with salt and pepper. Place the fillets, skinned-side down, on top of potato slices, spaced evenly apart. (Tuck thinner tail ends of fillets under themselves as needed to create uniform pieces.) Dot the fillets with the butter mixture and top with the lemon slices. Return the basket to the air fryer and air fry until the cod flakes apart when gently prodded with a paring knife and registers 140°F (60°C), 12 to 15 minutes, using a sling to rotate the potato slices and cod halfway through cooking.

5. Using a sling, carefully remove potatoes and cod from air fryer. Cut the potato slices into 2 portions between fillets using fish spatula. Slide spatula along underside of potato slices and transfer with cod to individual plates. Serve.

191

ROASTED SALMON FILLETS

Prep time: 5 minutes | **Cook time:** 10 minutes | **Serves** 2

2 (8-ounce / 227 -g) skin-on salmon fillets, 1½ inches thick

1 teaspoon vegetable oil

Salt and pepper, to taste

Vegetable oil spray

1. Press "Pre-Heat", set the temperature at 400°F (204°C).

2. Make foil sling for air fryer basket by folding 1 long sheet of aluminum foil so it is 4 inches wide. Lay sheet of foil widthwise across basket, pressing foil into and up sides of basket. Fold excess foil as needed so that edges of foil are flush with top of basket. Lightly spray foil and basket with vegetable oil spray.

3. Pat salmon dry with paper towels, rub with oil, and season with salt and pepper. Arrange fillets skin side down on sling in prepared basket, spaced evenly apart. Air fry salmon until center is still translucent when checked with the tip of a paring knife and registers 125°F (52°C) (for medium-rare), 10 to 14 minutes, using sling to rotate fillets halfway through cooking.

4. Using the sling, carefully remove salmon from air fryer. Slide fish spatula along underside of fillets and transfer to individual serving plates, leaving skin behind. Serve.

192

SALMON PATTIES

Prep time: 10 minutes | **Cook time:** 8 minutes | **Serves** 4

2 (5-ounce / 142 g) cans salmon, flaked
2 large eggs, beaten
1/3 cup minced onion
2/3 cup panko bread crumbs
1½ teaspoons Italian-Style seasoning
1 teaspoon garlic powder
Cooking spray

1. In a medium bowl, stir together the salmon, eggs, and onion.
2. In a small bowl, whisk the bread crumbs, Italian-Style seasoning, and garlic powder until blended. Add the bread crumb mixture to the salmon mixture and stir until blended. Shape the mixture into 8 patties.
3. Press "Pre-Heat", set the temperature at 350°F (177°C). Line the air fryer basket with parchment paper.
4. Working in batches as needed, place the patties on the parchment and spritz with oil.
5. Bake for 4 minutes. Flip, spritz the patties with oil, and bake for 4 to 8 minutes more, until browned and firm. Serve.

193

SHRIMP AND CHERRY TOMATO KEBABS

Prep time: 15 minutes | **Cook time:** 5 minutes | **Serves** 4

1½ pounds (680 g) jumbo shrimp, cleaned, shelled and deveined

1 pound (454 g) cherry tomatoes

2 tablespoons butter, melted

1 tablespoons Sriracha sauce

Sea salt and ground black pepper, to taste

1 teaspoon dried parsley flakes

½ teaspoon dried basil

½ teaspoon dried oregano

½ teaspoon mustard seeds

½ teaspoon marjoram

Special Equipment:

4 to 6 wooden skewers, soaked in water for 30 minutes

1.Press "Pre-Heat", set the temperature at 400°F (204°C).

2.Put all the ingredients in a large bowl and toss to coat well.

3.Make the kebabs: Thread, alternating jumbo shrimp and cherry tomatoes, onto the wooden skewers that fit into the air fryer.

4. Arrange the kebabs in the air fryer basket. You may need to cook in batches depending on the size of your air fryer basket.

5. Air fry for 5 minutes, or until the shrimp are pink and the cherry tomatoes are softened. Repeat with the remaining kebabs.

6. Let the shrimp and cherry tomato kebabs cool for 5 minutes and serve hot.

194

SHRIMP DEJONGHE SKEWERS

Prep time: 10 minutes | **Cook time:** 15 minutes | **Serves** 4

2 teaspoons sherry
3 tablespoons unsalted butter, melted
1 cup panko bread crumbs
3 cloves garlic, minced
1/3 cup minced flat-leaf parsley, plus more for garnish
1 teaspoon kosher salt
Pinch of cayenne pepper
1½ pounds (680 g) shrimp, peeled and deveined
Vegetable oil, for spraying
Lemon wedges, for serving

1. Stir the sherry and melted butter together in a shallow bowl or pie plate and whisk until combined. Set aside. Whisk together the panko, garlic, parsley, salt, and cayenne pepper on a large plate or shallow bowl.

2. Thread the shrimp onto metal skewers designed for the air fryer or bamboo skewers, 3 to 4 per skewer. Dip 1 shrimp skewer in the butter mixture, then dredge in the panko mixture until each shrimp is lightly coated. Place the skewer on a plate or rimmed baking sheet and repeat the process with the remaining skewers.

3. Press "Pre-Heat", set the temperature at 350°F (177°C). Arrange 4 skewers in the air fryer basket. Spray the skewers with oil and air fry for 8 minutes, until the bread crumbs are golden brown and the shrimp are cooked through. Transfer the cooked skewers to a serving plate and keep warm while cooking the remaining 4 skewers in the air fryer.

4. Sprinkle the cooked skewers with additional fresh parsley and serve with lemon wedges if desired.

195

SOLE AND ASPARAGUS BUNDLES

Prep time: 10 minutes | **Cook time:** 14 minutes | **Serves** 2

8 ounces (227 g) asparagus, trimmed

1 teaspoon extra-virgin olive oil, divided

Salt and pepper, to taste

4 (3-ounce / 85-g) skinless sole or flounder fillets, ⅛ to ¼ inch thick

4 tablespoons unsalted butter, softened

1 small shallot, minced

1 tablespoon chopped fresh tarragon

¼ teaspoon lemon zest plus ½ teaspoon juice

Vegetable oil spray

1. Press "Pre-Heat", set the temperature at 300°F (149°C).

2. Toss asparagus with ½ teaspoon oil, pinch salt, and pinch pepper in a bowl. Cover and microwave until bright green and just tender, about 3 minutes, tossing halfway through microwaving. Uncover and set aside to cool slightly.

3. Make foil sling for air fryer basket by folding 1 long sheet of aluminum foil so it is 4 inches wide. Lay sheet of foil widthwise across basket, pressing foil into and up sides of basket. Fold excess

foil as needed so that edges of foil are flush with top of basket. Lightly spray foil and basket with vegetable oil spray.

4. Pat sole dry with paper towels and season with salt and pepper. Arrange fillets skinned side up on cutting board, with thicker ends closest to you. Arrange asparagus evenly across base of each fillet, then tightly roll fillets away from you around asparagus to form tidy bundles.

5. Rub bundles evenly with remaining $\frac{1}{2}$ teaspoon oil and arrange seam side down on sling in prepared basket. Bake until asparagus is tender and sole flakes apart when gently prodded with a paring knife, 14 to 18 minutes, using a sling to rotate bundles halfway through cooking.

6. Combine butter, shallot, tarragon, and lemon zest and juice in a bowl. Using sling, carefully remove sole bundles from air fryer and transfer to individual plates. Top evenly with butter mixture and serve.

196

SWORDFISH SKEWERS WITH CAPONATA

Prep time: 15 minutes | **Cook time:** 20 minutes | **Serves** 2

1 (10-ounce / 283-g) small Italian eggplant, cut into 1-inch pieces

6 ounces (170 g) cherry tomatoes

3 scallions, cut into 2 inches long

2 tablespoons extra-virgin olive oil, divided

Salt and pepper, to taste

12 ounces (340 g) skinless swordfish steaks, 1¼ inches thick, cut into 1-inch pieces

2 teaspoons honey, divided

2 teaspoons ground coriander, divided

1 teaspoon grated lemon zest, divided

1 teaspoon juice

4 (6-inch) wooden skewers

1 garlic clove, minced

½ teaspoon ground cumin

1 tablespoon chopped fresh basil

1. Press "Pre-Heat", set the temperature at 400°F (204°C).

2. Toss eggplant, tomatoes, and scallions with 1 tablespoon oil, ¼ teaspoon salt, and ⅛ teaspoon pepper in bowl; transfer to air

fryer basket. Air fry until eggplant is softened and browned and tomatoes have begun to burst, about 14 minutes, tossing halfway through cooking. Transfer vegetables to cutting board and set aside to cool slightly.

3. Pat swordfish dry with paper towels. Combine 1 teaspoon oil, 1 teaspoon honey, 1 teaspoon coriander, ½ teaspoon lemon zest, ⅛ teaspoon salt, and pinch pepper in a clean bowl. Add swordfish and toss to coat. Thread swordfish onto skewers, leaving about ¼ inch between each piece (3 or 4 pieces per skewer).

4. Arrange skewers in air fryer basket, spaced evenly apart. (Skewers may overlap slightly.) Return basket to air fryer and air fry until swordfish is browned and registers 140°F (60°C), 6 to 8 minutes, flipping and rotating skewers halfway through cooking.

5. Meanwhile, combine remaining 2 teaspoons oil, remaining 1 teaspoon honey, remaining 1 teaspoon coriander, remaining ½ teaspoon lemon zest, lemon juice, garlic, cumin, ¼ teaspoon salt, and ⅛ teaspoon pepper in large bowl. Microwave, stirring once, until fragrant, about 30 seconds. Coarsely chop the cooked vegetables, transfer to bowl with dressing, along with any accumulated juices, and gently toss to combine. Stir in basil and season with salt and pepper to taste. Serve skewers with caponata.

197

TANDOORI-SPICED SALMON AND POTATOES

Prep time: 10 minutes | **Cook time:** 28 minutes | **Serves** 2

1 pound (454 g) fingerling potatoes

2 tablespoons vegetable oil, divided

Kosher salt and freshly ground black pepper, to taste

1 teaspoon ground turmeric

1 teaspoon ground cumin

1 teaspoon ground ginger

½ teaspoon smoked paprika

¼ teaspoon cayenne pepper

2 (6-ounce / 170-g) skin-on salmon fillets

1. Press "Pre-Heat", set the temperature at 375°F (191°C).

2. In a bowl, toss the potatoes with 1 tablespoon of the oil until evenly coated. Season with salt and pepper. Transfer the potatoes to the air fryer and air fry for 20 minutes.

3. Meanwhile, in a bowl, combine the remaining 1 tablespoon oil, the turmeric, cumin, ginger, paprika, and cayenne. Add the salmon fillets and turn in the spice mixture until fully coated all over.

4. After the potatoes have cooked for 20 minutes, place the

salmon fillets, skin-side up, on top of the potatoes, and continue cooking until the potatoes are tender, the salmon is cooked, and the salmon skin is slightly crisp.

5. Transfer the salmon fillets to two plates and serve with the potatoes while both are warm.

198

THAI SHRIMP SKEWERS WITH PEANUT DIPPING SAUCE

Prep time: 15 minutes | **Cook time:** 6 minutes | **Serves** 2

Salt and pepper, to taste
12 ounces (340 g) extra-large shrimp, peeled and deveined
1 tablespoon vegetable oil
1 teaspoon honey
½ teaspoon grated lime zest plus 1 tablespoon juice, plus lime wedges for serving
6 (6-inch) wooden skewers
3 tablespoons creamy peanut butter
3 tablespoons hot tap water
1 tablespoon chopped fresh cilantro
1 teaspoon fish sauce

1. Press "Pre-Heat", set the temperature at 400°F (204°C).
2. Dissolve 2 tablespoons salt in 1 quart cold water in a large container. Add shrimp, cover, and refrigerate for 15 minutes.
3. Remove shrimp from brine and pat dry with paper towels. Whisk oil, honey, lime zest, and ¼ teaspoon pepper together in a large bowl. Add shrimp and toss to coat. Thread shrimp onto skewers, leaving about ¼ inch between each shrimp (3 or 4 shrimp per skewer).

4. Arrange 3 skewers in air fryer basket, parallel to each other and spaced evenly apart. Arrange remaining 3 skewers on top, perpendicular to the bottom layer. Air fry until shrimp are opaque throughout, 6 to 8 minutes, flipping and rotating skewers halfway through cooking.

5. Whisk peanut butter, hot tap water, lime juice, cilantro, and fish sauce together in a bowl until smooth. Serveskewers with peanut dipping sauce and lime wedges.

199

TRADITIONAL TUNA MELT

Prep time: 10 minutes | **Cook time:** 12 minutes | **Serves** 2

2 cans unsalted albacore tuna, drained
½ cup mayonnaise
½ teaspoon salt
¼ teaspoon ground black pepper
4 slices sourdough bread
4 pieces sliced Cheddar cheese
2 tablespoons crispy fried onions
Cooking spray
¼ teaspoon granulated garlic

1. Press "Pre-Heat", set the temperature at 390°F (199°C).

2. In a medium bowl, combine the tuna, mayonnaise, salt, and pepper, and mix well. Set aside.

3. Assemble the sandwiches by laying out the bread and then adding 1 slice of cheese on top of each piece.

4. Sprinkle the fried onions on top of the cheese on 2 of the slices of bread.

5. Divide the tuna between the 2 slices of bread with the onions.

6. Take the remaining 2 slices of bread that have only cheese on them, and place them cheese-side down on top of the tuna.

7. Place one sandwich in the air fryer basket, spray with cooking spray, and air fry for 6 minutes.

8. Using a spatula, flip the sandwich over, spray it again, and air fry for another 6 minutes, or until golden brown. Sprinkle with the garlic immediately after removing from the air fryer basket. Repeat with the other sandwich.

9. Allow the sandwiches to sit for 1 to 2 minutes before cutting and serving.

TROUT AMANDINE WITH LEMON BUTTER SAUCE

Prep time: 20 minutes | **Cook time:** 8 minutes | **Serves** 4

Trout Amandine:
²/₃ cup toasted almonds
¹/₃ cup grated Parmesan cheese
1 teaspoon salt
½ teaspoon freshly ground black pepper
2 tablespoons butter, melted
4 (4-ounce / 113-g) trout fillets, or salmon fillets
Cooking spray
Lemon Butter Sauce:
8 tablespoons (1 stick) butter, melted
2 tablespoons freshly squeezed lemon juice
½ teaspoon Worcestershire sauce
½ teaspoon salt
½ teaspoon freshly ground black pepper
¼ teaspoon hot sauce

1. In a blender or food processor, pulse the almonds for 5 to 10 seconds until finely processed. Transfer to a shallow bowl and whisk in the Parmesan cheese, salt, and pepper. Place the melted butter in another shallow bowl.

2.One at a time, dip the fish in the melted butter, then the almond mixture, coating thoroughly.

3.Press "Pre-Heat", set the temperature at 300°F (149°C). Line the air fryer basket with parchment paper.

4.Place the coated fish on the parchment and spritz with oil.

5.Bake for 4 minutes. Flip the fish, spritz it with oil, and bake for 4 minutes more until the fish flakes easily with a fork.

6.In a small bowl, whisk the butter, lemon juice, Worcestershire sauce, salt, pepper, and hot sauce until blended.

7.Serve with the fish.

201

TUNA-STUFFED QUINOA PATTIES

Prep time: 10 minutes | **Cook time:** 15 minutes | **Serves** 4

12 ounces (340 g) quinoa
4 slices white bread with crusts removed
½ cup milk
3 eggs
10 ounces (283 g) tuna packed in olive oil, drained
2 to 3 lemons
Kosher salt and pepper, to taste
1¼ cups panko bread crumbs
Vegetable oil, for spraying
Lemon wedges, for serving

1.Rinse the quinoa in a fine-mesh sieve until the water runs clear. Bring 4 cups of salted water to a boil. Add the quinoa, cover, and reduce heat to low. Simmer the quinoa covered until most of the water is absorbed and the quinoa is tender, 15 to 20 minutes. Drain and allow to cool to room temperature. Meanwhile, soak the bread in the milk.

2.Mix the drained quinoa with the soaked bread and 2 of the eggs in a large bowl and mix thoroughly. In a medium bowl, combine the tuna, the remaining egg, and the juice and zest of 1 of the lemons. Season well with salt and pepper. Spread the panko on a plate.

3. Scoop up approximately ½ cup of the quinoa mixture and flatten into a patty. Place a heaping tablespoon of the tuna mixture in the center of the patty and close the quinoa around the tuna. Flatten the patty slightly to create an oval-shaped croquette. Dredge both sides of the croquette in the panko. Repeat with the remaining quinoa and tuna.

4. Spray the air fryer basket with oil to prevent sticking, and Press "Pre-Heat", set the temperature at 400°F (204°C). Arrange 4 or 5 of the croquettes in the basket, taking care to avoid overcrowding. Spray the tops of the croquettes with oil. Air fry for 8 minutes until the top side is browned and crispy. Carefully turn the croquettes over and spray the second side with oil. Air fry until the second side is browned and crispy, another 7 minutes. Repeat with the remaining croquettes.

5. Serve the croquetas warm with plenty of lemon wedges for spritzing.

POULTRY

202

AIR FRYER CHICKEN FAJITAS

Prep time: 15 minutes | **Cook time:** 10 to 15 minutes | **Serves** 4

4 (5-ounce / 142-g) low-sodium boneless, skinless chicken breasts, cut into 4-by-½-inch strips

1 tablespoon freshly squeezed lemon juice

2 teaspoons olive oil

2 teaspoons chili powder

2 red bell peppers, sliced

4 low-sodium whole-wheat tortillas

⅓ cup nonfat sour cream

1 cup grape tomatoes, sliced

1. Press "Pre-Heat", set the temperature at 380°F (193°C).

2. In a large bowl, mix the chicken, lemon juice, olive oil, and chili powder. Toss to coat. Transfer the chicken to the air fryer basket. Add the red bell peppers. Roast for 10 to 15 minutes, or until the chicken reaches an internal temperature of 165°F (74°C) on a meat thermometer.

3. Assemble the fajitas with the tortillas, chicken, bell peppers, sour cream, and tomatoes. Serve immediately.

203

ALMOND-CRUSTED CHICKEN NUGGETS

Prep time: 10 minutes | **Cook time:** 10 to 13 minutes | **Serves** 4

1 egg white

1 tablespoon freshly squeezed lemon juice

½ teaspoon dried basil

½ teaspoon ground paprika

1 pound (454 g) low-sodium boneless, skinless chicken breasts, cut into 1½-inch cubes

½ cup ground almonds

2 slices low-sodium whole-wheat bread, crumbled

1. Press "Pre-Heat", set the temperature at 400°F (204°C).

2. In a shallow bowl, beat the egg white, lemon juice, basil, and paprika with a fork until foamy.

3. Add the chicken and stir to coat.

4. On a plate, mix the almonds and bread crumbs.

5. Toss the chicken cubes in the almond and bread crumb mixture until coated.

6. Bake the nuggets in the air fryer, in two batches, for 10 to 13 minutes, or until the chicken reaches an internal temperature of 165°F (74°C) on a meat thermometer. Serve immediately.

204

APRICOT-GLAZED CHICKEN

Prep time: 5 minutes | **Cook time:** 12 minutes | **Serves** 2

2 tablespoons apricot preserves
½ teaspoon minced fresh thyme or ⅛ teaspoon dried
2 (8-ounce / 227-g) boneless, skinless chicken breasts, trimmed
1 teaspoon vegetable oil
Salt and pepper, to taste

1. Press "Pre-Heat", set the temperature at 400°F (204°C).
2. Microwave apricot preserves and thyme in bowl until fluid, about 30 seconds; set aside. Pound chicken to uniform thickness as needed. Pat dry with paper towels, rub with oil, and season with salt and pepper.
3. Arrange breasts skin-side down in air fryer basket, spaced evenly apart, alternating ends. Air fry the chicken for 4 minutes. Flip chicken and brush skin side with apricot-thyme mixture. Air fry until chicken registers 160°F (71°C), 8 to 12 minutes more.
4. Transfer chicken to serving platter, tent loosely with aluminum foil, and let rest for 5 minutes. Serve.

205

BARBECUE CHICKEN

Prep time: 10 minutes | **Cook time:** 18 to 20 minutes | **Serves** 4

1/3 cup no-salt-added tomato sauce

2 tablespoons low-sodium grainy mustard

2 tablespoons apple cider vinegar

1 tablespoon honey

2 garlic cloves, minced

1 jalapeño pepper, minced

3 tablespoons minced onion

4 (5-ounce / 142-g) low-sodium boneless, skinless chicken breasts

1.Press "Pre-Heat", set the temperature at 370°F (188°C).

2.In a small bowl, stir together the tomato sauce, mustard, cider vinegar, honey, garlic, jalapeño, and onion.

3.Brush the chicken breasts with some sauce and air fry for 10 minutes.

4.Remove the air fryer basket and turn the chicken; brush with more sauce. Air fry for 5 minutes more.

5.Remove the air fryer basket and turn the chicken again;

brush with more sauce. Air fry for 3 to 5 minutes more, or until the chicken reaches an internal temperature of 165°F (74°C) on a meat thermometer. Discard any remaining sauce. Serve immediately.

206

BARBECUED CHICKEN WITH CREAMY COLESLAW

Prep time: 10 minutes | **Cook time:** 20 minutes | **Serves** 2

3 cups shredded coleslaw mix

Salt and pepper

2 (12-ounce / 340-g) bone-in split chicken breasts, trimmed

1 teaspoon vegetable oil

2 tablespoons barbecue sauce, plus extra for serving

2 tablespoons mayonnaise

2 tablespoons sour cream

1 teaspoon distilled white vinegar, plus extra for seasoning

¼ teaspoon sugar

1. Press "Pre-Heat", set the temperature at 350°F (177°C).

2. Toss coleslaw mix and ¼ teaspoon salt in a colander set over bowl. Let sit until wilted slightly, about 30 minutes. Rinse, drain, and dry well with a dish towel.

3. Meanwhile, pat chicken dry with paper towels, rub with oil, and season with salt and pepper. Arrange breasts skin-side down in air fryer basket, spaced evenly apart, alternating ends. Bake for 10 minutes. Flip breasts and brush skin side with barbecue sauce. Return basket to air fryer and bake until well browned and chicken registers 160°F (71°C), 10 to 15 minutes.

4. Transfer chicken to serving platter, tent loosely with aluminum foil, and let rest for 5 minutes. While chicken rests, whisk mayonnaise, sour cream, vinegar, sugar, and pinch pepper together in a large bowl. Stir in coleslaw mix and season with salt, pepper, and additional vinegar to taste. Serve chicken with coleslaw, passing extra barbecue sauce separately.

207

BUTTERMILK PAPRIKA CHICKEN

Prep time: 7 minutes | **Cook time:** 17 to 23 minutes | **Serves** 4

4 (5-ounce / 142-g) low-sodium boneless, skinless chicken breasts, pounded to about ½ inch thick

½ cup buttermilk

½ cup all-purpose flour

2 tablespoons cornstarch

1 teaspoon dried thyme

1 teaspoon ground paprika

1 egg white

1 tablespoon olive oil

1. Press "Pre-Heat", set the temperature at 390°F (199°C).

2. In a shallow bowl, mix the chicken and buttermilk. Let stand for 10 minutes.

3. Meanwhile, in another shallow bowl, mix the flour, cornstarch, thyme, and paprika.

4. In a small bowl, whisk the egg white and olive oil. Quickly stir this egg mixture into the flour mixture so the dry ingredients are evenly moistened.

5. Remove the chicken from the buttermilk and shake off any

excess liquid. Dip each piece of chicken into the flour mixture to coat.

6.Air fry the chicken in the air fryer basket for 17 to 23 minutes, or until the chicken reaches an internal temperature of 165°F (74°C) on a meat thermometer. Serve immediately.

208

CHEESY CHICKEN TACOS

Prep time: 10 minutes | **Cook time:** 12 to 16 minutes | **Serves** 2 to 4

1 teaspoon chili powder
½ teaspoon ground cumin
½ teaspoon garlic powder
Salt and pepper, to taste
Pinch cayenne pepper
1 pound (454 g) boneless, skinless chicken thighs, trimmed
1 teaspoon vegetable oil
1 tomato, cored and chopped
2 tablespoons finely chopped red onion
2 teaspoons minced jalapeño chile
1½ teaspoons lime juice
6 to 12 (6-inch) corn tortillas, warmed
1 cup shredded iceberg lettuce
3 ounces (85 g) cheddar cheese, shredded (¾ cup)

1. Press "Pre-Heat", set the temperature at 400°F (204°C).
2. Combine chili powder, cumin, garlic powder, ½ teaspoon salt, ¼ teaspoon pepper, and cayenne in bowl. Pat chicken dry with paper towels, rub with oil, and sprinkle evenly with spice

Poultry

mixture. Place chicken in air fryer basket. Air fry until chicken registers 165°F (74°C), 12 to 16 minutes, flipping chicken halfway through cooking.

3. Meanwhile, combine tomato, onion, jalapeño, and lime juice in a bowl; season with salt and pepper to taste and set aside until ready to serve.

4. Transfer chicken to a cutting board, let cool slightly, then shred into bite-size pieces using 2 forks. Serve chicken on warm tortillas, topped with salsa, lettuce, and cheddar.

209

CHICKEN AND VEGETABLE FAJITAS

Prep time: 15 minutes | **Cook time:** 23 minutes | **Serves** 6

Chicken:
1 pound (454 g) boneless, skinless chicken thighs, cut crosswise into thirds
1 tablespoon vegetable oil
4½ teaspoons taco seasoning
Vegetables
1 cup sliced onion
1 cup sliced bell pepper
1 or 2 jalapeños, quartered lengthwise
1 tablespoon vegetable oil
½ teaspoon kosher salt
½ teaspoon ground cumin
For Serving:
Tortillas
Sour cream
Shredded cheese
Guacamole
Salsa

1. Press "Pre-Heat", set the temperature at 375°F (191°C).

2. For the chicken: In a medium bowl, toss together the chicken, vegetable oil, and taco seasoning to coat.

3. For the vegetables: In a separate bowl, toss together the onion, bell pepper, jalapeño (s), vegetable oil, salt, and cumin to coat.

4. Place the chicken in the air fryer basket. Air fry for 10 minutes. Add the vegetables to the basket, toss everything together to blend the seasonings, and air fry for 13 minutes more. Use a meat thermometer to ensure the chicken has reached an internal temperature of 165°F (74°C).

5. Transfer the chicken and vegetables to a serving platter. Serve with tortillas and the desired fajita fixings.

210

CHICKEN BURGERS WITH HAM AND CHEESE

Prep time: 12 minutes | **Cook time:** 13 to 16 minutes | **Serves** 4

- ⅓ cup soft bread crumbs
- 3 tablespoons milk
- 1 egg, beaten
- ½ teaspoon dried thyme
- Pinch salt
- Freshly ground black pepper, to taste
- 1¼ pounds (567 g) ground chicken
- ¼ cup finely chopped ham
- ⅓ cup grated Havarti cheese
- Olive oil for misting

1. Press "Pre-Heat", set the temperature at 350°F (177°C).
2. In a medium bowl, combine the bread crumbs, milk, egg, thyme, salt, and pepper. Add the chicken and mix gently but thoroughly with clean hands.
3. Form the chicken into eight thin patties and place on waxed paper.
4. Top four of the patties with the ham and cheese. Top with

Poultry

remaining four patties and gently press the edges together to seal, so the ham and cheese mixture is in the middle of the burger.

5. Place the burgers in the basket and mist with olive oil. Bake for 13 to 16 minutes or until the chicken is thoroughly cooked to 165°F (74°C) as measured with a meat thermometer. Serve immediately.

211

CHICKEN MANCHURIAN

Prep time: 10 minutes | **Cook time:** 20 minutes | **Serves** 2

1 pound (454 g) boneless, skinless chicken breasts, cut into 1-inch pieces

¼ cup ketchup

1 tablespoon tomato-based chili sauce, such as Heinz

1 tablespoon soy sauce

1 tablespoon rice vinegar

2 teaspoons vegetable oil

1 teaspoon hot sauce, such as Tabasco

½ teaspoon garlic powder

¼ teaspoon cayenne pepper

2 scallions, thinly sliced

Cooked white rice, for serving

1. Press "Pre-Heat", set the temperature at 350°F (177°C).

2. In a bowl, combine the chicken, ketchup, chili sauce, soy sauce, vinegar, oil, hot sauce, garlic powder, cayenne, and three-quarters of the scallions and toss until evenly coated.

3. Scrape the chicken and sauce into a metal cake pan and place the pan in the air fryer. Bake until the chicken is cooked

through and the sauce is reduced to a thick glaze, about 20 minutes, flipping the chicken pieces halfway through.

4.Remove the pan from the air fryer. Spoon the chicken and sauce over rice and top with the remaining scallions. Serve immediately.

212

CHICKEN WITH PINEAPPLE AND PEACH

Prep time: 10 minutes | **Cook time:** 14 to 15 minutes | **Serves** 4

1 pound (454 g) low-sodium boneless, skinless chicken breasts, cut into 1-inch pieces

1 medium red onion, chopped

1 (8-ounce / 227-g) can pineapple chunks, drained, ¼ cup juice reserved

1 tablespoon peanut oil or safflower oil

1 peach, peeled, pitted, and cubed

1 tablespoon cornstarch

½ teaspoon ground ginger

¼ teaspoon ground allspice

Brown rice, cooked (optional)

1. Press "Pre-Heat", set the temperature at 380°F (193°C).
2. In a medium metal bowl, mix the chicken, red onion, pineapple, and peanut oil. Bake in the air fryer for 9 minutes. Remove and stir.
3. Add the peach and return the bowl to the air fryer. Bake for 3 minutes more. Remove and stir again.
4. In a small bowl, whisk the reserved pineapple juice, the

cornstarch, ginger, and allspice well. Add to the chicken mixture and stir to combine.

5. Bake for 2 to 3 minutes more, or until the chicken reaches an internal temperature of 165°F (74°C) on a meat thermometer and the sauce is slightly thickened.

6. Serve immediately over hot cooked brown rice, if desired.

213

CHINA SPICY TURKEY THIGHS

Prep time: 10 minutes | **Cook time:** 25 minutes | **Serves** 6

2 pounds (907 g) turkey thighs

1 teaspoon Chinese five-spice powder

¼ teaspoon Sichuan pepper

1 teaspoon pink Himalayan salt

1 tablespoon Chinese rice vinegar

1 tablespoon mustard

1 tablespoon chili sauce

2 tablespoons soy sauce

Cooking spray

1. Press "Pre-Heat", set the temperature at 360°F (182°C). Spritz the air fryer basket with cooking spray.

2. Rub the turkey thighs with five-spice powder, Sichuan pepper, and salt on a clean work surface.

3. Put the turkey thighs in the preheated air fryer and spritz with cooking spray. You may need to work in batches to avoid overcrowding.

4. Air fry for 22 minutes or until well browned. Flip the thighs at least three times during the cooking.

5. Meanwhile, heat the remaining ingredients in a saucepan over medium-high heat. Cook for 3 minutes or until the sauce is thickened and reduces to two thirds.

6. Transfer the thighs onto a plate and baste with sauce before serving.

214

COCONUT CHICKEN MEATBALLS

Prep time: 10 minutes | **Cook time:** 14 minutes | **Serves** 4

1 pound (454 g) ground chicken
2 scallions, finely chopped
1 cup chopped fresh cilantro leaves
¼ cup unsweetened shredded coconut
1 tablespoon hoisin sauce
1 tablespoon soy sauce
2 teaspoons sriracha or other hot sauce
1 teaspoon toasted sesame oil
½ teaspoon kosher salt
1 teaspoon black pepper

1. Press "Pre-Heat", set the temperature at 350°F (177°C).

2. In a large bowl, gently mix the chicken, scallions, cilantro, coconut, hoisin, soy sauce, sriracha, sesame oil, salt, and pepper until thoroughly combined (the mixture will be wet and sticky).

3. Place a sheet of parchment paper in the air fryer basket. Using a small scoop or teaspoon, drop rounds of the mixture in a single layer onto the parchment paper.

4. Air fry for 10 minutes, turning the meatballs halfway through the cooking time. Increase the temperature to 400°F

(204°C) and air fry for 4 minutes more to brown the outsides of the meatballs. Use a meat thermometer to ensure the meatballs have reached an internal temperature of 165°F (74°C).

5. Transfer the meatballs to a serving platter. Repeat with any remaining chicken mixture. Serve.

215

CRANBERRY CURRY CHICKEN

Prep time: 12 minutes | **Cook time:** 18 minutes | **Serves** 4

3 (5-ounce / 142-g) low-sodium boneless, skinless chicken breasts, cut into 1½-inch cubes

2 teaspoons olive oil

2 tablespoons cornstarch

1 tablespoon curry powder

1 tart apple, chopped

½ cup low-sodium chicken broth

⅓ cup dried cranberries

2 tablespoons freshly squeezed orange juice

Brown rice, cooked (optional)

1. Press "Pre-Heat", set the temperature at 380°F (193°C).

2. In a medium bowl, mix the chicken and olive oil. Sprinkle with the cornstarch and curry powder. Toss to coat. Stir in the apple and transfer to a metal pan. Bake in the air fryer for 8 minutes, stirring once during cooking.

3. Add the chicken broth, cranberries, and orange juice. Bake for about 10 minutes more, or until the sauce is slightly thickened and the chicken reaches an internal temperature of 165°F (74°C)

on a meat thermometer. Serve over hot cooked brown rice, if desired.

216

CRISP CHICKEN WINGS

Prep time: 15 minutes | **Cook time:** 20 minutes | **Serves** 4

1 pound (454 g) chicken wings
3 tablespoons vegetable oil
½ cup all-purpose flour
½ teaspoon smoked paprika
½ teaspoon garlic powder
½ teaspoon kosher salt
1½ teaspoons freshly cracked black pepper

1. Press "Pre-Heat", set the temperature at 400°F (204°C).
2. Place the chicken wings in a large bowl. Drizzle the vegetable oil over wings and toss to coat.
3. In a separate bowl, whisk together the flour, paprika, garlic powder, salt, and pepper until combined.
4. Dredge the wings in the flour mixture one at a time, coating them well, and place in the air fryer basket. Air fry for 20 minutes, turning the wings halfway through the cooking time, until the breading is browned and crunchy.
5. Serve hot.

217

CRISPY CHICKEN CORDON BLEU

Prep time: 15 minutes | **Cook time:** 13 to 15 minutes | **Serves** 4

- 4 chicken breast fillets
- ¼ cup chopped ham
- ⅓ cup grated Swiss or Gruyère cheese
- ¼ cup flour
- Pinch salt
- Freshly ground black pepper, to taste
- ½ teaspoon dried marjoram
- 1 egg
- 1 cup panko bread crumbs
- Olive oil for misting

1. Press "Pre-Heat", set the temperature at 380°F (193°C).
2. Put the chicken breast fillets on a work surface and gently press them with the palm of your hand to make them a bit thinner. Don't tear the meat.
3. In a small bowl, combine the ham and cheese. Divide this mixture among the chicken fillets. Wrap the chicken around the filling to enclose it, using toothpicks to hold the chicken together.
4. In a shallow bowl, mix the flour, salt, pepper, and marjoram.

In another bowl, beat the egg. Spread the bread crumbs out on a plate.

5.Dip the chicken into the flour mixture, then into the egg, then into the bread crumbs to coat thoroughly.

6.Put the chicken in the air fryer basket and mist with olive oil.

7.Bake for 13 to 15 minutes or until the chicken is thoroughly cooked to 165°F (74°C). Carefully remove the toothpicks and serve.

218

CURRIED ORANGE HONEY CHICKEN

Prep time: 10 minutes | **Cook time:** 16 to 19 minutes | **Serves** 4

¾ pound (340 g) boneless, skinless chicken thighs, cut into 1-inch pieces

1 yellow bell pepper, cut into 1½-inch pieces

1 small red onion, sliced

Olive oil for misting

¼ cup chicken stock

2 tablespoons honey

¼ cup orange juice

1 tablespoon cornstarch

2 to 3 teaspoons curry powder

1. Press "Pre-Heat", set the temperature at 370°F (188°C).
2. Put the chicken thighs, pepper, and red onion in the air fryer basket and mist with olive oil.
3. Roast for 12 to 14 minutes or until the chicken is cooked to 165°F (74°C), shaking the basket halfway through cooking time.
4. Remove the chicken and vegetables from the air fryer basket and set aside.
5. In a metal bowl, combine the stock, honey, orange juice,

cornstarch, and curry powder, and mix well. Add the chicken and vegetables, stir, and put the bowl in the basket.

6.Return the basket to the air fryer and roast for 2 minutes. Remove and stir, then roast for 2 to 3 minutes or until the sauce is thickened and bubbly.

7.Serve warm.

219

DEEP FRIED DUCK LEG QUARTERS

Prep time: 5 minutes | **Cook time:** 45 minutes | **Serves** 4

4 (½-pound / 227-g) skin-on duck leg quarters
2 medium garlic cloves, minced
½ teaspoon salt
½ teaspoon ground black pepper

1. Press "Pre-Heat", set the temperature at 300°F (149°C). Spritz the air fryer basket with cooking spray.
2. On a clean work surface, rub the duck leg quarters with garlic, salt, and black pepper.
3. Arrange the leg quarters in the preheated air fryer and spritz with cooking spray.
4. Air fry for 30 minutes, then flip the leg quarters and increase the temperature to 375°F (191°C). Air fry for 15 more minutes or until well browned and crispy.
5. Remove the duck leg quarters from the air fryer and allow to cool for 10 minutes before serving.

220

DUCK BREASTS WITH MARMALADE BALSAMIC GLAZE

Prep time: 5 minutes | **Cook time:** 13 minutes | **Serves** 4

4 (6-ounce / 170-g) skin-on duck breasts
1 teaspoon salt
¼ cup orange marmalade
1 tablespoon white balsamic vinegar
¾ teaspoon ground black pepper

1. Press "Pre-Heat", set the temperature at 400°F (204°C).
2. Cut 10 slits into the skin of the duck breasts, then sprinkle with salt on both sides.
3. Place the breasts in the preheated air fryer, skin side up, and air fry for 10 minutes.
4. Meanwhile, combine the remaining ingredients in a small bowl. Stir to mix well.
5. When the frying is complete, brush the duck skin with the marmalade mixture. Flip the breast and air fry for 3 more minutes or until the skin is crispy and the breast is well browned.
6. Serve immediately.

221

EASY TANDOORI CHICKEN

Prep time: 5 minutes | **Cook time:** 18 to 23 minutes | **Serves** 4

²/₃ cup plain low-fat yogurt
2 tablespoons freshly squeezed lemon juice
2 teaspoons curry powder
½ teaspoon ground cinnamon
2 garlic cloves, minced
2 teaspoons olive oil
4 (5-ounce / 142-g) low-sodium boneless, skinless chicken breasts

1. In a medium bowl, whisk the yogurt, lemon juice, curry powder, cinnamon, garlic, and olive oil.

2. With a sharp knife, cut thin slashes into the chicken. Add it to the yogurt mixture and turn to coat. Let stand for 10 minutes at room temperature. You can also prepare this ahead of time and marinate the chicken in the refrigerator for up to 24 hours.

3. Press "Pre-Heat", set the temperature at 360°F (182°C).

4. Remove the chicken from the marinade and shake off any excess liquid. Discard any remaining marinade.

5. Roast the chicken for 10 minutes. With tongs, carefully turn each piece. Roast for 8 to 13 minutes more, or until the chicken reaches an internal temperature of 165°F (74°C) on a meat thermometer. Serve immediately.

222

GARLIC SOY CHICKEN THIGHS

Prep time: 10 minutes | **Cook time:** 30 minutes | **Serves** 1 to 2

2 tablespoons chicken stock

2 tablespoons reduced-sodium soy sauce

1½ tablespoons sugar

4 garlic cloves, smashed and peeled

2 large scallions, cut into 2- to 3-inch batons, plus more, thinly sliced, for garnish

2 bone-in, skin-on chicken thighs (7 to 8 ounces / 198 to 227 g each)

1. Press "Pre-Heat", set the temperature at 375°F (191°C).

2. In a metal cake pan, combine the chicken stock, soy sauce, and sugar and stir until the sugar dissolves. Add the garlic cloves, scallions, and chicken thighs, turning the thighs to coat them in the marinade, then resting them skin-side up. Place the pan in the air fryer and bake, flipping the thighs every 5 minutes after the first 10 minutes, until the chicken is cooked through and the marinade is reduced to a sticky glaze over the chicken, about 30 minutes.

3.Remove the pan from the air fryer and serve the chicken thighs warm, with any remaining glaze spooned over top and sprinkled with more sliced scallions.

223

GLAZED DUCK WITH CHERRY SAUCE

Prep time: 20 minutes | **Cook time:** 32 minutes | **Serves** 12

1 whole duck (about 5 pounds / 2.3 kg in total), split in half, back and rib bones removed, fat trimmed

1 teaspoon olive oil

Salt and freshly ground black pepper, to taste

Cherry Sauce:

1 tablespoon butter

1 shallot, minced

½ cup sherry

1 cup chicken stock

1 teaspoon white wine vinegar

¾ cup cherry preserves

1 teaspoon fresh thyme leaves

Salt and freshly ground black pepper, to taste

1. Press "Pre-Heat", set the temperature at 400°F (204°C).

2. On a clean work surface, rub the duck with olive oil, then sprinkle with salt and ground black pepper to season.

3. Place the duck in the preheated air fryer, breast side up, and air fry for 25 minutes or until well browned. Flip the duck during the last 10 minutes.

4. Meanwhile, make the cherry sauce: Heat the butter in a nonstick skillet over medium-high heat or until melted.

5. Add the shallot and sauté for 5 minutes or until lightly browned.

6. Add the sherry and simmer for 6 minutes or until it reduces in half.

7. Add the chicken stick, white wine vinegar, and cherry preserves. Stir to combine well. Simmer for 6 more minutes or until thickened.

8. Fold in the thyme leaves and sprinkle with salt and ground black pepper. Stir to mix well.

9. When the air frying of the duck is complete, glaze the duck with a quarter of the cherry sauce, then air fry for another 4 minutes.

10. Flip the duck and glaze with another quarter of the cherry sauce. Air fry for an additional 3 minutes.

11. Transfer the duck on a large plate and serve with remaining cherry sauce.

224

HAWAIIAN TROPICAL CHICKEN

Prep time: 10 minutes | **Cook time:** 15 minutes | **Serves** 4

4 boneless, skinless chicken thighs (about 1½ pounds / 680 g)

1 (8-ounce / 227-g) can pineapple chunks in juice, drained, ¼ cup juice reserved

¼ cup soy sauce

¼ cup sugar

2 tablespoons ketchup

1 tablespoon minced fresh ginger

1 tablespoon minced garlic

¼ cup chopped scallions

1.Use a fork to pierce the chicken all over to allow the marinade to penetrate better. Place the chicken in a large bowl or large resealable plastic bag.

2.Set the drained pineapple chunks aside. In a small microwave-safe bowl, combine the pineapple juice, soy sauce, sugar, ketchup, ginger, and garlic. Pour half the sauce over the chicken; toss to coat. Reserve the remaining sauce. Marinate the chicken at room temperature for 30 minutes, or cover and refrigerate for up to 24 hours.

3.Press "Pre-Heat", set the temperature at 350°F (177°C).

4. Place the chicken in the air fryer basket, discarding marinade. Bake for 15 minutes, turning halfway through the cooking time.

5. Meanwhile, microwave the reserved sauce on high for 45 to 60 seconds, stirring every 15 seconds, until the sauce has the consistency of a thick glaze.

6. At the end of the cooking time, use a meat thermometer to ensure the chicken has reached an internal temperature of 165°F (74°C).

7. Transfer the chicken to a serving platter. Pour the sauce over the chicken. Garnish with the pineapple chunks and scallions before serving.

225

HERB-BUTTERMILK CHICKEN BREAST

Prep time: 5 minutes | **Cook time:** 40 minutes | **Serves** 2

1 large bone-in, skin-on chicken breast
1 cup buttermilk
1½ teaspoons dried parsley
1½ teaspoons dried chives
¾ teaspoon kosher salt
½ teaspoon dried dill
½ teaspoon onion powder
¼ teaspoon garlic powder
¼ teaspoon dried tarragon
Cooking spray

1. Place the chicken breast in a bowl and pour over the buttermilk, turning the chicken in it to make sure it's completely covered. Let the chicken stand at room temperature for at least 20 minutes or in the refrigerator for up to 4 hours.

2. Meanwhile, in a bowl, stir together the parsley, chives, salt, dill, onion powder, garlic powder, and tarragon.

3. Press "Pre-Heat", set the temperature at 300°F (149°C).

4. Remove the chicken from the buttermilk, letting the excess drip off, then place the chicken skin-side up directly in the air

fryer. Sprinkle the seasoning mix all over the top of the chicken breast, then let stand until the herb mix soaks into the buttermilk, at least 5 minutes.

5. Spray the top of the chicken with cooking spray. Bake for 10 minutes, then increase the temperature to 350°F (177°C) and bake until an instant-read thermometer inserted into the thickest part of the breast reads 160°F (71°C) and the chicken is deep golden brown, 30 to 35 minutes.

6. Transfer the chicken breast to a cutting board, let rest for 10 minutes, then cut the meat off the bone and cut into thick slices for serving.

226

HERBED TURKEY BREAST WITH SIMPLE DIJON SAUCE

Prep time: 5 minutes | **Cook time:** 30 minutes | **Serves** 4

1 teaspoon chopped fresh sage
1 teaspoon chopped fresh tarragon
1 teaspoon chopped fresh thyme leaves
1 teaspoon chopped fresh rosemary leaves
1½ teaspoons sea salt
1 teaspoon ground black pepper
1 (2-pound / 907-g) turkey breast
3 tablespoons Dijon mustard
3 tablespoons butter, melted
Cooking spray

1. Press "Pre-Heat", set the temperature at 390°F (199°C). Spritz the air fryer basket with cooking spray.
2. Combine the herbs, salt, and black pepper in a small bowl. Stir to mix well. Set aside.
3. Combine the Dijon mustard and butter in a separate bowl. Stir to mix well.
4. Rub the turkey with the herb mixture on a clean work surface, then brush the turkey with Dijon mixture.
5. Arrange the turkey in the preheated air fryer basket. Air fry

for 30 minutes or until an instant-read thermometer inserted in the thickest part of the turkey breast reaches at least 165 °F (74 °C).

6. Transfer the cooked turkey breast on a large plate and slice to serve.

227

JERK CHICKEN LEG QUARTERS

Prep time: 8 minutes | **Cook time:** 27 minutes | **Serves** 2

1 tablespoon packed brown sugar
1 teaspoon ground allspice
1 teaspoon pepper
1 teaspoon garlic powder
¾ teaspoon dry mustard
¾ teaspoon dried thyme
½ teaspoon salt
¼ teaspoon cayenne pepper
2 (10-ounce / 284-g) chicken leg quarters, trimmed
1 teaspoon vegetable oil
1 scallion, green part only, sliced thin
Lime wedges

1. Press "Pre-Heat", set the temperature at 400°F (204°C).

2. Combine sugar, allspice, pepper, garlic powder, mustard, thyme, salt, and cayenne in a bowl. Pat chicken dry with paper towels. Using metal skewer, poke 10 to 15 holes in skin of each chicken leg. Rub with oil and sprinkle evenly with spice mixture.

3. Arrange chicken skin-side up in the air fryer basket, spaced evenly apart. Air fry until chicken is well browned and crisp, 27 to

30 minutes, rotating chicken halfway through cooking (do not flip).

4.Transfer chicken to plate, tent loosely with aluminum foil, and let rest for 5 minutes. Sprinkle with scallion. Serve with lime wedges.

228

KOREAN FLAVOR GLAZED CHICKEN WINGS

Prep time: 10 minutes | **Cook time:** 25 minutes | **Serves** 4

Wings:
2 pounds (907 g) chicken wings
1 teaspoon salt
1 teaspoon ground black pepper
Sauce:
2 tablespoons gochujang
1 tablespoon mayonnaise
1 tablespoon minced ginger
1 tablespoon minced garlic
1 teaspoon agave nectar
2 packets Splenda
1 tablespoon sesame oil
For Garnish:
2 teaspoons sesame seeds
¼ cup chopped green onions

1. Press "Pre-Heat", set the temperature at 400°F (204°C). Line a baking pan with aluminum foil, then arrange the rack on the pan.

2. On a clean work surface, rub the chicken wings with salt and

ground black pepper, then arrange the seasoned wings on the rack.

3.Air fry for 20 minutes or until the wings are well browned. Flip the wings halfway through. You may need to work in batches to avoid overcrowding.

4.Meanwhile, combine the ingredients for the sauce in a small bowl. Stir to mix well. Reserve half of the sauce in a separate bowl until ready to serve.

5.Remove the air fried chicken wings from the air fryer and toss with remaining half of the sauce to coat well.

6.Place the wings back to the air fryer and air fry for 5 more minutes or until the internal temperature of the wings reaches at least 165°F (74°C).

7.Remove the wings from the air fryer and place on a large plate. Sprinkle with sesame seeds and green onions. Serve with reserved sauce.

229

LEMON CHICKEN AND SPINACH SALAD

Prep time: 10 minutes | **Cook time:** 16 to 20 minutes | **Serves** 4

3 (5-ounce / 142-g) low-sodium boneless, skinless chicken breasts, cut into 1-inch cubes

5 teaspoons olive oil

½ teaspoon dried thyme

1 medium red onion, sliced

1 red bell pepper, sliced

1 small zucchini, cut into strips

3 tablespoons freshly squeezed lemon juice

6 cups fresh baby spinach

1.Press "Pre-Heat", set the temperature at 400°F (204°C).

2.In a large bowl, mix the chicken with the olive oil and thyme. Toss to coat. Transfer to a medium metal bowl and roast for 8 minutes in the air fryer.

3.Add the red onion, red bell pepper, and zucchini. Roast for 8 to 12 minutes more, stirring once during cooking, or until the chicken reaches an internal temperature of 165°F (74°C) on a meat thermometer.

4.Remove the bowl from the air fryer and stir in the lemon juice.

5.Put the spinach in a serving bowl and top with the chicken mixture. Toss to combine and serve immediately.

230

LEMON GARLIC CHICKEN

Prep time: 10 minutes | **Cook time:** 16 to 19 minutes | **Serves** 4

4 (5-ounce / 142-g) low-sodium boneless, skinless chicken breasts, cut into 4-by-½-inch strips

2 teaspoons olive oil

2 tablespoons cornstarch

3 garlic cloves, minced

½ cup low-sodium chicken broth

¼ cup freshly squeezed lemon juice

1 tablespoon honey

½ teaspoon dried thyme

Brown rice, cooked (optional)

1. Press "Pre-Heat", set the temperature at 400°F (204°C).

2. In a large bowl, mix the chicken and olive oil. Sprinkle with the cornstarch. Toss to coat.

3. Add the garlic and transfer to a metal pan. Bake in the air fryer for 10 minutes, stirring once during cooking.

4. Add the chicken broth, lemon juice, honey, and thyme to the chicken mixture. Bake for 6 to 9 minutes more, or until the

sauce is slightly thickened and the chicken reaches an internal temperature of 165°F (74°C) on a meat thermometer. Serve over hot cooked brown rice, if desired.

231

LETTUCE CHICKEN TACOS WITH PEANUT SAUCE

Prep time: 10 minutes | **Cook time:** 6 minutes | **Serves** 4

1 pound (454 g) ground chicken
2 cloves garlic, minced
¼ cup diced onions
¼ teaspoon sea salt
Cooking spray
Peanut Sauce:
¼ cup creamy peanut butter, at room temperature
2 tablespoons tamari
1½ teaspoons hot sauce
2 tablespoons lime juice
2 tablespoons grated fresh ginger
2 tablespoons chicken broth
2 teaspoons sugar
For Serving:
2 small heads butter lettuce, leaves separated
Lime slices (optional)

1. Press "Pre-Heat", set the temperature at 350°F (177°C). Spritz a baking pan with cooking spray.
2. Combine the ground chicken, garlic, and onions in the

baking pan, then sprinkle with salt. Use a fork to break the ground chicken and combine them well.

3. Place the pan in the preheated air fryer. Bake in the preheated air fryer for 5 minutes or until the chicken is lightly browned. Stir them halfway through the cooking time.

4. Meanwhile, combine the ingredients for the sauce in a small bowl. Stir to mix well.

5. Pour the sauce in the pan of chicken, then cook for 1 more minute or until heated through.

6. Unfold the lettuce leaves on a large serving plate, then divide the chicken mixture on the lettuce leaves. Drizzle with lime juice and serve immediately.

232

LETTUCE-WRAPPED TURKEY AND MUSHROOM MEATBALLS

Prep time: 10 minutes | **Cook time:** 15 minutes | **Serves** 6

Sauce:
2 tablespoons tamari
2 tablespoons tomato sauce
1 tablespoon lime juice
¼ teaspoon peeled and grated fresh ginger
1 clove garlic, smashed to a paste
½ cup chicken broth
⅓ cup sugar
2 tablespoons toasted sesame oil
Cooking spray
Meatballs:
2 pounds (907 g) ground turkey
¾ cup finely chopped button mushrooms
2 large eggs, beaten
1½ teaspoons tamari
¼ cup finely chopped green onions, plus more for garnish
2 teaspoons peeled and grated fresh ginger
1 clove garlic, smashed
2 teaspoons toasted sesame oil

2 tablespoons sugar

For Serving:

Lettuce leaves, for serving

Sliced red chiles, for garnish (optional)

Toasted sesame seeds, for garnish (optional)

1. Press "Pre-Heat", set the temperature at 350°F (177°C). Spritz a baking pan with cooking spray.

2. Combine the ingredients for the sauce in a small bowl. Stir to mix well. Set aside.

3. Combine the ingredients for the meatballs in a large bowl. Stir to mix well, then shape the mixture in twelve 1½-inch meatballs.

4. Arrange the meatballs in a single layer on the baking pan, then baste with the sauce. You may need to work in batches to avoid overcrowding.

5. Arrange the pan in the air fryer. Air fry for 15 minutes or until the meatballs are golden brown. Flip the balls halfway through the cooking time.

6. Unfold the lettuce leaves on a large serving plate, then transfer the cooked meatballs on the leaves. Spread the red chiles and sesame seeds over the balls, then serve.

233

LIME CHICKEN WITH CILANTRO

Prep time: 35 minutes | **Cook time:** 20 minutes | **Serves** 4

4 (4-ounce / 113-g) boneless, skinless chicken breasts
½ cup chopped fresh cilantro
Juice of 1 lime
Chicken seasoning or rub, to taste
Salt and ground black pepper, to taste
Cooking spray

1. Put the chicken breasts in the large bowl, then add the cilantro, lime juice, chicken seasoning, salt, and black pepper. Toss to coat well.
2. Wrap the bowl in plastic and refrigerate to marinate for at least 30 minutes.
3. Press "Pre-Heat", set the temperature at 400°F (204°C). Spritz the air fryer basket with cooking spray.
4. Remove the marinated chicken breasts from the bowl and place in the preheated air fryer. Spritz with cooking spray. You may need to work in batches to avoid overcrowding.
5. Air fry for 10 minutes or until the internal temperature of the chicken reaches at least 165°F (74°C). Flip the breasts halfway through.

6. Serve immediately.

234

MERGUEZ MEATBALLS

Prep time: 10 minutes | **Cook time:** 10 minutes | **Serves** 4

1 pound (454 g) ground chicken
2 garlic cloves, finely minced
1 tablespoon sweet Hungarian paprika
1 teaspoon kosher salt
1 teaspoon sugar
1 teaspoon ground cumin
½ teaspoon black pepper
½ teaspoon ground fennel
½ teaspoon ground coriander
½ teaspoon cayenne pepper
¼ teaspoon ground allspice

1. In a large bowl, gently mix the chicken, garlic, paprika, salt, sugar, cumin, black pepper, fennel, coriander, cayenne, and allspice until all the ingredients are incorporated. Let stand for 30 minutes at room temperature, or cover and refrigerate for up to 24 hours.

2. Press "Pre-Heat", set the temperature at 400°F (204°C).

3. Form the mixture into 16 meatballs. Arrange them in a

single layer in the air fryer basket. Air fry for 10 minutes, turning the meatballs halfway through the cooking time. Use a meat thermometer to ensure the meatballs have reached an internal temperature of 165°F (74°C).

4.Serve warm.

235

NICE GOULASH

Prep time: 5 minutes | **Cook time:** 17 minutes | **Serves** 2

2 red bell peppers, chopped
1 pound (454 g) ground chicken
2 medium tomatoes, diced
½ cup chicken broth
Salt and ground black pepper, to taste
Cooking spray

1. Press "Pre-Heat", set the temperature at 365°F (185°C). Spritz a baking pan with cooking spray.
2. Set the bell pepper in the baking pan and put in the air fry to broil for 5 minutes or until the bell pepper is tender. Shake the basket halfway through.
3. Add the ground chicken and diced tomatoes in the baking pan and stir to mix well. Broil for 6 more minutes or until the chicken is lightly browned.
4. Pour the chicken broth over and sprinkle with salt and ground black pepper. Stir to mix well. Broil for an additional 6 minutes.
5. Serve immediately.

236

PAPRIKA INDIAN FENNEL CHICKEN

Prep time: 10 minutes | **Cook time:** 15 minutes | **Serves** 4

1 pound (454 g) boneless, skinless chicken thighs, cut crosswise into thirds

1 yellow onion, cut into 1½-inch-thick slices

1 tablespoon coconut oil, melted

2 teaspoons minced fresh ginger

2 teaspoons minced garlic

1 teaspoon smoked paprika

1 teaspoon ground fennel

1 teaspoon garam masala

1 teaspoon ground turmeric

1 teaspoon kosher salt

½ to 1 teaspoon cayenne pepper

Vegetable oil spray

2 teaspoons fresh lemon juice

¼ cup chopped fresh cilantro or parsley

1. Use a fork to pierce the chicken all over to allow the marinade to penetrate better.

2. In a large bowl, combine the onion, coconut oil, ginger, garlic, paprika, fennel, garam masala, turmeric, salt, and cayenne.

Add the chicken, toss to combine, and marinate at room temperature for 30 minutes, or cover and refrigerate for up to 24 hours.

3. Press "Pre-Heat", set the temperature at 350°F (177°C).

4. Place the chicken and onion in the air fryer basket. (Discard remaining marinade.) Spray with some vegetable oil spray. Air fry for 15 minutes. Halfway through the cooking time, remove the basket, spray the chicken and onion with more vegetable oil spray, and toss gently to coat. At the end of the cooking time, use a meat thermometer to ensure the chicken has reached an internal temperature of 165°F (74°C).

5. Transfer the chicken and onion to a serving platter. Sprinkle with the lemon juice and cilantro and serve.

237

PARMESAN CHICKEN WINGS

Prep time: 15 minutes | **Cook time:** 16 to 18 minutes | **Serves** 4

1¼ cups grated Parmesan cheese

1 tablespoon garlic powder

1 teaspoon salt

½ teaspoon freshly ground black pepper

¾ cup all-purpose flour

1 large egg, beaten

12 chicken wings (about 1 pound / 454 g)

Cooking spray

1.Press "Pre-Heat", set the temperature at 390°F (199°C). Line the air fryer basket with parchment paper.

2.In a shallow bowl, whisk the Parmesan cheese, garlic powder, salt, and pepper until blended. Place the flour in a second shallow bowl and the beaten egg in a third shallow bowl.

3.One at a time, dip the chicken wings into the flour, the beaten egg, and the Parmesan cheese mixture, coating thoroughly.

4.Place the chicken wings on the parchment and spritz with cooking spray.

5. Air fry for 8 minutes. Flip the chicken, spritz it with cooking spray, and air fry for 8 to 10 minutes more until the internal temperature reaches 165°F (74°C) and the insides are no longer pink. Let sit for 5 minutes before serving.

238

POMEGRANATE-GLAZED CHICKEN WITH COUSCOUS SALAD

Prep time: 25 minutes | **Cook time:** 20 minutes | **Serves** 4

3 tablespoons plus 2 teaspoons pomegranate molasses
½ teaspoon ground cinnamon
1 teaspoon minced fresh thyme
Salt and ground black pepper, to taste
2 (12-ounce / 340-g) bone-in split chicken breasts, trimmed
¼ cup chicken broth
¼ cup water
½ cup couscous
1 tablespoon minced fresh parsley
2 ounces (57 g) cherry tomatoes, quartered
1 scallion, white part minced, green part sliced thin on bias
1 tablespoon extra-virgin olive oil
1 ounce (28 g) feta cheese, crumbled
Cooking spray

1. Press "Pre-Heat", set the temperature at 350°F (177°C). Spritz the air fryer basket with cooking spray.
2. Combine 3 tablespoons of pomegranate molasses, cinnamon, thyme, and ⅛ teaspoon of salt in a small bowl. Stir to mix well. Set aside.

3. Place the chicken breasts in the preheated air fryer, skin side down, and spritz with cooking spray. Sprinkle with salt and ground black pepper.

4. Air fry the chicken for 10 minutes, then brush the chicken with half of pomegranate molasses mixture and flip. Air fry for 5 more minutes.

5. Brush the chicken with remaining pomegranate molasses mixture and flip. Air fry for another 5 minutes or until the internal temperature of the chicken breasts reaches at least 165°F (74°C).

6. Meanwhile, pour the broth and water in a pot and bring to a boil over medium-high heat. Add the couscous and sprinkle with salt. Cover and simmer for 7 minutes or until the liquid is almost absorbed.

7. Combine the remaining ingredients, except for the cheese, with cooked couscous in a large bowl. Toss to mix well. Scatter with the feta cheese.

8. When the air frying is complete, remove the chicken from the air fryer and allow to cool for 10 minutes. Serve with vegetable and couscous salad.

239

ROASTED CHICKEN AND VEGETABLE SALAD

Prep time: 10 minutes | **Cook time:** 10 to 13 minutes | **Serves** 4

3 (4-ounce / 113-g) low-sodium boneless, skinless chicken breasts, cut into 1-inch cubes

1 small red onion, sliced

1 red bell pepper, sliced

1 cup green beans, cut into 1-inch pieces

2 tablespoons low-fat ranch salad dressing

2 tablespoons freshly squeezed lemon juice

½ teaspoon dried basil

4 cups mixed lettuce

1. Press "Pre-Heat", set the temperature at 400°F (204°C).
2. In the air fryer basket, roast the chicken, red onion, red bell pepper, and green beans for 10 to 13 minutes, or until the chicken reaches an internal temperature of 165°F (74°C) on a meat thermometer, tossing the food in the basket once during cooking.
3. While the chicken cooks, in a serving bowl, mix the ranch dressing, lemon juice, and basil.
4. Transfer the chicken and vegetables to a serving bowl and toss with the dressing to coat. Serve immediately on lettuce leaves.

240

ROASTED CHICKEN WITH GARLIC

Prep time: 5 minutes | **Cook time:** 25 minutes | **Serves** 4

4 (5-ounce / 142-g) low-sodium bone-in skinless chicken breasts

1 tablespoon olive oil

1 tablespoon freshly squeezed lemon juice

3 tablespoons cornstarch

1 teaspoon dried basil leaves

⅛ teaspoon freshly ground black pepper

20 garlic cloves, unpeeled

1. Press "Pre-Heat", set the temperature at 370°F (188°C).

2. Rub the chicken with the olive oil and lemon juice on both sides and sprinkle with the cornstarch, basil, and pepper.

3. Place the seasoned chicken in the air fryer basket and top with the garlic cloves. Roast for about 25 minutes, or until the garlic is soft and the chicken reaches an internal temperature of 165°F (74°C) on a meat thermometer. Serve immediately.

241

ROSEMARY TURKEY BREAST

Prep time: 2 hours 20 minutes | **Cook time:** 30 minutes | **Serves** 6

½ teaspoon dried rosemary

2 minced garlic cloves

2 teaspoons salt

1 teaspoon ground black pepper

¼ cup olive oil

2½ pounds (1.1 kg) turkey breast

¼ cup pure maple syrup

1 tablespoon stone-ground brown mustard

1 tablespoon melted vegan butter

1. Combine the rosemary, garlic, salt, ground black pepper, and olive oil in a large bowl. Stir to mix well.

2. Dunk the turkey breast in the mixture and wrap the bowl in plastic. Refrigerate for 2 hours to marinate.

3. Remove the bowl from the refrigerator and let sit for half an hour before cooking.

4. Press "Pre-Heat", set the temperature at 400°F (204°C). Spritz the air fryer basket with cooking spray.

5. Remove the turkey from the marinade and place in the

preheated air fry and air fry for 20 minutes or until well browned. Flip the breast halfway through.

6.Meanwhile, combine the remaining ingredients in a small bowl. Stir to mix well.

7.Pour half of the butter mixture over the turkey breast in the air fryer and air fry for 10 more minutes. Flip the breast and pour the remaining half of butter mixture over halfway through.

8.Transfer the turkey on a plate and slice to serve.

242

ROSEMARY TURKEY SCOTCH EGGS

Prep time: 15 minutes | **Cook time:** 12 minutes | **Serves** 4

1 egg
1 cup panko breadcrumbs
½ teaspoon rosemary
1 pound (454 g) ground turkey
4 hard-boiled eggs, peeled
Salt and ground black pepper, to taste
Cooking spray

1. Press "Pre-Heat", set the temperature at 400°F (204°C). Spritz the air fryer basket with cooking spray.

2. Whisk the egg with salt in a bowl. Combine the breadcrumbs with rosemary in a shallow dish.

3. Stir the ground turkey with salt and ground black pepper in a separate large bowl, then divide the ground turkey into four portions.

4. Wrap each hard-boiled egg with a portion of ground turkey. Dredge in the whisked egg, then roll over the breadcrumb mixture.

5. Place the wrapped eggs in the preheated air fryer and spritz

with cooking spray. Air fry for 12 minutes or until golden brown and crunchy. Flip the eggs halfway through.

6.Serve immediately.

243

SIMPLE AIR FRIED CHICKEN WINGS

Prep time: 10 minutes | **Cook time:** 15 minutes | **Serves** 4

1 tablespoon olive oil
8 whole chicken wings
Chicken seasoning or rub, to taste
1 teaspoon garlic powder
Freshly ground black pepper, to taste

1. Press "Pre-Heat", set the temperature at 400°F (204°C). Grease the air fryer basket with olive oil.
2. On a clean work surface, rub the chicken wings with chicken seasoning and rub, garlic powder, and ground black pepper.
3. Arrange the well-coated chicken wings in the preheated air fryer. Air fry for 15 minutes or until the internal temperature of the chicken wings reaches at least 165°F (74°C). Flip the chicken wings halfway through.
4. Remove the chicken wings from the air fryer. Serve immediately.

244

SIMPLE CHICKEN NUGGETS

Prep time: 10 minutes | **Cook time:** 20 minutes | **Serves** 4

1 pound (454 g) boneless, skinless chicken breasts, cut into 1-inch pieces

2 tablespoons panko breadcrumbs

6 tablespoons breadcrumbs

Chicken seasoning or rub, to taste

Salt and ground black pepper, to taste

2 eggs

Cooking spray

1. Press "Pre-Heat", set the temperature at 400°F (204°C). Spritz the air fryer basket with cooking spray.

2. Combine the breadcrumbs, chicken seasoning, salt, and black pepper in a large bowl. Stir to mix well. Whisk the eggs in a separate bowl.

3. Dunk the chicken pieces in the egg mixture, then in the breadcrumb mixture. Shake the excess off.

4. Arrange the well-coated chicken pieces in the preheated air fryer. Spritz with cooking spray and air fry for 8 minutes or until crispy and golden brown. Shake the basket halfway through. You may need to work in batches to avoid overcrowding.

5. Serve immediately.

245

SIMPLE CHICKEN SHAWARMA

Prep time: 10 minutes | **Cook time:** 15 minutes | **Serves** 4

Shawarma Spice:
2 teaspoons dried oregano
1 teaspoon ground cinnamon
1 teaspoon ground cumin
1 teaspoon ground coriander
1 teaspoon kosher salt
½ teaspoon ground allspice
½ teaspoon cayenne pepper

Chicken:
1 pound (454 g) boneless, skinless chicken thighs, cut into large bite-size chunks
2 tablespoons vegetable oil

For Serving:
Tzatziki
Pita bread

1. For the shawarma spice: In a small bowl, combine the oregano, cayenne, cumin, coriander, salt, cinnamon, and allspice.

2. For the chicken: In a large bowl, toss together the chicken, vegetable oil, and shawarma spice to coat. Marinate at room

temperature for 30 minutes or cover and refrigerate for up to 24 hours.

3.Press "Pre-Heat", set the temperature at 350°F (177°C). Place the chicken in the air fryer basket. Air fry for 15 minutes, or until the chicken reaches an internal temperature of 165°F (74°C).

4.Transfer the chicken to a serving platter. Serve with tzatziki and pita bread.

246

SIMPLE WHOLE CHICKEN BAKE

Prep time: 10 minutes | **Cook time:** 1 hour | **Serves** 2 to 4

½ cup melted butter

3 tablespoons garlic, minced

Salt, to taste

1 teaspoon ground black pepper

1 (1-pound / 454-g) whole chicken

1. Press "Pre-Heat", set the temperature at 350°F (177°C).
2. Combine the butter with garlic, salt, and ground black pepper in a small bowl.
3. Brush the butter mixture over the whole chicken, then place the chicken in the preheated air fryer, skin side down.
4. Bake the chicken for an hour or until an instant-read thermometer inserted in the thickest part of the chicken registers at least 165°F (74°C). Flip the chicken halfway through.
5. Remove the chicken from the air fryer and allow to cool for 15 minutes before serving.

247

SPANISH CHICKEN AND MINI SWEET PEPPER BAGUETTE

Prep time: 10 minutes | **Cook time:** 20 minutes | **Serves** 2

1¼ pounds (567 g) assorted small chicken parts, breasts cut into halves

¼ teaspoon salt

¼ teaspoon ground black pepper

2 teaspoons olive oil

½ pound (227 g) mini sweet peppers

¼ cup light mayonnaise

¼ teaspoon smoked paprika

½ clove garlic, crushed

Baguette, for serving

Cooking spray

1. Preheat air fryer to 375°F (191°C). Spritz the air fryer basket with cooking spray.

2. Toss the chicken with salt, ground black pepper, and olive oil in a large bowl.

3. Arrange the sweet peppers and chicken in the preheated air fryer and air fry for 10 minutes, then transfer the peppers on a plate.

4.Flip the chicken and air fry for 10 more minutes or until well browned.

5.Meanwhile, combine the mayo, paprika, and garlic in a small bowl. Stir to mix well.

6.Assemble the baguette with chicken and sweet pepper, then spread with mayo mixture and serve.

248

SPICY CHICKEN SKEWERS WITH SATAY SAUCE

Prep time: 5 minutes | **Cook time:** 10 minutes | **Serves** 4

4 (6-ounce / 170-g) boneless, skinless chicken breasts, sliced into strips

1 teaspoon sea salt

1 teaspoon paprika

Cooking spray

Satay Sauce:

¼ cup creamy almond butter

½ teaspoon hot sauce

1½ tablespoons coconut vinegar

2 tablespoons chicken broth

1 teaspoon peeled and minced fresh ginger

1 clove garlic, minced

1 teaspoon sugar

For Serving:

¼ cup chopped cilantro leaves

Red pepper flakes, to taste

Thinly sliced red, orange, or / and yellow bell peppers

Special Equipment:

16 wooden or bamboo skewers, soaked in water for 15 minutes

1. Press "Pre-Heat", set the temperature at 400°F (204°C). Spritz the air fryer basket with cooking spray.

2. Run the bamboo skewers through the chicken strips, then arrange the chicken skewers in the air fryer and sprinkle with salt and paprika.

3. Air fry for 10 minutes or until lightly browned on all sides. Flip the chicken skewers halfway during the cooking.

4. Meanwhile, combine the ingredients for the sauce in a small bowl. Stir to mix well.

5. Transfer the cooked chicken skewers on a large plate, then top with cilantro, sliced bell peppers, red pepper flakes. Serve with the sauce or just baste the sauce over before serving.

249

SPICY TANDOORI CHICKEN DRUMSTICKS

Prep time: 70 minutes | **Cook time:** 14 minutes | **Serves** 4

8 (4- to 5-ounce / 113- to 142-g) skinless bone-in chicken drumsticks

½ cup plain full-fat or low-fat yogurt

¼ cup buttermilk

2 teaspoons minced garlic

2 teaspoons minced fresh ginger

2 teaspoons ground cinnamon

2 teaspoons ground coriander

2 teaspoons mild paprika

1 teaspoon salt

1 teaspoon Tabasco hot red pepper sauce

1.Press "Pre-Heat", set the temperature at 375°F (191°C).

2.In a large bowl, stir together all the ingredients except for chicken drumsticks until well combined. Add the chicken drumsticks to the bowl and toss until well coated. Cover in plastic and set in the refrigerator to marinate for 1 hour, tossing once.

3.Arrange the marinated drumsticks in a single layer in the air fryer basket, leaving enough space between them. Air fry for 14 minutes, or until the internal temperature of the chicken drumsticks reaches 160°F (71°C) on a meat thermometer. Flip the drumsticks once halfway through to ensure even cooking.

4. Transfer the drumsticks to plates. Rest for 5 minutes before serving.

250

STRAWBERRY-GLAZED TURKEY

Prep time: 15 minutes | **Cook time:** 37 minutes | **Serves** 2

2 pounds (907 g) turkey breast
1 tablespoon olive oil
Salt and ground black pepper, to taste
1 cup fresh strawberries

1. Press "Pre-Heat", set the temperature at 375°F (191°C).
2. Rub the turkey bread with olive oil on a clean work surface, then sprinkle with salt and ground black pepper.
3. Transfer the turkey in the preheated air fryer and air fry for 30 minutes or until the internal temperature of the turkey reaches at least 165°F (74°C). flip the turkey breast halfway through.
4. Meanwhile, put the strawberries in a food processor and pulse until smooth.
5. When the frying of the turkey is complete, spread the puréed strawberries over the turkey and fry for 7 more minutes.
6. Serve immediately.

251

SWEET-AND-SOUR CHICKEN NUGGETS

Prep time: 15 minutes | **Cook time:** 15 minutes | **Serves** 4

1 cup cornstarch
Chicken seasoning or rub, to taste
Salt and ground black pepper, to taste
2 eggs
2 (4-ounce/ 113-g) boneless, skinless chicken breasts, cut into 1-inch pieces
1½ cups sweet-and-sour sauce
Cooking spray

1. Press "Pre-Heat", set the temperature at 360°F (182°C). Spritz the air fryer basket with cooking spray.
2. Combine the cornstarch, chicken seasoning, salt, and pepper in a large bowl. Stir to mix well. Whisk the eggs in a separate bowl.
3. Dredge the chicken pieces in the bowl of cornstarch mixture first, then in the bowl of whisked eggs, and then in the cornstarch mixture again.
4. Arrange the well-coated chicken pieces in the air fryer basket. Spritz with cooking spray.

5. Air fry for 15 minutes or until golden brown and crispy. Shake the basket halfway through the cooking time.

6. Transfer the chicken pieces on a large serving plate, then baste with sweet-and-sour sauce before serving.

252

TERIYAKI CHICKEN THIGHS WITH LEMONY SNOW PEAS

Prep time: 30 minutes | **Cook time:** 34 minutes | **Serves** 4

¼ cup chicken broth
½ teaspoon grated fresh ginger
⅛ teaspoon red pepper flakes
1½ tablespoons soy sauce
4 (5-ounce / 142-g) bone-in chicken thighs, trimmed
1 tablespoon mirin
½ teaspoon cornstarch
1 tablespoon sugar
6 ounces (170 g) snow peas, strings removed
⅛ teaspoon lemon zest
1 garlic clove, minced
¼ teaspoon salt
Ground black pepper, to taste
½ teaspoon lemon juice

1. Combine the broth, ginger, pepper flakes, and soy sauce in a large bowl. Stir to mix well.
2. Pierce 10 to 15 holes into the chicken skin. Put the chicken in the broth mixture and toss to coat well. Let sit for 10 minutes to marinate.

3. Press "Pre-Heat", set the temperature at 400°F (205°C).

4. Transfer the marinated chicken on a plate and pat dry with paper towels.

5. Scoop 2 tablespoons of marinade in a microwave-safe bowl and combine with mirin, cornstarch and sugar. Stir to mix well. Microwave for 1 minute or until frothy and has a thick consistency. Set aside.

6. Arrange the chicken in the preheated air fryer, skin side up, and air fry for 25 minutes or until the internal temperature of the chicken reaches at least 165°F (74°C). Gently turn the chicken over halfway through.

7. When the frying is complete, brush the chicken skin with marinade mixture. Air fryer the chicken for 5 more minutes or until glazed.

8. Remove the chicken from the air fryer and reserve ½ teaspoon of chicken fat remains in the air fryer. Allow the chicken to cool for 10 minutes.

9. Meanwhile, combine the reserved chicken fat, snow peas, lemon zest, garlic, salt, and ground black pepper in a small bowl. Toss to coat well.

10. Transfer the snow peas in the air fryer and air fry for 3 minutes or until soft. Remove the peas from the air fryer and toss with lemon juice.

11. Serve the chicken with lemony snow peas.

253

TEX-MEX CHICKEN BREASTS

Prep time: 10 minutes | **Cook time:** 17 to 20 minutes | **Serves** 4

1 pound (454 g) low-sodium boneless, skinless chicken breasts, cut into 1-inch cubes

1 medium onion, chopped

1 red bell pepper, chopped

1 jalapeño pepper, minced

2 teaspoons olive oil

²⁄₃ cup canned low-sodium black beans, rinsed and drained

½ cup low-sodium salsa

2 teaspoons chili powder

1. Press "Pre-Heat", set the temperature at 400°F (204°C).

2. In a medium metal bowl, mix the chicken, onion, bell pepper, jalapeño, and olive oil. Roast for 10 minutes, stirring once during cooking.

3. Add the black beans, salsa, and chili powder. Roast for 7 to 10 minutes more, stirring once, until the chicken reaches an internal temperature of 165°F (74°C) on a meat thermometer. Serve immediately.

254

THAI CORNISH GAME HENS

Prep time: 15 minutes | **Cook time:** 20 minutes | **Serves** 4

1 cup chopped fresh cilantro leaves and stems
¼ cup fish sauce
1 tablespoon soy sauce
1 serrano chile, seeded and chopped
8 garlic cloves, smashed
2 tablespoons sugar
2 tablespoons lemongrass paste
2 teaspoons black pepper
2 teaspoons ground coriander
1 teaspoon kosher salt
1 teaspoon ground turmeric
2 Cornish game hens, giblets removed, split in half lengthwise

1. In a blender, combine the cilantro, fish sauce, soy sauce, serrano, garlic, sugar, lemongrass, black pepper, coriander, salt, and turmeric. Blend until smooth.

2. Place the game hen halves in a large bowl. Pour the cilantro mixture over the hen halves and toss to coat. Marinate at room temperature for 30 minutes, or cover and refrigerate for up to 24 hours.

3.Press "Pre-Heat", set the temperature at 400°F (204°C).

4.Arrange the hen halves in a single layer in the air fryer basket. Roast for 20 minutes. Use a meat thermometer to ensure the game hens have reached an internal temperature of 165°F (74°C). Serve warm.

255

THAI CURRY MEATBALLS

Prep time: 10 minutes | **Cook time:** 10 minutes | **Serves** 4

1 pound (454 g) ground chicken
¼ cup chopped fresh cilantro
1 teaspoon chopped fresh mint
1 tablespoon fresh lime juice
1 tablespoon Thai red, green, or yellow curry paste
1 tablespoon fish sauce
2 garlic cloves, minced
2 teaspoons minced fresh ginger
½ teaspoon kosher salt
½ teaspoon black pepper
¼ teaspoon red pepper flakes

1. Press "Pre-Heat", set the temperature at 400°F (204°C).

2. In a large bowl, gently mix the ground chicken, cilantro, mint, lime juice, curry paste, fish sauce, garlic, ginger, salt, black pepper, and red pepper flakes until thoroughly combined.

3. Form the mixture into 16 meatballs. Place the meatballs in a single layer in the air fryer basket. Air fry for 10 minutes, turning the meatballs halfway through the cooking time. Use a meat ther-

mometer to ensure the meatballs have reached an internal temperature of 165°F (74°C). Serve immediately.

256

THAI GAME HENS WITH CUCUMBER AND CHILE SALAD

Prep time: 25 minutes | **Cook time:** 25 minutes | **Serves** 6

2 (1¼-pound / 567-g) Cornish game hens, giblets discarded
1 tablespoon fish sauce
6 tablespoons chopped fresh cilantro
2 teaspoons lime zest
1 teaspoon ground coriander
2 garlic cloves, minced
2 tablespoons packed light brown sugar
2 teaspoons vegetable oil
Salt and ground black pepper, to taste
1 English cucumber, halved lengthwise and sliced thin
1 Thai chile, stemmed, deseeded, and minced
2 tablespoons chopped dry-roasted peanuts
1 small shallot, sliced thinly
1 tablespoon lime juice
Lime wedges, for serving
Cooking spray

1. Arrange a game hen on a clean work surface, remove the backbone with kitchen shears, then pound the hen breast to flat. Cut the breast in half. Repeat with the remaining game hen.

2. Loose the breast and thigh skin with your fingers, then pat the game hens dry and pierce about 10 holes into the fat deposits of the hens. Tuck the wings under the hens.

3. Combine 2 teaspoons of fish sauce, ¼ cup of cilantro, lime zest, coriander, garlic, 4 teaspoons of sugar, 1 teaspoon of vegetable oil, ½ teaspoon of salt, and ⅛ teaspoon of ground black pepper in a small bowl. Stir to mix well.

4. Rub the fish sauce mixture under the breast and thigh skin of the game hens, then let sit for 10 minutes to marinate.

5. Press "Pre-Heat", set the temperature at 400°F (204°C). Spritz the air fryer basket with cooking spray.

6. Arrange the marinated game hens in the preheated air fryer, skin side down.

7. Air fry for 15 minutes, then gently turn the game hens over and air fry for 10 more minutes or until the skin is golden brown and the internal temperature of the hens reads at least 165°F (74°C).

8. Meanwhile, combine all the remaining ingredients, except for the lime wedges, in a large bowl and sprinkle with salt and black pepper. Toss to mix well.

9. Transfer the fried hens on a large plate, then sit the salad aside and squeeze the lime wedges over before serving.

257

TURKEY AND CAULIFLOWER MEATLOAF

Prep time: 15 minutes | **Cook time:** 50 minutes | **Serves** 6

2 pounds (907 g) lean ground turkey
1⅓ cups riced cauliflower
2 large eggs, lightly beaten
¼ cup almond flour
⅔ cup chopped yellow or white onion
1 teaspoon ground dried turmeric
1 teaspoon ground cumin
1 teaspoon ground coriander
1 tablespoon minced garlic
1 teaspoon salt
1 teaspoon ground black pepper
Cooking spray

1. Press "Pre-Heat", set the temperature at 350°F (177°C). Spritz a loaf pan with cooking spray.

2. Combine all the ingredients in a large bowl. Stir to mix well. Pour half of the mixture in the prepared loaf pan and press with a spatula to coat the bottom evenly. Spritz the mixture with cooking spray.

3. Arrange the loaf pan in the preheated air fryer and bake for

25 minutes or until the meat is well browned and the internal temperature reaches at least 165°F (74°C). Repeat with remaining mixture.

4.Remove the loaf pan from the air fryer and serve immediately.

258

TURKISH CHICKEN KEBABS

Prep time: 15 minutes | **Cook time:** 15 minutes | **Serves** 4

¼ cup plain Greek yogurt

1 tablespoon minced garlic

1 tablespoon tomato paste

1 tablespoon fresh lemon juice

1 tablespoon vegetable oil

1 teaspoon kosher salt

1 teaspoon ground cumin

1 teaspoon sweet Hungarian paprika

½ teaspoon ground cinnamon

½ teaspoon black pepper

½ teaspoon cayenne pepper

1 pound (454 g) boneless, skinless chicken thighs, quartered crosswise

1. In a large bowl, combine the yogurt, garlic, tomato paste, lemon juice, vegetable oil, salt, cumin, paprika, cinnamon, black pepper, and cayenne. Stir until the spices are blended into the yogurt.

2. Add the chicken to the bowl and toss until well coated.

Poultry

Marinate at room temperature for 30 minutes, or cover and refrigerate for up to 24 hours.

3. Press "Pre-Heat", set the temperature at 375°F (191°C).

4. Arrange the chicken in a single layer in the air fryer basket. Air fry for 10 minutes. Turn the chicken and air fry for 5 minutes more. Use a meat thermometer to ensure the chicken has reached an internal temperature of 165°F (74°C).

5. Serve warm.

259

YAKITORI

Prep time: 10 minutes | **Cook time:** 15 minutes | **Serves** 4

½ cup mirin
¼ cup dry white wine
½ cup soy sauce
1 tablespoon light brown sugar
1½ pounds (680 g) boneless, skinless chicken thighs, cut into 1½-inch pieces, fat trimmed
4 medium scallions, trimmed, cut into 1½-inch pieces
Cooking spray
Special Equipment:
4 (4-inch) bamboo skewers, soaked in water for at least 30 minutes

1. Combine the mirin, dry white wine, soy sauce, and brown sugar in a saucepan. Bring to a boil over medium heat. Keep stirring.
2. Boil for another 2 minutes or until it has a thick consistency. Turn off the heat.
3. Press "Pre-Heat", set the temperature at 400°F (204°C). Spritz the air fryer basket with cooking spray.

4. Run the bamboo skewers through the chicken pieces and scallions alternatively.

5. Arrange the skewers in the preheated air fryer, then brush with mirin mixture on both sides. Spritz with cooking spray.

6. Air fry for 10 minutes or until the chicken and scallions are glossy. Flip the skewers halfway through.

7. Serve immediately.

260

YELLOW CURRY CHICKEN THIGHS WITH PEANUTS

Prep time: 10 minutes | **Cook time:** 20 minutes | **Serves** 6

½ cup unsweetened full-fat coconut milk

2 tablespoons yellow curry paste

1 tablespoon minced fresh ginger

1 tablespoon minced garlic

1 teaspoon kosher salt

1 pound (454 g) boneless, skinless chicken thighs, halved crosswise

2 tablespoons chopped peanuts

1. In a large bowl, stir together the coconut milk, curry paste, ginger, garlic, and salt until well blended. Add the chicken; toss well to coat. Marinate at room temperature for 30 minutes, or cover and refrigerate for up to 24 hours.

2. Press "Pre-Heat", set the temperature at 375°F (191°C).

3. Place the chicken (along with marinade) in a baking pan. Place the pan in the air fryer basket. Bake for 20 minutes, turning the chicken halfway through the cooking time. Use a meat thermometer to ensure the chicken has reached an internal temperature of 165°F (74°C).

4. Sprinkle the chicken with the chopped peanuts and serve.

MEATS

261

AIR FRIED BABY BACK RIBS

Prep time: 5 minutes | **Cook time:** 30 minutes | **Serves** 2

2 teaspoons red pepper flakes
¾ ground ginger
3 cloves minced garlic
Salt and ground black pepper, to taste
2 baby back ribs

1. Press "Pre-Heat", set the temperature at 350°F (177°C).
2. Combine the red pepper flakes, ginger, garlic, salt and pepper in a bowl, making sure to mix well. Massage the mixture into the baby back ribs.
3. Air fry the ribs in the air fryer for 30 minutes.
4. Take care when taking the rubs out of the air fryer. Put them on a serving dish and serve.

262

AIR FRIED BEEF RIBS

Prep time: 20 minutes | **Cook time:** 8 minutes | **Serves** 4

1 pound (454 g) meaty beef ribs, rinsed and drained
3 tablespoons apple cider vinegar
1 cup coriander, finely chopped
1 tablespoon fresh basil leaves, chopped
2 garlic cloves, finely chopped
1 chipotle powder
1 teaspoon fennel seeds
1 teaspoon hot paprika
Kosher salt and black pepper, to taste
½ cup vegetable oil

1. Coat the ribs with the remaining ingredients and refrigerate for at least 3 hours.
2. Press "Pre-Heat", set the temperature at 360°F (182°C).
3. Separate the ribs from the marinade and put them in the air fryer basket. Air fry for 8 minutes.
4. Pour the remaining marinade over the ribs before serving.

AIR FRIED GOLDEN WASABI SPAM

Prep time: 5 minutes | **Cook time:** 12 minutes | **Serves** 3

2/3 cup all-purpose flour
2 large eggs
1½ tablespoons wasabi paste
2 cups panko breadcrumbs
6 ½-inch-thick spam slices
Cooking spray

1. Press "Pre-Heat", set the temperature at 400°F (204°C) and spritz with cooking spray.
2. Pour the flour in a shallow plate. Whisk the eggs with wasabi in a large bowl. Pour the panko in a separate shallow plate.
3. Dredge the spam slices in the flour first, then dunk in the egg mixture, and then roll the spam over the panko to coat well. Shake the excess off.
4. Arrange the spam slices in a single layer in the preheated air fryer and spritz with cooking spray.
5. Air fry for 12 minutes or until the spam slices are golden and crispy. Flip the spam slices halfway through.
6. Serve immediately.

264

APPLE-GLAZED PORK

Prep time: 15 minutes | **Cook time:** 19 minutes | **Serves** 4

1 sliced apple
1 small onion, sliced
2 tablespoons apple cider vinegar, divided
½ teaspoon thyme
½ teaspoon rosemary
¼ teaspoon brown sugar
3 tablespoons olive oil, divided
¼ teaspoon smoked paprika
4 pork chops
Salt and ground black pepper, to taste

1. Press "Pre-Heat", set the temperature at 350°F (177°C).

2. Combine the apple slices, onion, 1 tablespoon of vinegar, thyme, rosemary, brown sugar, and 2 tablespoons of olive oil in a baking pan. Stir to mix well.

3. Arrange the pan in the preheated air fryer and bake for 4 minutes.

4. Meanwhile, combine the remaining vinegar and olive oil, and paprika in a large bowl. Sprinkle with salt and ground black

pepper. Stir to mix well. Dredge the pork in the mixture and toss to coat well.

5. Remove the baking pan from the air fryer and put in the pork. Air fry for 10 minutes to lightly brown the pork. Flip the pork chops halfway through.

6. Remove the pork from the air fryer and baste with baked apple mixture on both sides. Put the pork back to the air fryer and air fry for an additional 5 minutes. Flip halfway through.

7. Serve immediately.

265

AVOCADO BUTTERED FLANK STEAK

Prep time: 5 minutes | **Cook time:** 12 minutes | **Serves** 1

1 flank steak
Salt and ground black pepper, to taste
2 avocados
2 tablespoons butter, melted
½ cup chimichurri sauce

1. Rub the flank steak with salt and pepper to taste and leave to sit for 20 minutes.
2. Press "Pre-Heat", set the temperature at 400°F (204°C).
3. Halve the avocados and take out the pits. Spoon the flesh into a bowl and mash with a fork. Mix in the melted butter and chimichurri sauce, making sure everything is well combined.
4. Put the steak in the air fryer basket and air fry for 6 minutes. Flip over and allow to air fry for another 6 minutes.
5. Serve the steak with the avocado butter.

266

BACON AND PEAR STUFFED PORK CHOPS

Prep time: 20 minutes | **Cook time:** 24 minutes | **Serves** 3

4 slices bacon, chopped
1 tablespoon butter
½ cup finely diced onion
⅓ cup chicken stock
1½ cups seasoned stuffing cubes
1 egg, beaten
½ teaspoon dried thyme
½ teaspoon salt
⅛ teaspoon freshly ground black pepper
1 pear, finely diced
⅓ cup crumbled blue cheese
3 boneless center-cut pork chops (2-inch thick)
Olive oil, for greasing
Salt and freshly ground black pepper, to taste

1. Press "Pre-Heat", set the temperature at 400°F (204°C).
2. Put the bacon into the air fryer basket and air fry for 6 minutes, stirring halfway through the cooking time. Remove the bacon and set it aside on a paper towel. Pour out the grease from the bottom of the air fryer.

3. To make the stuffing, melt the butter in a medium saucepan over medium heat on the stovetop. Add the onion and sauté for a few minutes until it starts to soften. Add the chicken stock and simmer for 1 minute. Remove the pan from the heat and add the stuffing cubes. Stir until the stock has been absorbed. Add the egg, dried thyme, salt and freshly ground black pepper, and stir until combined. Fold in the diced pear and crumbled blue cheese.

4. Put the pork chops on a cutting board. Using the palm of the hand to hold the chop flat and steady, slice into the side of the pork chop to make a pocket in the center of the chop. Leave about an inch of chop uncut and make sure you don't cut all the way through the pork chop. Brush both sides of the pork chops with olive oil and season with salt and freshly ground black pepper. Stuff each pork chop with a third of the stuffing, packing the stuffing tightly inside the pocket.

5. Adjust the temperature to 360°F (182°C).

6. Spray or brush the sides of the air fryer basket with oil. Put the pork chops in the air fryer basket with the open, stuffed edge of the pork chop facing the outside edges of the basket.

7. Air fry the pork chops for 18 minutes, turning the pork chops over halfway through the cooking time. When the chops are done, let them rest for 5 minutes and then transfer to a serving platter.

267

BACON WRAPPED PORK WITH APPLE GRAVY

Prep time: 10 minutes | **Cook time:** 25 minutes | **Serves** 4

Pork:
1 tablespoons Dijon mustard
1 pork tenderloin
3 strips bacon

Apple Gravy:
3 tablespoons ghee, divided
1 small shallot, chopped
2 apples
1 tablespoon almond flour
1 cup vegetable broth
½ teaspoon Dijon mustard

1. Press "Pre-Heat", set the temperature at 360°F (182°C).
2. Spread Dijon mustard all over tenderloin and wrap with strips of bacon.
3. Put into air fryer and air fry for 12 minutes. Use a meat thermometer to check for doneness.
4. To make sauce, heat 1 tablespoons of ghee in a pan and add shallots. Cook for 1 minute.
5. Then add apples, cooking for 4 minutes until softened.

6. Add flour and 2 tablespoons of ghee to make a roux. Add broth and mustard, stirring well to combine.

7. When sauce starts to bubble, add 1 cup of sautéed apples, cooking until sauce thickens.

8. Once pork tenderloin is cooked, allow to sit 8 minutes to rest before slicing.

9. Serve topped with apple gravy.

268

BACON-WRAPPED HOT DOGS WITH MAYO-KETCHUP SAUCE

Prep time: 5 minutes | **Cook time:** 10 to 12 minutes | **Serves** 5

10 thin slices of bacon
5 pork hot dogs, halved
1 teaspoon cayenne pepper
Sauce:
¼ cup mayonnaise
4 tablespoons low-carb ketchup
1 teaspoon rice vinegar
1 teaspoon chili powder

1. Press "Pre-Heat", set the temperature at 390°F (199°C).
2. Arrange the slices of bacon on a clean work surface. One by one, place the halved hot dog on one end of each slice, season with cayenne pepper and wrap the hot dog with the bacon slices and secure with toothpicks as needed.
3. Work in batches, place half the wrapped hot dogs in the air fryer basket and air fry for 10 to 12 minutes or until the bacon becomes browned and crispy.
4. Make the sauce: Stir all the ingredients for the sauce in a

small bowl. Wrap the bowl in plastic and set in the refrigerator until ready to serve.

5. Transfer the hot dogs to a platter and serve hot with the sauce.

269

BACON-WRAPPED SAUSAGE WITH TOMATO RELISH

Prep time: 1 hour 15 minutes | **Cook time:** 32 minutes | **Serves** 4

8 pork sausages

8 bacon strips

Relish:

8 large tomatoes, chopped

1 small onion, peeled

1 clove garlic, peeled

1 tablespoon white wine vinegar

3 tablespoons chopped parsley

1 teaspoon smoked paprika

2 tablespoons sugar

Salt and ground black pepper, to taste

1. Purée the tomatoes, onion, and garlic in a food processor until well mixed and smooth.

2. Pour the purée in a saucepan and drizzle with white wine vinegar. Sprinkle with salt and ground black pepper. Simmer over medium heat for 10 minutes.

3. Add the parsley, paprika, and sugar to the saucepan and

cook for 10 more minutes or until it has a thick consistency. Keep stirring during the cooking. Refrigerate for an hour to chill.

4. Press "Pre-Heat", set the temperature at 350°F (177°C).

5. Wrap the sausage with bacon strips and secure with toothpicks, then place them in the preheated air fryer.

6. Air fry for 12 minutes or until the bacon is crispy and browned. Flip the bacon-wrapped sausage halfway through.

7. Transfer the bacon-wrapped sausage on a plate and baste with the relish or just serve with the relish alongside.

270

BBQ PORK STEAKS

Prep time: 5 minutes | **Cook time:** 15 minutes | **Serves** 4

4 pork steaks
1 tablespoon Cajun seasoning
2 tablespoons BBQ sauce
1 tablespoon vinegar
1 teaspoon soy sauce
½ cup brown sugar
½ cup ketchup

1. Press "Pre-Heat", set the temperature at 290°F (143°C).
2. Sprinkle pork steaks with Cajun seasoning.
3. Combine remaining ingredients and brush onto steaks.
4. Add coated steaks to air fryer. Air fry 15 minutes until just browned.
5. Serve immediately.

271

BEEF AND PORK SAUSAGE MEATLOAF

Prep time: 20 minutes | **Cook time:** 25 minutes | **Serves** 4

¾ pound (340 g) ground chuck
4 ounces (113 g) ground pork sausage
1 cup shallots, finely chopped
2 eggs, well beaten
3 tablespoons plain milk
1 tablespoon oyster sauce
1 teaspoon porcini mushrooms
½ teaspoon cumin powder
1 teaspoon garlic paste
1 tablespoon fresh parsley
Salt and crushed red pepper flakes, to taste
1 cup crushed saltines
Cooking spray

1.Press "Pre-Heat", set the temperature at 360°F (182°C). Spritz a baking dish with cooking spray.

2.Mix all the ingredients in a large bowl, combining everything well.

3.Transfer to the baking dish and bake in the air fryer for 25 minutes.

4. Serve hot.

272

BEEF AND SPINACH ROLLS

Prep time: 10 minutes | **Cook time:** 14 minutes | **Serves** 2

3 teaspoons pesto

2 pounds (907 g) beef flank steak

6 slices provolone cheese

3 ounces (85 g) roasted red bell peppers

¾ cup baby spinach

1 teaspoon sea salt

1 teaspoon black pepper

1. Press "Pre-Heat", set the temperature at 400°F (204°C).

2. Spoon equal amounts of the pesto onto each flank steak and spread it across evenly.

3. Put the cheese, roasted red peppers and spinach on top of the meat, about three-quarters of the way down.

4. Roll the steak up, holding it in place with toothpicks. Sprinkle with the sea salt and pepper.

5. Put inside the air fryer and air fry for 14 minutes, turning halfway through the cooking time.

6. Allow the beef to rest for 10 minutes before slicing up and serving.

273

BEEF CHEESEBURGER EGG ROLLS

Prep time: 15 minutes | **Cook time:** 8 minutes | Makes 6 egg rolls

8 ounces (227 g) raw lean ground beef
½ cup chopped onion
½ cup chopped bell pepper
¼ teaspoon onion powder
¼ teaspoon garlic powder
3 tablespoons cream cheese
1 tablespoon yellow mustard
3 tablespoons shredded Cheddar cheese
6 chopped dill pickle chips
6 egg roll wrappers

1. Press "Pre-Heat", set the temperature at 392°F (200°C).
2. In a skillet, add the beef, onion, bell pepper, onion powder, and garlic powder. Stir and crumble beef until fully cooked, and vegetables are soft.
3. Take skillet off the heat and add cream cheese, mustard, and Cheddar cheese, stirring until melted.
4. Pour beef mixture into a bowl and fold in pickles.
5. Lay out egg wrappers and divide the beef mixture into each

one. Moisten egg roll wrapper edges with water. Fold sides to the middle and seal with water.

6. Repeat with all other egg rolls.

7. Put rolls into air fryer, one batch at a time. Air fry for 8 minutes.

8. Serve immediately.

274

BEEF CHUCK CHEESEBURGERS

Prep time: 10 minutes | **Cook time:** 15 minutes | **Serves** 4

¾ pound (340 g) ground beef chuck

1 envelope onion soup mix

Kosher salt and freshly ground black pepper, to taste

1 teaspoon paprika

4 slices Monterey Jack cheese

4 ciabatta rolls

1. In a bowl, stir together the ground chuck, onion soup mix, salt, black pepper, and paprika to combine well.

2. Press "Pre-Heat", set the temperature at 385°F (196°C).

3. Take four equal portions of the mixture and mold each one into a patty. Transfer to the air fryer and air fry for 10 minutes.

4. Put the slices of cheese on the top of the burgers.

5. Air fry for another minute before serving on ciabatta rolls.

275

BEEF CHUCK WITH BRUSSELS SPROUTS

Prep time: 20 minutes | **Cook time:** 15 minutes | **Serves** 4

1 pound (454 g) beef chuck shoulder steak
2 tablespoons vegetable oil
1 tablespoon red wine vinegar
1 teaspoon fine sea salt
½ teaspoon ground black pepper
1 teaspoon smoked paprika
1 teaspoon onion powder
½ teaspoon garlic powder
½ pound (227 g) Brussels sprouts, cleaned and halved
½ teaspoon fennel seeds
1 teaspoon dried basil
1 teaspoon dried sage

1. Massage the beef with the vegetable oil, wine vinegar, salt, black pepper, paprika, onion powder, and garlic powder, coating it well.
2. Allow to marinate for a minimum of 3 hours.
3. Press "Pre-Heat", set the temperature at 390°F (199°C).
4. Remove the beef from the marinade and put in the

preheated air fryer. Air fry for 10 minutes. Flip the beef halfway through.

5.Put the prepared Brussels sprouts in the air fryer along with the fennel seeds, basil, and sage.

6.Lower the heat to 380°F (193°C) and air fry everything for another 5 minutes.

7.Give them a good stir. Air fry for an additional 10 minutes.

8.Serve immediately.

276

BEEF EGG ROLLS

Prep time: 15 minutes | **Cook time:** 12 minutes | Makes 8 egg rolls

½ chopped onion
2 garlic cloves, chopped
½ packet taco seasoning
Salt and ground black pepper, to taste
1 pound (454 g) lean ground beef
½ can cilantro lime rotel
16 egg roll wrappers
1 cup shredded Mexican cheese
1 tablespoon olive oil
1 teaspoon cilantro

1. Press "Pre-Heat", set the temperature at 400°F (205°C).
2. Add onions and garlic to a skillet, cooking until fragrant. Then add taco seasoning, pepper, salt, and beef, cooking until beef is broke up into tiny pieces and cooked thoroughly.
3. Add rotel and stir well.
4. Lay out egg wrappers and brush with a touch of water to soften a bit.
5. Load wrappers with beef filling and add cheese to each.

6. Fold diagonally to close and use water to secure edges.

7. Brush filled egg wrappers with olive oil and add to the air fryer.

8. Air fry 8 minutes, flip, and air fry for another 4 minutes.

9. Serve sprinkled with cilantro.

277

BEEF LOIN WITH THYME AND PARSLEY

Prep time: 5 minutes | **Cook time:** 15 minutes | **Serves** 4

1 tablespoon butter, melted
¼ dried thyme
1 teaspoon garlic salt
¼ teaspoon dried parsley
1 pound (454 g) beef loin

1. Press "Pre-Heat", set the temperature at 400°F (204°C).
2. In a bowl, combine the melted butter, thyme, garlic salt, and parsley.
3. Cut the beef loin into slices and generously apply the seasoned butter using a brush. Transfer to the air fryer basket.
4. Air fry the beef for 15 minutes.
5. Take care when removing it and serve hot.

278

CARNE ASADA TACOS

Prep time: 5 minutes | **Cook time:** 14 minutes | **Serves** 4

- ⅓ cup olive oil
- 1½ pounds (680 g) flank steak
- Salt and freshly ground black pepper, to taste
- ⅓ cup freshly squeezed lime juice
- ½ cup chopped fresh cilantro
- 4 teaspoons minced garlic
- 1 teaspoon ground cumin
- 1 teaspoon chili powder

1. Brush the air fryer basket with olive oil.
2. Put the flank steak in a large mixing bowl. Season with salt and pepper.
3. Add the lime juice, cilantro, garlic, cumin, and chili powder and toss to coat the steak.
4. For the best flavor, let the steak marinate in the refrigerator for about 1 hour.
5. Press "Pre-Heat", set the temperature at 400°F (204°C)
6. Put the steak in the air fryer basket. Air fry for 7 minutes. Flip the steak. Air fry for 7 minutes more or until an internal temperature reaches at least 145°F (63°C).

7. Let the steak rest for about 5 minutes, then cut into strips to serve.

CHAR SIU

Prep time: 8 hours 10 minutes | **Cook time:** 15 minutes | **Serves** 4

¼ cup honey

1 teaspoon Chinese five-spice powder

1 tablespoon Shaoxing wine (rice cooking wine)

1 tablespoon hoisin sauce

2 teaspoons minced garlic

2 teaspoons minced fresh ginger

2 tablespoons soy sauce

1 tablespoon sugar

1 pound (454 g) fatty pork shoulder, cut into long, 1-inch-thick pieces

Cooking spray

1.Combine all the ingredients, except for the pork should, in a microwave-safe bowl. Stir to mix well. Microwave until the honey has dissolved. Stir periodically.

2.Pierce the pork pieces generously with a fork, then put the pork in a large bowl. Pour in half of the honey mixture. Set the remaining sauce aside until ready to serve.

3. Press the pork pieces into the mixture to coat and wrap the bowl in plastic and refrigerate to marinate for at least 8 hours.

4. Press "Pre-Heat", set the temperature at 400°F (204°C). Spritz the air fryer basket with cooking spray.

5. Discard the marinade and transfer the pork pieces in the preheated air fryer basket.

6. Air fry for 15 minutes or until well browned. Flip the pork pieces halfway through the cooking time.

7. Meanwhile, microwave the remaining marinade on high for a minute or until it has a thick consistency. Stir periodically.

8. Remove the pork from the air fryer and allow to cool for 10 minutes before serving with the thickened marinade.

280

CHEDDAR BACON BURST WITH SPINACH

Prep time: 5 minutes | **Cook time:** 60 minutes | **Serves** 8

30 slices bacon

1 tablespoon Chipotle seasoning

2 teaspoons Italian seasoning

2½ cups Cheddar cheese

4 cups raw spinach

1. Press "Pre-Heat", set the temperature at 375°F (191°C).
2. Weave the bacon into 15 vertical pieces and 12 horizontal pieces. Cut the extra 3 in half to fill in the rest, horizontally.
3. Season the bacon with Chipotle seasoning and Italian seasoning.
4. Add the cheese to the bacon.
5. Add the spinach and press down to compress.
6. Tightly roll up the woven bacon.
7. Line a baking sheet with kitchen foil and add plenty of salt to it.
8. Put the bacon on top of a cooling rack and put that on top of the baking sheet.
9. Bake for 60 minutes.
10. Let cool for 15 minutes before slicing and serving.

281

CHEESE CRUSTED CHOPS

Prep time: 10 minutes | **Cook time:** 12 minutes | **Serves** 4 to 6

- ¼ teaspoon pepper
- ½ teaspoons salt
- 4 to 6 thick boneless pork chops
- 1 cup pork rind crumbs
- ¼ teaspoon chili powder
- ½ teaspoons onion powder
- 1 teaspoon smoked paprika
- 2 beaten eggs
- 3 tablespoons grated Parmesan cheese
- Cooking spray

1. Press "Pre-Heat", set the temperature at 400°F (205°C).
2. Rub the pepper and salt on both sides of pork chops.
3. In a food processor, pulse pork rinds into crumbs. Mix crumbs with chili powder, onion powder, and paprika in a bowl.
4. Beat eggs in another bowl.
5. Dip pork chops into eggs then into pork rind crumb mixture.
6. Spritz the air fryer basket with cooking spray and add pork chops to the basket.

7. Air fry for 12 minutes.
8. Serve garnished with the Parmesan cheese.

282

CHICKEN FRIED STEAK

Prep time: 15 minutes | **Cook time:** 10 minutes | **Serves** 4

½ cup flour
2 teaspoons salt, divided
Freshly ground black pepper, to taste
¼ teaspoon garlic powder
1 cup buttermilk
1 cup fine bread crumbs
4 (6-ounce / 170-g) tenderized top round steaks, ½-inch thick
Vegetable or canola oil
For the Gravy:
2 tablespoons butter or bacon drippings
¼ onion, minced
1 clove garlic, smashed
¼ teaspoon dried thyme
3 tablespoons flour
1 cup milk
Salt and freshly ground black pepper, to taste
Dashes of Worcestershire sauce

1.Set up a dredging station. Combine the flour, 1 teaspoon of salt, black pepper and garlic powder in a shallow bowl. Pour the buttermilk into a second shallow bowl. Finally, put the bread crumbs and 1 teaspoon of salt in a third shallow bowl.

2. Dip the tenderized steaks into the flour, then the buttermilk, and then the bread crumb mixture, pressing the crumbs onto the steak. Put them on a baking sheet and spray both sides generously with vegetable or canola oil.

3. Press "Pre-Heat", set the temperature at 400°F (204°C).

4. Transfer the steaks to the air fryer basket, two at a time, and air fry for 10 minutes, flipping the steaks over halfway through the cooking time. Hold the first batch of steaks warm in a 170°F (77°C) oven while you air fry the second batch.

5. While the steaks are cooking, make the gravy. Melt the butter in a small saucepan over medium heat on the stovetop. Add the onion, garlic and thyme and cook for five minutes, until the onion is soft and just starting to brown. Stir in the flour and cook for another five minutes, stirring regularly, until the mixture starts to brown. Whisk in the milk and bring the mixture to a boil to thicken. Season to taste with salt, lots of freshly ground black pepper, and a few dashes of Worcestershire sauce.

6. Pour the gravy over the chicken fried steaks and serve.

283

CITRUS CARNITAS

Prep time: 1 hour 10 minutes | **Cook time:** 25 minutes | **Serves** 6

2½ pounds (1.1 kg) boneless country-style pork ribs, cut into 2-inch pieces

3 tablespoons olive brine

1 tablespoon minced fresh oregano leaves

⅓ cup orange juice

1 teaspoon ground cumin

1 tablespoon minced garlic

1 teaspoon salt

1 teaspoon ground black pepper

Cooking spray

1. Combine all the ingredients in a large bowl. Toss to coat the pork ribs well. Wrap the bowl in plastic and refrigerate for at least an hour to marinate.

2. Press "Pre-Heat", set the temperature at 400°F (204°C) and spritz with cooking spray.

3. Arrange the marinated pork ribs in a single layer in the preheated air fryer and spritz with cooking spray.

4. Air fry for 25 minutes or until well browned. Flip the ribs halfway through.

5. Serve immediately.

284

CLASSIC WALLISER SCHNITZEL

Prep time: 5 minutes | **Cook time:** 14 minutes | **Serves** 2

½ cup pork rinds

½ tablespoon fresh parsley

½ teaspoon fennel seed

½ teaspoon mustard

⅓ tablespoon cider vinegar

1 teaspoon garlic salt

⅓ teaspoon ground black pepper

2 eggs

2 pork schnitzel, halved

Cooking spray

1. Press "Pre-Heat", set the temperature at 350°F (177°C) and spritz with cooking spray.

2. Put the pork rinds, parsley, fennel seeds, and mustard in a food processor. Pour in the vinegar and sprinkle with salt and ground black pepper. Pulse until well combined and smooth.

3. Pour the pork rind mixture in a large bowl. Whisk the eggs in a separate bowl.

4. Dunk the pork schnitzel in the whisked eggs, then dunk in the pork rind mixture to coat well. Shake the excess off.

5. Arrange the schnitzel in the preheated air fryer and spritz with cooking spray. Air fry for 14 minutes or until golden and crispy. Flip the schnitzel halfway through.

6. Serve immediately.

CRISPY PORK TENDERLOIN

Prep time: 5 minutes | **Cook time:** 10 minutes | **Serves** 6

2 large egg whites

1½ tablespoons Dijon mustard

2 cups crushed pretzel crumbs

1½ pounds (680 g) pork tenderloin, cut into ¼-pound (113-g) sections

Cooking spray

1. Press "Pre-Heat", set the temperature at 350°F (177°C). Spritz the air fryer basket with cooking spray.
2. Whisk the egg whites with Dijon mustard in a bowl until bubbly. Pour the pretzel crumbs in a separate bowl.
3. Dredge the pork tenderloin in the egg white mixture and press to coat. Shake the excess off and roll the tenderloin over the pretzel crumbs.
4. Arrange the well-coated pork tenderloin in batches in a single layer in the air fryer basket and spritz with cooking spray.
5. Air fry for 10 minutes or until the pork is golden brown and crispy. Flip the pork halfway through. Repeat with remaining pork sections.
6. Serve immediately.

286

CRUMBED GOLDEN FILET MIGNON

Prep time: 15 minutes | **Cook time:** 12 minutes | **Serves** 4

½ pound (227 g) filet mignon
Sea salt and ground black pepper, to taste
½ teaspoon cayenne pepper
1 teaspoon dried basil
1 teaspoon dried rosemary
1 teaspoon dried thyme
1 tablespoon sesame oil
1 small egg, whisked
½ cup bread crumbs

1. Press "Pre-Heat", set the temperature at 360°F (182°C).
2. Cover the filet mignon with the salt, black pepper, cayenne pepper, basil, rosemary, and thyme. Coat with sesame oil.
3. Put the egg in a shallow plate.
4. Pour the bread crumbs in another plate.
5. Dip the filet mignon into the egg. Roll it into the crumbs.
6. Transfer the steak to the air fryer and air fry for 12 minutes or until it turns golden.
7. Serve immediately.

287

GREEK LAMB PITA POCKETS

Prep time: 15 minutes | **Cook time:** 6 minutes | **Serves** 4

Dressing:
1 cup plain yogurt
1 tablespoon lemon juice
1 teaspoon dried dill weed, crushed
1 teaspoon ground oregano
½ teaspoon salt

Meatballs:
½ pound (227 g) ground lamb
1 tablespoon diced onion
1 teaspoon dried parsley
1 teaspoon dried dill weed, crushed
¼ teaspoon oregano
¼ teaspoon coriander
¼ teaspoon ground cumin
¼ teaspoon salt
4 pita halves

Suggested Toppings:
1 red onion, slivered
1 medium cucumber, deseeded, thinly sliced

Crumbled feta cheese
Sliced black olives
Chopped fresh peppers

1. Press "Pre-Heat", set the temperature at 390°F (199°C).
2. Stir the dressing ingredients together in a small bowl and refrigerate while preparing lamb.
3. Combine all meatball ingredients in a large bowl and stir to distribute seasonings.
4. Shape meat mixture into 12 small meatballs, rounded or slightly flattened if you prefer.
5. Transfer the meatballs in the preheated air fryer and air fry for 6 minutes, until well done. Remove and drain on paper towels.
6. To serve, pile meatballs and the choice of toppings in pita pockets and drizzle with dressing.

288

GREEK LAMB RACK

Prep time: 5 minutes | **Cook time:** 10 minutes | **Serves** 4

¼ cup freshly squeezed lemon juice
1 teaspoon oregano
2 teaspoons minced fresh rosemary
1 teaspoon minced fresh thyme
2 tablespoons minced garlic
Salt and freshly ground black pepper, to taste
2 to 4 tablespoons olive oil
1 lamb rib rack (7 to 8 ribs)

1. Press "Pre-Heat", set the temperature at 360°F (182°C).
2. In a small mixing bowl, combine the lemon juice, oregano, rosemary, thyme, garlic, salt, pepper, and olive oil and mix well.
3. Rub the mixture over the lamb, covering all the meat. Put the rack of lamb in the air fryer. Roast for 10 minutes. Flip the rack halfway through.
4. After 10 minutes, measure the internal temperature of the rack of lamb reaches at least 145°F (63°C).
5. Serve immediately.

289

HERBED BEEF

Prep time: 5 minutes | **Cook time:** 22 minutes | **Serves** 6

1 teaspoon dried dill
1 teaspoon dried thyme
1 teaspoon garlic powder
2 pounds (907 g) beef steak
3 tablespoons butter

1. Press "Pre-Heat", set the temperature at 360°F (182°C).
2. Combine the dill, thyme, and garlic powder in a small bowl, and massage into the steak.
3. Air fry the steak in the air fryer for 20 minutes, then remove, shred, and return to the air fryer.
4. Add the butter and air fry the shredded steak for a further 2 minutes at 365°F (185°C). Make sure the beef is coated in the butter before serving.

HOMEMADE TERIYAKI PORK RIBS

Prep time: 5 minutes | **Cook time:** 30 minutes | **Serves** 4

¼ cup soy sauce
¼ cup honey
1 teaspoon garlic powder
1 teaspoon ground dried ginger
4 (8-ounce / 227-g) boneless country-style pork ribs
Cooking spray

1. Press "Pre-Heat", set the temperature at 350°F (177°C). Spritz the air fryer basket with cooking spray.
2. Make the teriyaki sauce: combine the soy sauce, honey, garlic powder, and ginger in a bowl. Stir to mix well.
3. Brush the ribs with half of the teriyaki sauce, then arrange the ribs in the preheated air fryer. Spritz with cooking spray. You may need to work in batches to avoid overcrowding.
4. Air fry for 30 minutes or until the internal temperature of the ribs reaches at least 145°F (63°C). Brush the ribs with remaining teriyaki sauce and flip halfway through.
5. Serve immediately.

291

ITALIAN LAMB CHOPS WITH AVOCADO MAYO

Prep time: 5 minutes | **Cook time:** 12 minutes | **Serves** 2

2 lamp chops
2 teaspoons Italian herbs
2 avocados
½ cup mayonnaise
1 tablespoon lemon juice

1. Season the lamb chops with the Italian herbs, then set aside for 5 minutes.
2. Press "Pre-Heat", set the temperature at 400°F (204°C) and place the rack inside.
3. Put the chops on the rack and air fry for 12 minutes.
4. In the meantime, halve the avocados and open to remove the pits. Spoon the flesh into a blender.
5. Add the mayonnaise and lemon juice and pulse until a smooth consistency is achieved.
6. Take care when removing the chops from the air fryer, then plate up and serve with the avocado mayo.

292

KALE AND BEEF OMELET

Prep time: 15 minutes | **Cook time:** 16 minutes | **Serves** 4

½ pound (227 g) leftover beef, coarsely chopped
2 garlic cloves, pressed
1 cup kale, torn into pieces and wilted
1 tomato, chopped
¼ teaspoon sugar
4 eggs, beaten
4 tablespoons heavy cream
½ teaspoon turmeric powder
Salt and ground black pepper, to taste
⅛ teaspoon ground allspice
Cooking spray

1. Press "Pre-Heat", set the temperature at 360°F (182°C). Spritz four ramekins with cooking spray.
2. Put equal amounts of each of the ingredients into each ramekin and mix well.
3. Air fry for 16 minutes. Serve immediately.

293

KIELBASA SAUSAGE WITH PIEROGIES

Prep time: 15 minutes | **Cook time:** 30 minutes | **Serves** 3 to 4

1 sweet onion, sliced
1 teaspoon olive oil
Salt and freshly ground black pepper, to taste
2 tablespoons butter, cut into small cubes
1 teaspoon sugar
1 pound (454 g) light Polish kielbasa sausage, cut into 2-inch chunks
1 (13-ounce / 369-g) package frozen mini pierogies
2 teaspoons vegetable or olive oil
Chopped scallions, for garnish

1. Press "Pre-Heat", set the temperature at 400°F (204°C).
2. Toss the sliced onions with olive oil, salt and pepper and transfer them to the air fryer basket. Dot the onions with pieces of butter and air fry for 2 minutes. Then sprinkle the sugar over the onions and stir. Pour any melted butter from the bottom of the air fryer drawer over the onions. Continue to air fry for another 13 minutes, stirring or shaking the basket every few minutes to air fry the onions evenly.

3. Add the kielbasa chunks to the onions and toss. Air fry for another 5 minutes, shaking the basket halfway through the cooking time. Transfer the kielbasa and onions to a bowl and cover with aluminum foil to keep warm.

4. Toss the frozen pierogies with the vegetable or olive oil and transfer them to the air fryer basket. Air fry at 400°F (204°C) for 8 minutes, shaking the basket twice during the cooking time.

5. When the pierogies have finished cooking, return the kielbasa and onions to the air fryer and gently toss with the pierogies. Air fry for 2 more minutes and then transfer everything to a serving platter. Garnish with the chopped scallions and serve hot.

294

KIELBASA SAUSAGE WITH PINEAPPLE AND BELL PEPPERS

Prep time: 15 minutes | **Cook time:** 10 minutes | **Serves** 2 to 4

- ¾ pound (340 g) kielbasa sausage, cut into ½-inch slices
- 1 (8-ounce / 227-g) can pineapple chunks in juice, drained
- 1 cup bell pepper chunks
- 1 tablespoon barbecue seasoning
- 1 tablespoon soy sauce
- Cooking spray

1. Press "Pre-Heat", set the temperature at 390°F (199°C). Spritz the air fryer basket with cooking spray.
2. Combine all the ingredients in a large bowl. Toss to mix well.
3. Pour the sausage mixture in the preheated air fryer.
4. Air fry for 10 minutes or until the sausage is lightly browned and the bell pepper and pineapple are soft. Shake the basket halfway through.
5. Serve immediately.

295

LAHMACUN (TURKISH PIZZA)

Prep time: 20 minutes | **Cook time:** 10 minutes per batch | **Serves** 4

4 (6-inch) flour tortillas
For the Meat Topping:
4 ounces (113 g) ground lamb or 85% lean ground beef
¼ cup finely chopped green bell pepper
¼ cup chopped fresh parsley
1 small plum tomato, deseeded and chopped
2 tablespoons chopped yellow onion
1 garlic clove, minced
2 teaspoons tomato paste
¼ teaspoon sweet paprika
¼ teaspoon ground cumin
⅛ to ¼ teaspoon red pepper flakes
⅛ teaspoon ground allspice
⅛ teaspoon kosher salt
⅛ teaspoon black pepper
For Serving:
¼ cup chopped fresh mint
1 teaspoon extra-virgin olive oil

1 lemon, cut into wedges

1. Press "Pre-Heat", set the temperature at 400°F (204°C).
2. Combine all the ingredients for the meat topping in a medium bowl until well mixed.
3. Lay the tortillas on a clean work surface. Spoon the meat mixture on the tortillas and spread all over.
4. Place the tortillas in the air fryer basket. Air fry in batches, one at a time, for 10 minutes, or until the edge of the tortilla is golden and the meat is lightly browned.
5. Transfer them to a serving dish. Top with chopped fresh mint and drizzle with olive oil. Squeeze the lemon wedges on top and serve.

296

LAMB KOFTA

Prep time: 25 minutes | **Cook time:** 10 minutes | **Serves** 4

1 pound (454 g) ground lamb
1 tablespoon ras el hanout (North African spice)
½ teaspoon ground coriander
1 teaspoon onion powder
1 teaspoon garlic powder
1 teaspoon cumin
2 tablespoons mint, chopped
Salt and ground black pepper, to taste
Special Equipment:
4 bamboo skewers

1. Combine the ground lamb, ras el hanout, coriander, onion powder, garlic powder, cumin, mint, salt, and ground black pepper in a large bowl. Stir to mix well.

2. Transfer the mixture into sausage molds and sit the bamboo skewers in the mixture. Refrigerate for 15 minutes.

3. Preheat air fryer to 380°F (193°C). Spritz the basket with cooking spray.

4. Place the lamb skewers in the preheated air fryer and spritz with cooking spray.

5. Air fry for 10 minutes or until the lamb is well browned. Flip the lamb skewers halfway through.

6. Serve immediately.

LAMB LOIN CHOPS WITH HORSERADISH CREAM SAUCE

Prep time: 10 minutes | **Cook time:** 13 minutes | **Serves** 4

For the Lamb:
4 lamb loin chops
2 tablespoons vegetable oil
1 clove garlic, minced
½ teaspoon kosher salt
½ teaspoon black pepper
For the Horseradish Cream Sauce:
1 to 1½ tablespoons prepared horseradish
1 tablespoon Dijon mustard
½ cup mayonnaise
2 teaspoons sugar
Cooking spray

1. Press "Pre-Heat", set the temperature at 325°F (163°C). Spritz the air fryer basket with cooking spray.

2. Place the lamb chops on a plate. Rub with the oil and sprinkle with the garlic, salt and black pepper. Let sit to marinate for 30 minutes at room temperature.

3. Make the horseradish cream sauce: Mix the horseradish,

mustard, mayonnaise, and sugar in a bowl until well combined. Set half of the sauce aside until ready to serve.

4. Arrange the marinated chops in the prepared basket. Set the time to 10 minutes, flipping the chops halfway through..

5. Transfer the chops from the air fryer to the bowl of the horseradish sauce. Roll to coat well.

6. Put the coated chops in the air fryer basket again. Set the temperature to 400°F (204°C) and the time to 3 minutes. Air fry until the internal temperature reaches 145°F (63°C) on a meat thermometer (for medium-rare).

7. Serve hot with the horseradish cream sauce.

298

LAMB RACK WITH PISTACHIO

Prep time: 10 minutes | **Cook time:** 20 minutes | **Serves** 2

½ cup finely chopped pistachios

1 teaspoon chopped fresh rosemary

3 tablespoons panko breadcrumbs

2 teaspoons chopped fresh oregano

1 tablespoon olive oil

Salt and freshly ground black pepper, to taste

1 lamb rack, bones fat trimmed and frenched

1 tablespoon Dijon mustard

1. Press "Pre-Heat", set the temperature at 380°F (193°C).

2. Put the pistachios, rosemary, breadcrumbs, oregano, olive oil, salt, and black pepper in a food processor. Pulse to combine until smooth.

3. Rub the lamb rack with salt and black pepper on a clean work surface, then place it in the preheated air fryer.

4. Air fry for 12 minutes or until lightly browned. Flip the lamb halfway through the cooking time.

5. Transfer the lamb on a plate and brush with Dijon mustard on the fat side, then sprinkle with the pistachios mixture over the lamb rack to coat well.

6. Put the lamb rack back to the air fryer and air fry for 8 more minutes or until the internal temperature of the rack reaches at least 145°F (63°C).

7. Remove the lamb rack from the air fryer with tongs and allow to cool for 5 minutes before sling to serve.

LECHON KAWALI

Prep time: 10 minutes | **Cook time:** 30 minutes | **Serves** 4

1 pound (454 g) pork belly, cut into three thick chunks
6 garlic cloves
2 bay leaves
2 tablespoons soy sauce
1 teaspoon kosher salt
1 teaspoon ground black pepper
3 cups water
Cooking spray

1. Put all the ingredients in a pressure cooker, then put the lid on and cook on high for 15 minutes.

2. Natural release the pressure and release any remaining pressure, transfer the tender pork belly on a clean work surface. Allow to cool under room temperature until you can handle.

3. Press "Pre-Heat", set the temperature at 400°F (204°C). Generously spritz the air fryer basket with cooking spray.

4. Cut each chunk into two slices, then put the pork slices in the preheated air fryer.

5. Air fry for 15 minutes or until the pork fat is crispy. Spritz the pork with more cooking spray, if necessary.

6. Serve immediately.

300

LEMONY PORK LOIN CHOP SCHNITZEL

Prep time: 15 minutes | **Cook time:** 15 minutes | **Serves** 4

4 thin boneless pork loin chops
2 tablespoons lemon juice
½ cup flour
¼ teaspoon marjoram
1 teaspoon salt
1 cup panko breadcrumbs
2 eggs
Lemon wedges, for serving
Cooking spray

1. Press "Pre-Heat", set the temperature at 390°F (199°C) and spritz with cooking spray.
2. On a clean work surface, drizzle the pork chops with lemon juice on both sides.
3. Combine the flour with marjoram and salt on a shallow plate. Pour the breadcrumbs on a separate shallow dish. Beat the eggs in a large bowl.
4. Dredge the pork chops in the flour, then dunk in the beaten eggs to coat well. Shake the excess off and roll over the breadcrumbs.

5.Arrange the chops in the preheated air fryer and spritz with cooking spray. Air fry for 15 minutes or until the chops are golden and crispy. Flip the chops halfway through.

6.Squeeze the lemon wedges over the fried chops and serve immediately.

301

MACADAMIA NUTS CRUSTED PORK RACK

Prep time: 5 minutes | **Cook time:** 35 minutes | **Serves** 2

1 clove garlic, minced
2 tablespoons olive oil
1 pound (454 g) rack of pork
1 cup chopped macadamia nuts
1 tablespoon breadcrumbs
1 tablespoon rosemary, chopped
1 egg
Salt and ground black pepper, to taste

1. Press "Pre-Heat", set the temperature at 350°F (177°C).
2. Combine the garlic and olive oil in a small bowl. Stir to mix well.
3. On a clean work surface, rub the pork rack with the garlic oil and sprinkle with salt and black pepper on both sides.
4. Combine the macadamia nuts, breadcrumbs, and rosemary in a shallow dish. Whisk the egg in a large bowl.
5. Dredge the pork in the egg, then roll the pork over the macadamia nut mixture to coat well. Shake the excess off.
6. Arrange the pork in the preheated air fryer and air fry for 30

minutes on both sides. Increase to 390°F (199°C) and fry for 5 more minutes or until the pork is well browned.

7. Serve immediately.

302

MARINATED PORK TENDERLOIN

Prep time: 10 minutes | **Cook time:** 30 minutes | **Serves** 4 to 6

- ¼ cup olive oil
- ¼ cup soy sauce
- ¼ cup freshly squeezed lemon juice
- 1 garlic clove, minced
- 1 tablespoon Dijon mustard
- 1 teaspoon salt
- ½ teaspoon freshly ground black pepper
- 2 pounds (907 g) pork tenderloin

1. In a large mixing bowl, make the marinade: Mix the olive oil, soy sauce, lemon juice, minced garlic, Dijon mustard, salt, and pepper. Reserve ¼ cup of the marinade.

2. Put the tenderloin in a large bowl and pour the remaining marinade over the meat. Cover and marinate in the refrigerator for about 1 hour.

3. Press "Pre-Heat", set the temperature at 400°F (204°C).

4. Put the marinated pork tenderloin into the air fryer basket. Roast for 10 minutes. Flip the pork and baste it with half of the reserved marinade. Roast for 10 minutes more.

5. Flip the pork, then baste with the remaining marinade. Roast for another 10 minutes, for a total cooking time of 30 minutes.

6. Serve immediately.

303

MEXICAN PORK CHOPS

Prep time: 5 minutes | **Cook time:** 15 minutes | **Serves** 2

¼ teaspoon dried oregano

1½ teaspoons taco seasoning mix

2 (4-ounce / 113-g) boneless pork chops

2 tablespoons unsalted butter, divided

1. Press "Pre-Heat", set the temperature at 400°F (204°C).

2. Combine the dried oregano and taco seasoning in a small bowl and rub the mixture into the pork chops. Brush the chops with 1 tablespoon butter.

3. In the air fryer, air fry the chops for 15 minutes, turning them over halfway through to air fry on the other side.

4. When the chops are a brown color, check the internal temperature has reached 145°F (63°C) and remove from the air fryer. Serve with a garnish of remaining butter.

304

PEPPERCORN CRUSTED BEEF TENDERLOIN

Prep time: 5 minutes | **Cook time:** 25 minutes | **Serves** 6

2 pounds (907 g) beef tenderloin
2 teaspoons roasted garlic, minced
2 tablespoons salted butter, melted
3 tablespoons ground 4-peppercorn blend

1. Press "Pre-Heat", set the temperature at 400°F (204°C).
2. Remove any surplus fat from the beef tenderloin.
3. Combine the roasted garlic and melted butter to apply to the tenderloin with a brush.
4. On a plate, spread out the peppercorns and roll the tenderloin in them, making sure they are covering and clinging to the meat.
5. Air fry the tenderloin in the air fryer for 25 minutes, turning halfway through cooking.
6. Let the tenderloin rest for ten minutes before slicing and serving.

305

PORK AND TRICOLOR VEGETABLES KEBABS

Prep time: 1 hour 20 minutes | **Cook time:** 8 minutes per batch | **Serves** 4

For the Pork:
1 pound (454 g) pork steak, cut in cubes
1 tablespoon white wine vinegar
3 tablespoons steak sauce
¼ cup soy sauce
1 teaspoon powdered chili
1 teaspoon red chili flakes
2 teaspoons smoked paprika
1 teaspoon garlic salt

For the Vegetable:
1 green squash, deseeded and cut in cubes
1 yellow squash, deseeded and cut in cubes
1 red pepper, cut in cubes
1 green pepper, cut in cubes
Salt and ground black pepper, to taste
Cooking spray

Special Equipment:
4 bamboo skewers, soaked in water for at least 30 minutes

1.Combine the ingredients for the pork in a large bowl. Press the pork to dunk in the marinade. Wrap the bowl in plastic and refrigerate for at least an hour.

2.Press "Pre-Heat", set the temperature at 370°F (188°C) and spritz with cooking spray.

3.Remove the pork from the marinade and run the skewers through the pork and vegetables alternatively. Sprinkle with salt and pepper to taste.

4.Arrange the skewers in the preheated air fryer and spritz with cooking spray. Air fry for 8 minutes or until the pork is browned and the vegetables are lightly charred and tender. Flip the skewers halfway through. You may need to work in batches to avoid overcrowding.

5.Serve immediately.

306

PORK BUTT WITH GARLICKY CORIANDER-PARSLEY SAUCE

Prep time: 1 hour 15 minutes | **Cook time:** 30 minutes | **Serves** 4

    1 teaspoon golden flaxseed meal
    1 egg white, well whisked
    1 tablespoon soy sauce
    1 teaspoon lemon juice, preferably freshly squeezed
    1 tablespoon olive oil
    1 pound (454 g) pork butt, cut into pieces 2-inches long
    Salt and ground black pepper, to taste
    Garlicky Coriander-Parsley Sauce:
    3 garlic cloves, minced
    1/3 cup fresh coriander leaves
    1/3 cup fresh parsley leaves
    1 teaspoon lemon juice
    1/2 tablespoon salt
    1/3 cup extra-virgin olive oil

    1.Combine the flaxseed meal, egg white, soy sauce, lemon juice, salt, black pepper, and olive oil in a large bowl. Dunk the pork strips in and press to submerge.

2. Wrap the bowl in plastic and refrigerate to marinate for at least an hour.

3. Press "Pre-Heat", set the temperature at 380°F (193°C).

4. Arrange the marinated pork strips in the preheated air fryer and air fry for 30 minutes or until cooked through and well browned. Flip the strips halfway through.

5. Meanwhile, combine the ingredients for the sauce in a small bowl. Stir to mix well. Arrange the bowl in the refrigerator to chill until ready to serve.

6. Serve the air fried pork strips with the chilled sauce.

307

PORK CHOP STIR FRY

Prep time: 10 minutes | **Cook time:** 20 minutes | **Serves** 4

1 tablespoon olive oil
¼ teaspoon ground black pepper
½ teaspoon salt
1 egg white
4 (4-ounce / 113-g) pork chops
¾ cup almond flour
2 sliced jalapeño peppers
2 sliced scallions
2 tablespoons olive oil
¼ teaspoon ground white pepper
1 teaspoon sea salt

1. Coat the air fryer basket with olive oil.
2. Whisk black pepper, salt, and egg white together until foamy.
3. Cut pork chops into pieces, leaving just a bit on bones. Pat dry.
4. Add pieces of pork to egg white mixture, coating well. Let sit for marinade 20 minutes.
5. Press "Pre-Heat", set the temperature at 360°F (182°C).

6. Put marinated chops into a large bowl and add almond flour. Dredge and shake off excess and place into air fryer.

7. Air fry the chops in the preheated air fryer for 12 minutes.

8. Turn up the heat to 400°F (205°C) and air fry for another 6 minutes until pork chops are nice and crisp.

9. Meanwhile, remove jalapeño seeds and chop up. Chop scallions and mix with jalapeño pieces.

10. Heat a skillet with olive oil. Stir-fry the white pepper, salt, scallions, and jalapeños 60 seconds. Then add fried pork pieces to skills and toss with scallion mixture. Stir-fry 1 to 2 minutes until well coated and hot.

11. Serve immediately.

308

PORK CHOPS WITH RINDS

Prep time: 5 minutes | **Cook time:** 15 minutes | **Serves** 4

- 1 teaspoon chili powder
- ½ teaspoon garlic powder
- 1½ ounces (43 g) pork rinds, finely ground
- 4 (4-ounce / 113-g) pork chops
- 1 tablespoon coconut oil, melted

1. Press "Pre-Heat", set the temperature at 400°F (204°C).
2. Combine the chili powder, garlic powder, and ground pork rinds.
3. Coat the pork chops with the coconut oil, followed by the pork rind mixture, taking care to cover them completely. Then place the chops in the air fryer basket.
4. Air fry the chops for 15 minutes or until the internal temperature of the chops reaches at least 145°F (63°C), turning halfway through.
5. Serve immediately.

309

PORK MEDALLIONS WITH RADICCHIO AND ENDIVE SALAD

Prep time: 25 minutes | **Cook time:** 7 minutes | **Serves** 4

1 (8-ounce / 227-g) pork tenderloin
Salt and freshly ground black pepper, to taste
¼ cup flour
2 eggs, lightly beaten
¾ cup cracker meal
1 teaspoon paprika
1 teaspoon dry mustard
1 teaspoon garlic powder
1 teaspoon dried thyme
1 teaspoon salt
vegetable or canola oil, in spray bottle
Vinaigrette:
¼ cup white balsamic vinegar
2 tablespoons agave syrup (or honey or maple syrup)
1 tablespoon Dijon mustard
juice of ½ lemon
2 tablespoons chopped chervil or flat-leaf parsley
salt and freshly ground black pepper
½ cup extra-virgin olive oil

Radicchio and Endive Salad:
1 heart romaine lettuce, torn into large pieces
½ head radicchio, coarsely chopped
2 heads endive, sliced
½ cup cherry tomatoes, halved
3 ounces (85 g) fresh Mozzarella, diced
Salt and freshly ground black pepper, to taste

1. Slice the pork tenderloin into 1-inch slices. Using a meat pounder, pound the pork slices into thin ½-inch medallions. Generously season the pork with salt and freshly ground black pepper on both sides.

2. Set up a dredging station using three shallow dishes. Put the flour in one dish and the beaten eggs in a second dish. Combine the cracker meal, paprika, dry mustard, garlic powder, thyme and salt in a third dish.

3. Press "Pre-Heat", set the temperature at 400°F (204°C).

4. Dredge the pork medallions in flour first and then into the beaten egg. Let the excess egg drip off and coat both sides of the medallions with the cracker meal crumb mixture. Spray both sides of the coated medallions with vegetable or canola oil.

5. Air fry the medallions in two batches at 400°F (204°C) for 5 minutes. Once you have air-fried all the medallions, flip them all over and return the first batch of medallions back into the air fryer on top of the second batch. Air fry at 400°F (204°C) for an additional 2 minutes.

6. While the medallions are cooking, make the salad and dressing. Whisk the white balsamic vinegar, agave syrup, Dijon mustard, lemon juice, chervil, salt and pepper together in a small bowl. Whisk in the olive oil slowly until combined and thickened.

7. Combine the romaine lettuce, radicchio, endive, cherry tomatoes, and Mozzarella cheese in a large salad bowl. Drizzle the dressing over the vegetables and toss to combine. Season with salt and freshly ground black pepper.

8. Serve the pork medallions warm on or beside the salad.

310

PORK SAUSAGE WITH CAULIFLOWER MASH

Prep time: 5 minutes | **Cook time:** 27 minutes | **Serves** 6

1 pound (454 g) cauliflower, chopped
6 pork sausages, chopped
½ onion, sliced
3 eggs, beaten
⅓ cup Colby cheese
1 teaspoon cumin powder
½ teaspoon tarragon
½ teaspoon sea salt
½ teaspoon ground black pepper
Cooking spray

1. Press "Pre-Heat", set the temperature at 365°F (185°C). Spritz a baking pan with cooking spray.

2. In a saucepan over medium heat, boil the cauliflower until tender. Place the boiled cauliflower in a food processor and pulse until puréed. Transfer to a large bowl and combine with remaining ingredients until well blended.

3. Pour the cauliflower and sausage mixture into the baking pan. Bake in the preheated air fryer for 27 minutes, or until lightly browned.

4. Divide the mixture among six serving dishes and serve warm.

311

PORK SCHNITZELS WITH SOUR CREAM AND DILL SAUCE

Prep time: 5 minutes | **Cook time:** 24 minutes | **Serves** 4 to 6

½ cup flour
1½ teaspoons salt
Freshly ground black pepper, to taste
2 eggs
½ cup milk
1½ cups toasted breadcrumbs
1 teaspoon paprika
6 boneless, center cut pork chops (about 1½ pounds / 680 g), fat trimmed, pound to ½-inch thick
2 tablespoons olive oil
3 tablespoons melted butter
Lemon wedges, for serving
Sour Cream and Dill Sauce:
1 cup chicken stock
1½ tablespoons cornstarch
⅓ cup sour cream
1½ tablespoons chopped fresh dill
Salt and ground black pepper, to taste

1. Press "Pre-Heat", set the temperature at 400°F (204°C).
2. Combine the flour with salt and black pepper in a large bowl. Stir to mix well. Whisk the egg with milk in a second bowl. Stir the breadcrumbs and paprika in a third bowl.
3. Dredge the pork chops in the flour bowl, then in the egg milk, and then into the breadcrumbs bowl. Press to coat well. Shake the excess off.
4. Arrange one pork chop in the preheated air fryer each time, then brush with olive oil and butter on all sides.
5. Air fry each pork chop for 4 minutes or until golden brown and crispy. Flip the chop halfway through the cooking time.
6. Transfer the cooked pork chop (schnitzel) to a baking pan in the oven and keep warm over low heat while air frying the remaining pork chops.
7. Meanwhile, combine the chicken stock and cornstarch in a small saucepan and bring to a boil over medium-high heat. Simmer for 2 more minutes.
8. Turn off the heat, then mix in the sour cream, fresh dill, salt, and black pepper.
9. Remove the schnitzels from the air fryer to a plate and baste with sour cream and dill sauce. Squeeze the lemon wedges over and slice to serve.

312

SAUSAGE RATATOUILLE

Prep time: 10 minutes | **Cook time:** 25 minutes | **Serves** 4

4 pork sausages
Ratatouille:
2 zucchinis, sliced
1 eggplant, sliced
15 ounces (425 g) tomatoes, sliced
1 red bell pepper, sliced
1 medium red onion, sliced
1 cup canned butter beans, drained
1 tablespoon balsamic vinegar
2 garlic cloves, minced
1 red chili, chopped
2 tablespoons fresh thyme, chopped
2 tablespoons olive oil

1.Press "Pre-Heat", set the temperature at 390°F (199°C).

2.Place the sausages in the preheated air fryer and air fry for 10 minutes or until the sausage is lightly browned. Flip the sausages halfway through.

3.Meanwhile, make the ratatouille: arrange the vegetable

slices on the prepared baking pan alternatively, then add the remaining ingredients on top.

4. Transfer the air fried sausage to a plate, then arrange the baking pan in the air fryer and bake for 15 minutes or until the vegetables are tender.

5. Serve the ratatouille with the sausage on top.

313

SIMPLE PORK MEATBALLS WITH RED CHILI

Prep time: 5 minutes | **Cook time:** 15 minutes | **Serves** 4

1 pound (454 g) ground pork
2 cloves garlic, finely minced
1 cup scallions, finely chopped
1½ tablespoons Worcestershire sauce
½ teaspoon freshly grated ginger root
1 teaspoon turmeric powder
1 tablespoon oyster sauce
1 small sliced red chili, for garnish
Cooking spray

1. Press "Pre-Heat", set the temperature at 350°F (177°C). Spritz the air fryer basket with cooking spray.
2. Combine all the ingredients, except for the red chili in a large bowl. Toss to mix well.
3. Shape the mixture into equally sized balls, then arrange them in the preheated air fryer and spritz with cooking spray.
4. Air fry for 15 minutes or until the balls are lightly browned. Flip the balls halfway through.
5. Serve the pork meatballs with red chili on top.

314

SMOKY PAPRIKA PORK AND VEGETABLE KABOBS

Prep time: 25 minutes | **Cook time:** 15 minutes | **Serves** 4

1 pound (454 g) pork tenderloin, cubed
1 teaspoon smoked paprika
Salt and ground black pepper, to taste
1 green bell pepper, cut into chunks
1 zucchini, cut into chunks
1 red onion, sliced
1 tablespoon oregano
Cooking spray
Special Equipment:
Small bamboo skewers, soaked in water for 20 minutes to keep them from burning while cooking

1. Press "Pre-Heat", set the temperature at 350°F (177°C). Spritz the air fryer basket with cooking spray.
2. Add the pork to a bowl and season with the smoked paprika, salt and black pepper. Thread the seasoned pork cubes and vegetables alternately onto the soaked skewers.
3. Arrange the skewers in the prepared air fryer basket and spray with cooking spray. Air fry for 15 minutes, or until the pork

is well browned and the vegetables are tender, flipping once halfway through.

4. Transfer the skewers to the serving dishes and sprinkle with oregano. Serve hot.

315

SPICY PORK CHOPS WITH CARROTS AND MUSHROOMS

Prep time: 10 minutes | **Cook time:** 15 to 18 minutes | **Serves** 4

- 2 carrots, cut into sticks
- 1 cup mushrooms, sliced
- 2 garlic cloves, minced
- 2 tablespoons olive oil
- 1 pound (454 g) boneless pork chops
- 1 teaspoon dried oregano
- 1 teaspoon dried thyme
- 1 teaspoon cayenne pepper
- Salt and ground black pepper, to taste
- Cooking spray

1. Preheat air fryer to 360°F (182°C). Spritz the air fryer basket with cooking spray.
2. In a mixing bowl, toss together the carrots, mushrooms, garlic, olive oil and salt until well combined.
3. Add the pork chops to a different bowl and season with oregano, thyme, cayenne pepper, salt and black pepper.
4. Lower the vegetable mixture in the prepared air fryer basket. Place the seasoned pork chops on top. Air fry for 15 to 18

minutes, or until the pork is well browned and the vegetables are tender, flipping the pork and shaking the basket once halfway through.

5. Transfer the pork chops to the serving dishes and let cool for 5 minutes. Serve warm with vegetable on the side.

316

SPICY PORK WITH CANDY ONIONS

Prep time: 10 minutes | **Cook time:** 52 minutes | **Serves** 4

2 teaspoons sesame oil

1 teaspoon dried sage, crushed

1 teaspoon cayenne pepper

1 rosemary sprig, chopped

1 thyme sprig, chopped

Sea salt and ground black pepper, to taste

2 pounds (907 g) pork leg roast, scored

½ pound (227 g) candy onions, sliced

4 cloves garlic, finely chopped

2 chili peppers, minced

1. Press "Pre-Heat", set the temperature at 400°F (204°C).

2. In a mixing bowl, combine the sesame oil, sage, cayenne pepper, rosemary, thyme, salt and black pepper until well mixed. In another bowl, place the pork leg and brush with the seasoning mixture.

3. Place the seasoned pork leg in a baking pan and air fry for 40 minutes, or until lightly browned, flipping halfway through. Add the candy onions, garlic and chili peppers to the pan and air fry for another 12 minutes.

4. Transfer the pork leg to a plate. Let cool for 5 minutes and slice. Spread the juices left in the pan over the pork and serve warm with the candy onions.

317

SPINACH AND BEEF BRACIOLE

Prep time: 25 minutes | **Cook time:** 1 hour 32 minutes | **Serves** 4

½ onion, finely chopped
1 teaspoon olive oil
⅓ cup red wine
2 cups crushed tomatoes
1 teaspoon Italian seasoning
½ teaspoon garlic powder
¼ teaspoon crushed red pepper flakes
2 tablespoons chopped fresh parsley
2 top round steaks (about 1½ pounds / 680 g)
salt and freshly ground black pepper
2 cups fresh spinach, chopped
1 clove minced garlic
½ cup roasted red peppers, julienned
½ cup grated pecorino cheese
¼ cup pine nuts, toasted and roughly chopped
2 tablespoons olive oil

1. Press "Pre-Heat", set the temperature at 400°F (204°C).
2. Toss the onions and olive oil together in a baking pan or

casserole dish. Air fry at 400°F (204°C) for 5 minutes, stirring a couple times during the cooking process. Add the red wine, crushed tomatoes, Italian seasoning, garlic powder, red pepper flakes and parsley and stir. Cover the pan tightly with aluminum foil, lower the air fryer temperature to 350°F (177°C) and continue to air fry for 15 minutes.

3. While the sauce is simmering, prepare the beef. Using a meat mallet, pound the beef until it is ¼-inch thick. Season both sides of the beef with salt and pepper. Combine the spinach, garlic, red peppers, pecorino cheese, pine nuts and olive oil in a medium bowl. Season with salt and freshly ground black pepper. Disperse the mixture over the steaks. Starting at one of the short ends, roll the beef around the filling, tucking in the sides as you roll to ensure the filling is completely enclosed. Secure the beef rolls with toothpicks.

4. Remove the baking pan with the sauce from the air fryer and set it aside. Press "Pre-Heat", set the temperature at 400°F (204°C).

5. Brush or spray the beef rolls with a little olive oil and air fry at 400°F (204°C) for 12 minutes, rotating the beef during the cooking process for even browning. When the beef is browned, submerge the rolls into the sauce in the baking pan, cover the pan with foil and return it to the air fryer. Reduce the temperature of the air fryer to 250°F (121°C) and air fry for 60 minutes.

6. Remove the beef rolls from the sauce. Cut each roll into slices and serve, ladling some sauce overtop.

318

SUN-DRIED TOMATO CRUSTED CHOPS

Prep time: 15 minutes | **Cook time:** 10 minutes | **Serves** 4

½ cup oil-packed sun-dried tomatoes
½ cup toasted almonds
¼ cup grated Parmesan cheese
½ cup olive oil, plus more for brushing the air fryer basket
2 tablespoons water
½ teaspoon salt
Freshly ground black pepper, to taste
4 center-cut boneless pork chops (about 1¼ pounds / 567 g)

1. Put the sun-dried tomatoes into a food processor and pulse them until they are coarsely chopped. Add the almonds, Parmesan cheese, olive oil, water, salt and pepper. Process into a smooth paste. Spread most of the paste (leave a little in reserve) onto both sides of the pork chops and then pierce the meat several times with a needle-style meat tenderizer or a fork. Let the pork chops sit and marinate for at least 1 hour (refrigerate if marinating for longer than 1 hour).

2. Press "Pre-Heat", set the temperature at 370°F (188°C).

3. Brush more olive oil on the bottom of the air fryer basket. Transfer the pork chops into the air fryer basket, spooning a little

more of the sun-dried tomato paste onto the pork chops if there are any gaps where the paste may have been rubbed off. Air fry the pork chops for 10 minutes, turning the chops over halfway through.

4.When the pork chops have finished cooking, transfer them to a serving plate and serve.

319

SUPER BACON WITH MEAT

Prep time: 5 minutes | **Cook time:** 1 hour | **Serves** 4

30 slices thick-cut bacon

4 ounces (113 g) Cheddar cheese, shredded

12 ounces (340 g) steak

10 ounces (283 g) pork sausage

Salt and ground black pepper, to taste

1. Press "Pre-Heat", set the temperature at 400°F (204°C).
2. Lay out 30 slices of bacon in a woven pattern and bake for 20 minutes until crisp. Put the cheese in the center of the bacon.
3. Combine the steak and sausage to form a meaty mixture.
4. Lay out the meat in a rectangle of similar size to the bacon strips. Season with salt and pepper.
5. Roll the meat into a tight roll and refrigerate.
6. Press "Pre-Heat", set the temperature at 400°F (204°C).
7. Make a 7× 7 bacon weave and roll the bacon weave over the meat, diagonally.
8. Bake for 60 minutes or until the internal temperature reaches at least 165°F (74°C).
9. Let rest for 5 minutes before serving.

320

TONKATSU

Prep time: 5 minutes | **Cook time:** 10 minutes per batch | **Serves** 4

2/3 cup all-purpose flour

2 large egg whites

1 cup panko breadcrumbs

4 (4-ounce / 113-g) center-cut boneless pork loin chops (about ½ inch thick)

Cooking spray

1. Press "Pre-Heat", set the temperature at 375°F (191°C). Spritz the air fryer basket with cooking spray.

2. Pour the flour in a bowl. Whisk the egg whites in a separate bowl. Spread the breadcrumbs on a large plate.

3. Dredge the pork loin chops in the flour first, press to coat well, then shake the excess off and dunk the chops in the eggs whites, and then roll the chops over the breadcrumbs. Shake the excess off.

4. Arrange the pork chops in batches in a single layer in the preheated air fryer and spritz with cooking spray.

5. Air fry for 10 minutes or until the pork chops are lightly

browned and crunchy. Flip the chops halfway through. Repeat with remaining chops.

6.Serve immediately.

APPETIZERS AND SNACKS

321

AIR FRIED POT STICKERS

Prep time: 10 minutes | **Cook time:** 18 to 20 minutes | Makes 30 pot stickers

- ½ cup finely chopped cabbage
- ¼ cup finely chopped red bell pepper
- 2 green onions, finely chopped
- 1 egg, beaten
- 2 tablespoons cocktail sauce
- 2 teaspoons low-sodium soy sauce
- 30 wonton wrappers
- 1 tablespoon water, for brushing the wrappers

1. Press "Pre-Heat", set the temperature at 360°F (182°C).
2. In a small bowl, combine the cabbage, pepper, green onions, egg, cocktail sauce, and soy sauce, and mix well.
3. Put about 1 teaspoon of the mixture in the center of each wonton wrapper. Fold the wrapper in half, covering the filling; dampen the edges with water, and seal. You can crimp the edges of the wrapper with your fingers so they look like the pot stickers you get in restaurants. Brush them with water.
4. Place the pot stickers in the air fryer basket and air fry in 2

batches for 9 to 10 minutes, or until the pot stickers are hot and the bottoms are lightly browned.

5. Serve hot.

322

AIR FRYER CHICKEN WINGS

Prep time: 1 hour 20 minutes | **Cook time:** 17 to 19 minutes | **Serves** 4

2 pounds (907 g) chicken wings
Marinade:
1 cup buttermilk
½ teaspoon salt
½ teaspoon black pepper
Coating:
1 cup flour
1 cup panko bread crumbs
2 tablespoons poultry seasoning
2 teaspoons salt
Cooking spray

1. Whisk together all the ingredients for the marinade in a large bowl.
2. Add the chicken wings to the marinade and toss well. Transfer to the refrigerator to marinate for at least an hour.
3. Press "Pre-Heat", set the temperature at 360°F (182°C). Spritz the air fryer basket with cooking spray.

4. Thoroughly combine all the ingredients for the coating in a shallow bowl.

5. Remove the chicken wings from the marinade and shake off any excess. Roll them in the coating mixture.

6. Place the chicken wings in the air fryer basket in a single layer. You'll need to work in batches to avoid overcrowding.

7. Mist the wings with cooking spray and air fry for 17 to 19 minutes, or until the wings are crisp and golden brown on the outside. Flip the wings halfway through the cooking time.

8. Remove from the basket to a plate and repeat with the remaining wings.

9. Serve hot.

323

BACON-WRAPPED SHRIMP AND JALAPEÑO

Prep time: 20 minutes | **Cook time:** 26 minutes | **Serves** 8

24 large shrimp, peeled and deveined, about ¾ pound (340 g)
5 tablespoons barbecue sauce, divided
12 strips bacon, cut in half
24 small pickled jalapeño slices

1. Toss together the shrimp and 3 tablespoons of the barbecue sauce. Let stand for 15 minutes. Soak 24 wooden toothpicks in water for 10 minutes. Wrap 1 piece bacon around the shrimp and jalapeño slice, then secure with a toothpick.
2. Press "Pre-Heat", set the temperature at 350°F (177°C).
3. Working in batches, place half of the shrimp in the air fryer basket, spacing them ½ inch apart. Air fry for 10 minutes. Turn shrimp over with tongs and air fry for 3 minutes more, or until bacon is golden brown and shrimp are cooked through.
4. Brush with the remaining barbecue sauce and serve.

324

BAKED RICOTTA

Prep time: 10 minutes | **Cook time:** 15 minutes | Makes 2 cups

1 (15-ounce / 425-g) container whole milk Ricotta cheese
3 tablespoons grated Parmesan cheese, divided
2 tablespoons extra-virgin olive oil
1 teaspoon chopped fresh thyme leaves
1 teaspoon grated lemon zest
1 clove garlic, crushed with press
¼ teaspoon salt
¼ teaspoon pepper
Toasted baguette slices or crackers, for serving

1. Press "Pre-Heat", set the temperature at 380°F (193°C).
2. To get the baking dish in and out of the air fryer, create a sling using a 24-inch length of foil, folded lengthwise into thirds.
3. Whisk together the Ricotta, 2 tablespoons of the Parmesan, oil, thyme, lemon zest, garlic, salt, and pepper. Pour into a baking dish. Cover the dish tightly with foil.
4. Place the sling under dish and lift by the ends into the air fryer, tucking the ends of the sling around the dish. Bake for 10

minutes. Remove the foil cover and sprinkle with the remaining 1 tablespoon of the Parmesan. Air fry for 5 more minutes, or until bubbly at edges and the top is browned.

5. Serve warm with toasted baguette slices or crackers.

325

BBQ PORK RIBS

Prep time: 5 minutes | **Cook time:** 35 minutes | **Serves** 2

1 tablespoon kosher salt

1 tablespoon dark brown sugar

1 tablespoon sweet paprika

1 teaspoon garlic powder

1 teaspoon onion powder

1 teaspoon poultry seasoning

½ teaspoon mustard powder

½ teaspoon freshly ground black pepper

2¼ pounds (1 kg) individually cut St. Louis–style pork spareribs

1. Press "Pre-Heat", set the temperature at 350°F (177°C).

2. In a large bowl, whisk together the salt, brown sugar, paprika, garlic powder, onion powder, poultry seasoning, mustard powder, and pepper. Add the ribs and toss. Rub the seasonings into them with your hands until they're fully coated.

3. Arrange the ribs in the air fryer basket, standing up on their ends and leaned up against the wall of the basket and each other. Roast for 35 minutes, or until the ribs are tender inside and

golden brown and crisp on the outside. Transfer the ribs to plates and serve hot.

326

BEEF AND MANGO SKEWERS

Prep time: 10 minutes | **Cook time:** 4 to 7 minutes | **Serves** 4

- ¾ pound (340 g) beef sirloin tip, cut into 1-inch cubes
- 2 tablespoons balsamic vinegar
- 1 tablespoon olive oil
- 1 tablespoon honey
- ½ teaspoon dried marjoram
- Pinch of salt
- Freshly ground black pepper, to taste
- 1 mango

1. Press "Pre-Heat", set the temperature at 390°F (199°C).
2. Put the beef cubes in a medium bowl and add the balsamic vinegar, olive oil, honey, marjoram, salt, and pepper. Mix well, then massage the marinade into the beef with your hands. Set aside.
3. To prepare the mango, stand it on end and cut the skin off, using a sharp knife. Then carefully cut around the oval pit to remove the flesh. Cut the mango into 1-inch cubes.
4. Thread metal skewers alternating with three beef cubes and two mango cubes.

5. Roast the skewers in the air fryer basket for 4 to 7 minutes, or until the beef is browned and at least 145°F (63°C).

6. Serve hot.

BRUSCHETTA WITH BASIL PESTO

Prep time: 10 minutes | **Cook time:** 5 to 11 minutes | **Serves** 4

8 slices French bread, ½ inch thick
2 tablespoons softened butter
1 cup shredded Mozzarella cheese
½ cup basil pesto
1 cup chopped grape tomatoes
2 green onions, thinly sliced

1. Press "Pre-Heat", set the temperature at 350°F (177°C).
2. Spread the bread with the butter and place butter-side up in the air fryer basket. Bake for 3 to 5 minutes, or until the bread is light golden brown.
3. Remove the bread from the basket and top each piece with some of the cheese. Return to the basket in 2 batches and bake for 1 to 3 minutes, or until the cheese melts.
4. Meanwhile, combine the pesto, tomatoes, and green onions in a small bowl.
5. When the cheese has melted, remove the bread from the air fryer and place on a serving plate. Top each slice with some of the pesto mixture and serve.

328

BRUSCHETTA WITH TOMATO AND BASIL

Prep time: 5 minutes | **Cook time:** 6 minutes | **Serves** 6

4 tomatoes, diced
1/3 cup shredded fresh basil
1/4 cup shredded Parmesan cheese
1 tablespoon balsamic vinegar
1 tablespoon minced garlic
1 teaspoon olive oil
1 teaspoon salt
1 teaspoon freshly ground black pepper
1 loaf French bread, cut into 1-inch-thick slices
Cooking spray

1. Press "Pre-Heat", set the temperature at 250°F (121°C).

2. Mix together the tomatoes and basil in a medium bowl. Add the cheese, vinegar, garlic, olive oil, salt, and pepper and stir until well incorporated. Set aside.

3. Spritz the air fryer basket with cooking spray. Working in batches, lay the bread slices in the basket in a single layer. Spray the slices with cooking spray.

4. Bake for 3 minutes until golden brown.

5. Remove from the basket to a plate. Repeat with the remaining bread slices.

6. Top each slice with a generous spoonful of the tomato mixture and serve.

329

BUFFALO CAULIFLOWER WITH SOUR DIP

Prep time: 10 minutes | **Cook time:** 10 to 14 minutes | **Serves** 6

1 large head cauliflower, separated into small florets
1 tablespoon olive oil
½ teaspoon garlic powder
⅓ cup low-sodium hot wing sauce, divided
⅔ cup nonfat Greek yogurt
½ teaspoons Tabasco sauce
1 celery stalk, chopped
1 tablespoon crumbled blue cheese

1. Press "Pre-Heat", set the temperature at 380°F (193°C).

2. In a large bowl, toss the cauliflower florets with the olive oil. Sprinkle with the garlic powder and toss again to coat. Put half of the cauliflower in the air fryer basket. Air fry for 5 to 7 minutes, or until the cauliflower is browned, shaking the basket once during cooking.

3. Transfer to a serving bowl and toss with half of the wing sauce. Repeat with the remaining cauliflower and wing sauce.

4. In a small bowl, stir together the yogurt, Tabasco sauce, celery, and blue cheese. Serve the cauliflower with the dip.

330

CARAMELIZED PEACHES

Prep time: 10 minutes | **Cook time:** 10 to 13 minutes | **Serves** 4

2 tablespoons sugar

¼ teaspoon ground cinnamon

4 peaches, cut into wedges

Cooking spray

1. Press "Pre-Heat", set the temperature at 350°F (177°C). Lightly spray the air fryer basket with cooking spray.

2. Toss the peaches with the sugar and cinnamon in a medium bowl until evenly coated.

3. Arrange the peaches in the air fryer basket in a single layer. You may need to work in batches to avoid overcrowding.

4. Lightly mist the peaches with cooking spray and air fry for 5 minutes. Flip the peaches and air fry for another 5 to 8 minutes, or until the peaches are caramelized.

5. Repeat with the remaining peaches.

6. Let the peaches cool for 5 minutes and serve warm.

331

CHEESE AND HAM STUFFED BABY BELLA

Prep time: 15 minutes | **Cook time:** 12 minutes | **Serves** 8

4 ounces (113 g) Mozzarella cheese, cut into pieces
½ cup diced ham
2 green onions, chopped
2 tablespoons bread crumbs
½ teaspoon garlic powder
¼ teaspoon ground oregano
¼ teaspoon ground black pepper
1 to 2 teaspoons olive oil
16 fresh Baby Bella mushrooms, stemmed removed

1. Process the cheese, ham, green onions, bread crumbs, garlic powder, oregano, and pepper in a food processor until finely chopped.

2. With the food processor running, slowly drizzle in 1 to 2 teaspoons olive oil until a thick paste has formed. Transfer the mixture to a bowl.

3. Evenly divide the mixture into the mushroom caps and lightly press down the mixture.

4. Press "Pre-Heat", set the temperature at 390°F (199°C).

5. Lay the mushrooms in the air fryer basket in a single layer. You'll need to work in batches to avoid overcrowding.

6. Roast for 12 minutes until the mushrooms are lightly browned and tender.

7. Remove from the basket to a plate and repeat with the remaining mushrooms.

8. Let the mushrooms cool for 5 minutes and serve warm.

332

CHEESY CRAB TOASTS

Prep time: 10 minutes | **Cook time:** 5 minutes | Makes 15 to 18 toasts

1 (6-ounce / 170-g) can flaked crab meat, well drained
3 tablespoons light mayonnaise
¼ cup shredded Parmesan cheese
¼ cup shredded Cheddar cheese
1 teaspoon Worcestershire sauce
½ teaspoon lemon juice
1 loaf artisan bread, French bread, or baguette, cut into ⅜-inch-thick slices

1. Press "Pre-Heat", set the temperature at 360°F (182°C).
2. In a large bowl, stir together all the ingredients except the bread slices.
3. On a clean work surface, lay the bread slices. Spread ½ tablespoon of crab mixture onto each slice of bread.
4. Arrange the bread slices in the air fryer basket in a single layer. You'll need to work in batches to avoid overcrowding.
5. Bake for 5 minutes until the tops are lightly browned.
6. Transfer to a plate and repeat with the remaining bread slices.

PAMELA KENDRICK

7. Serve warm.

333

CHEESY STUFFED MUSHROOMS

Prep time: 10 minutes | **Cook time:** 8 to 12 minutes | **Serves** 4

16 medium button mushrooms, rinsed and patted dry
$1/3$ cup low-sodium salsa
3 garlic cloves, minced
1 medium onion, finely chopped
1 jalapeño pepper, minced
$1/8$ teaspoon cayenne pepper
3 tablespoons shredded Pepper Jack cheese
2 teaspoons olive oil

1. Press "Pre-Heat", set the temperature at 350°F (177°C).
2. Remove the stems from the mushrooms and finely chop them, reserving the whole caps.
3. In a medium bowl, mix the salsa, garlic, onion, jalapeño, cayenne, and Pepper Jack cheese. Stir in the chopped mushroom stems.
4. Stuff this mixture into the mushroom caps, mounding the filling. Drizzle the olive oil on the mushrooms. Air fry the mushrooms in the air fryer basket for 8 to 12 minutes, or until the filling is hot and the mushrooms are tender.

5. Serve immediately.

334

COCONUT-CRUSTED SHRIMP

Prep time: 10 minutes | **Cook time:** 4 minutes | **Serves** 2 to 4

½ pound (227 g) medium shrimp, peeled and deveined (tails intact)
1 cup canned coconut milk
Finely grated zest of 1 lime
Kosher salt, to taste
½ cup panko bread crumbs
½ cup unsweetened shredded coconut
Freshly ground black pepper, to taste
Cooking spray
1 small or ½ medium cucumber, halved and deseeded
1 cup coconut yogurt
1 serrano chile, deseeded and minced

1. Press "Pre-Heat", set the temperature at 400°F (204°C).
2. In a bowl, combine the shrimp, coconut milk, lime zest, and ½ teaspoon kosher salt. Let the shrimp stand for 10 minutes.
3. Meanwhile, in a separate bowl, stir together the bread crumbs and shredded coconut and season with salt and pepper.
4. A few at a time, add the shrimp to the bread crumb mixture

and toss to coat completely. Transfer the shrimp to a wire rack set over a baking sheet. Spray the shrimp all over with cooking spray.

5. Transfer the shrimp to the air fryer and air fry for 4 minutes, or until golden brown and cooked through. Transfer the shrimp to a serving platter and season with more salt.

6. Grate the cucumber into a small bowl. Stir in the coconut yogurt and chile and season with salt and pepper. Serve alongside the shrimp while they're warm.

335

CREAMY SPINACH-BROCCOLI DIP

Prep time: 10 minutes | **Cook time:** 9 to 14 minutes | **Serves** 4

½ cup low-fat Greek yogurt

¼ cup nonfat cream cheese

½ cup frozen chopped broccoli, thawed and drained

½ cup frozen chopped spinach, thawed and drained

⅓ cup chopped red bell pepper

1 garlic clove, minced

½ teaspoon dried oregano

2 tablespoons grated low-sodium Parmesan cheese

1. Press "Pre-Heat", set the temperature at 340°F (171°C).

2. In a medium bowl, blend the yogurt and cream cheese until well combined.

3. Stir in the broccoli, spinach, red bell pepper, garlic, and oregano. Transfer to a baking pan. Sprinkle with the Parmesan cheese.

4. Place the pan in the air fryer basket. Bake for 9 to 14 minutes, or until the dip is bubbly and the top starts to brown.

5. Serve immediately.

336

CRIPSY ARTICHOKE BITES

Prep time: 10 minutes | **Cook time:** 8 minutes | **Serves** 4

14 whole artichoke hearts packed in water
½ cup all-purpose flour
1 egg
⅓ cup panko bread crumbs
1 teaspoon Italian seasoning
Cooking spray

1. Press "Pre-Heat", set the temperature at 375°F (191°C)
2. Drain the artichoke hearts and dry thoroughly with paper towels.
3. Place the flour on a plate. Beat the egg in a shallow bowl until frothy. Thoroughly combine the bread crumbs and Italian seasoning in a separate shallow bowl.
4. Dredge the artichoke hearts in the flour, then in the beaten egg, and finally roll in the bread crumb mixture until evenly coated.
5. Place the artichoke hearts in the air fryer basket and mist them with cooking spray.
6. Air fry for 8 minutes, flipping the artichoke hearts halfway through, or until they begin to brown and edges are crispy.

7. Let the artichoke hearts sit for 5 minutes before serving.

337

CRISPY APPLE CHIPS

Prep time: 5 minutes | **Cook time:** 25 to 35 minutes | **Serves** 1

1 Honeycrisp or Pink Lady apple

1. Press "Pre-Heat", set the temperature at 300°F (149°C).

2. Core the apple with an apple corer, leaving apple whole. Cut the apple into ⅛-inch-thick slices.

3. Arrange the apple slices in the basket, staggering slices as much as possible. Air fry for 25 to 35 minutes, or until the chips are dry and some are lightly browned, turning 4 times with tongs to separate and rotate them from top to bottom.

4. Place the chips in a single layer on a wire rack to cool. Apples will become crisper as they cool. Serve immediately.

338

CRISPY COD FINGERS

Prep time: 5 minutes | **Cook time:** 12 minutes | **Serves** 4

2 eggs
2 tablespoons milk
2 cups flour
1 cup cornmeal
1 teaspoon seafood seasoning
Salt and black pepper, to taste
1 cup bread crumbs
1 pound (454 g) cod fillets, cut into 1-inch strips

1. Preheat air fryer to 400°F (204°C).
2. Beat the eggs with the milk in a shallow bowl. In another shallow bowl, combine the flour, cornmeal, seafood seasoning, salt, and pepper. On a plate, place the bread crumbs.
3. Dredge the cod strips, one at a time, in the flour mixture, then in the egg mixture, finally in the bread crumb to coat evenly.
4. Arrange the cod strips in the air fryer basket and air fry for 12 minutes until crispy.
5. Transfer the cod strips to a paper towel-lined plate and serve warm.

339

CRISPY GREEN TOMATOES WITH HORSERADISH

Prep time: 18 minutes | **Cook time:** 10 to 15 minutes | **Serves** 4

 2 eggs
 ¼ cup buttermilk
 ½ cup bread crumbs
 ½ cup cornmeal
 ¼ teaspoon salt
 1½ pounds (680 g) firm green tomatoes, cut into ¼-inch slices
 Cooking spray
 Horseradish Sauce:
 ¼ cup sour cream
 ¼ cup mayonnaise
 2 teaspoons prepared horseradish
 ½ teaspoon lemon juice
 ½ teaspoon Worcestershire sauce
 ⅛ teaspoon black pepper

 1.Preheat air fryer to 390°F (199°C). Spritz the air fryer basket with cooking spray.

 2.In a small bowl, whisk together all the ingredients for the horseradish sauce until smooth. Set aside.

3. In a shallow dish, beat the eggs and buttermilk.

4. In a separate shallow dish, thoroughly combine the bread crumbs, cornmeal, and salt.

5. Dredge the tomato slices, one at a time, in the egg mixture, then roll in the bread crumb mixture until evenly coated.

6. Working in batches, place the tomato slices in the air fryer basket in a single layer. Spray them with cooking spray.

7. Air fry for 10 to 15 minutes, flipping the slices halfway through, or until the tomato slices are nicely browned and crisp.

8. Remove from the basket to a platter and repeat with the remaining tomato slices.

9. Serve drizzled with the prepared horseradish sauce.

340

CRISPY PHYLLO ARTICHOKE TRIANGLES

Prep time: 15 minutes | **Cook time:** 9 to 12 minutes | Makes 18 triangles

- ¼ cup Ricotta cheese
- 1 egg white
- ⅓ cup minced and drained artichoke hearts
- 3 tablespoons grated Mozzarella cheese
- ½ teaspoon dried thyme
- 6 sheets frozen phyllo dough, thawed
- 2 tablespoons melted butter

1. Press "Pre-Heat", set the temperature at 400°F (204°C).

2. In a small bowl, combine the Ricotta cheese, egg white, artichoke hearts, Mozzarella cheese, and thyme, and mix well.

3. Cover the phyllo dough with a damp kitchen towel while you work so it doesn't dry out. Using one sheet at a time, place on the work surface and cut into thirds lengthwise.

4. Put about 1½ teaspoons of the filling on each strip at the base. Fold the bottom right-hand tip of phyllo over the filling to meet the other side in a triangle, then continue folding in a triangle. Brush each triangle with butter to seal the edges. Repeat with the remaining phyllo dough and filling.

5. Place the triangles in the air fryer basket. Bake, 6 at a time, for about 3 to 4 minutes, or until the phyllo is golden brown and crisp.

6. Serve hot.

341

CRISPY SPICED CHICKPEAS

Prep time: 5 minutes | **Cook time:** 6 to 12 minutes | Makes 1½ cups

1 can (15-ounce / 425-g) chickpeas, rinsed and dried with paper towels
1 tablespoon olive oil
½ teaspoon dried rosemary
½ teaspoon dried parsley
½ teaspoon dried chives
¼ teaspoon mustard powder
¼ teaspoon sweet paprika
¼ teaspoon cayenne pepper
Kosher salt and freshly ground black pepper, to taste

1. Press "Pre-Heat", set the temperature at 350°F (177°C).
2. In a large bowl, combine all the ingredients, except for the kosher salt and black pepper, and toss until the chickpeas are evenly coated in the herbs and spices.
3. Scrape the chickpeas and seasonings into the air fryer and air fry for 6 to 12 minutes, or until browned and crisp, shaking the basket halfway through.

4. Transfer the crispy chickpeas to a bowl, sprinkle with kosher salt and black pepper, and serve warm.

342

CUBAN SANDWICHES

Prep time: 20 minutes | **Cook time:** 8 minutes | Makes 4 sandwiches

    8 slices ciabatta bread, about ¼-inch thick

    Cooking spray

    1 tablespoon brown mustard

    Toppings:

    6 to 8 ounces (170 to 227 g) thinly sliced leftover roast pork

    4 ounces (113 g) thinly sliced deli turkey

    ⅓ cup bread and butter pickle slices

    2 to 3 ounces (57 to 85 g) Pepper Jack cheese slices

1. Press "Pre-Heat", set the temperature at 390°F (199°C).

2. On a clean work surface, spray one side of each slice of bread with cooking spray. Spread the other side of each slice of bread evenly with brown mustard.

3. Top 4 of the bread slices with the roast pork, turkey, pickle slices, cheese, and finish with remaining bread slices. Transfer to the air fryer basket.

4. Air fry for about 8 minutes until golden brown.

5. Cool for 5 minutes and serve warm.

343

DELUXE CHEESE SANDWICHES

Prep time: 10 minutes | **Cook time:** 5 to 6 minutes | **Serves** 4 to 8

8 ounces (227 g) Brie
8 slices oat nut bread
1 large ripe pear, cored and cut into ½-inch-thick slices
2 tablespoons butter, melted

1. Press "Pre-Heat", set the temperature at 360°F (182°C).
2. Make the sandwiches: Spread each of 4 slices of bread with ¼ of the Brie. Top the Brie with the pear slices and remaining 4 bread slices.
3. Brush the melted butter lightly on both sides of each sandwich.
4. Arrange the sandwiches in the air fryer basket. You may need to work in batches to avoid overcrowding.
5. Bake for 5 to 6 minutes until the cheese is melted. Repeat with the remaining sandwiches.
6. Serve warm.

344

EASY MUFFULETTA SLIDERS WITH OLIVES

Prep time: 10 minutes | **Cook time:** 5 to 7 minutes | Makes 8 sliders

¼ pound (113 g) thinly sliced deli ham
¼ pound (113 g) thinly sliced pastrami
4 ounces (113 g) low-fat Mozzarella cheese, grated
8 slider buns, split in half
Cooking spray
1 tablespoon sesame seeds
Olive Mix:
½ cup sliced green olives with pimentos
¼ cup sliced black olives
¼ cup chopped kalamata olives
1 teaspoon red wine vinegar
¼ teaspoon basil
⅛ teaspoon garlic powder

1. Press "Pre-Heat", set the temperature at 360°F (182°C).
2. Combine all the ingredients for the olive mix in a small bowl and stir well.
3. Stir together the ham, pastrami, and cheese in a medium bowl and divide the mixture into 8 equal portions.

Appetizers and Snacks

4. Assemble the sliders: Top each bottom bun with 1 portion of meat and cheese, 2 tablespoons of olive mix, finished by the remaining buns. Lightly spritz the tops with cooking spray. Scatter the sesame seeds on top.

5. Working in batches, arrange the sliders in the air fryer basket. Bake for 5 t0 7 minutes until the cheese melts.

6. Transfer to a large plate and repeat with the remaining sliders.

7. Serve immediately.

345

HOMEMADE BBQ CHICKEN PIZZA

Prep time: 5 minutes | **Cook time:** 8 minutes | **Serves** 1

1 piece naan bread
¼ cup Barbecue sauce
¼ cup shredded Monterrey Jack cheese
¼ cup shredded Mozzarella cheese
½ chicken herby sausage, sliced
2 tablespoons red onion, thinly sliced
Chopped cilantro or parsley, for garnish
Cooking spray

1. Press "Pre-Heat", set the temperature at 400°F (204°C).
2. Spritz the bottom of naan bread with cooking spray, then transfer to the air fryer basket.
3. Brush with the Barbecue sauce. Top with the cheeses, sausage, and finish with the red onion.
4. Air fry for 8 minutes until the cheese is melted.
5. Garnish with the chopped cilantro or parsley before slicing to serve.

346

ITALIAN RICE BALLS

Prep time: 20 minutes | **Cook time:** 10 minutes | Makes 8 rice balls

1½ cups cooked sticky rice
½ teaspoon Italian seasoning blend
¾ teaspoon salt, divided
8 black olives, pitted
1 ounce (28 g) Mozzarella cheese, cut into tiny pieces (small enough to stuff into olives)
2 eggs
⅓ cup Italian bread crumbs
¾ cup panko bread crumbs
Cooking spray

1. Preheat air fryer to 390°F (199°C).
2. Stuff each black olive with a piece of Mozzarella cheese. Set aside.
3. In a bowl, combine the cooked sticky rice, Italian seasoning blend, and ½ teaspoon of salt and stir to mix well. Form the rice mixture into a log with your hands and divide it into 8 equal portions. Mold each portion around a black olive and roll into a ball.

4. Transfer to the freezer to chill for 10 to 15 minutes until firm.

5. In a shallow dish, place the Italian bread crumbs. In a separate shallow dish, whisk the eggs. In a third shallow dish, combine the panko bread crumbs and remaining salt.

6. One by one, roll the rice balls in the Italian bread crumbs, then dip in the whisked eggs, finally coat them with the panko bread crumbs.

7. Arrange the rice balls in the air fryer basket and spritz both sides with cooking spray.

8. Air fry for 10 minutes until the rice balls are golden brown. Flip the balls halfway through the cooking time.

9. Serve warm.

347

KALE CHIPS WITH SESAME

Prep time: 15 minutes | **Cook time:** 8 minutes | **Serves** 5

8 cups deribbed kale leaves, torn into 2-inch pieces
1½ tablespoons olive oil
¾ teaspoon chili powder
¼ teaspoon garlic powder
½ teaspoon paprika
2 teaspoons sesame seeds

1. Preheat air fryer to 350°F (177°C).
2. In a large bowl, toss the kale with the olive oil, chili powder, garlic powder, paprika, and sesame seeds until well coated.
3. Put the kale in the air fryer basket and air fry for 8 minutes, flipping the kale twice during cooking, or until the kale is crispy.
4. Serve warm.

348

LEMONY CHICKEN DRUMSTICKS

Prep time: 5 minutes | **Cook time:** 30 minutes | **Serves** 2

2 teaspoons freshly ground coarse black pepper
1 teaspoon baking powder
½ teaspoon garlic powder
4 chicken drumsticks (4 ounces / 113 g each)
Kosher salt, to taste
1 lemon

1. In a small bowl, stir together the pepper, baking powder, and garlic powder. Place the drumsticks on a plate and sprinkle evenly with the baking powder mixture, turning the drumsticks so they're well coated. Let the drumsticks stand in the refrigerator for at least 1 hour or up to overnight.
2. Press "Pre-Heat", set the temperature at 375°F (191°C).
3. Sprinkle the drumsticks with salt, then transfer them to the air fryer, standing them bone-end up and leaning against the wall of the air fryer basket. Air fry for 30 minutes, or until cooked through and crisp on the outside.
4. Transfer the drumsticks to a serving platter and finely grate the zest of the lemon over them while they're hot. Cut the lemon into wedges and serve with the warm drumsticks.

349

LEMONY PEAR CHIPS

Prep time: 15 minutes | **Cook time:** 9 to 13 minutes | **Serves** 4

2 firm Bosc pears, cut crosswise into ⅛-inch-thick slices
1 tablespoon freshly squeezed lemon juice
½ teaspoon ground cinnamon
⅛ teaspoon ground cardamom

1. Press "Pre-Heat", set the temperature at 380°F (193°C).
2. Separate the smaller stem-end pear rounds from the larger rounds with seeds. Remove the core and seeds from the larger slices. Sprinkle all slices with lemon juice, cinnamon, and cardamom.
3. Put the smaller chips into the air fryer basket. Air fry for 3 to 5 minutes, or until light golden brown, shaking the basket once during cooking. Remove from the air fryer.
4. Repeat with the larger slices, air frying for 6 to 8 minutes, or until light golden brown, shaking the basket once during cooking.
5. Remove the chips from the air fryer. Cool and serve or store in an airtight container at room temperature up for to 2 days.

350

MOZZARELLA ARANCINI

Prep time: 5 minutes | **Cook time:** 8 to 11 minutes | Makes 16 arancini

2 cups cooked rice, cooled

2 eggs, beaten

1½ cups panko bread crumbs, divided

½ cup grated Parmesan cheese

2 tablespoons minced fresh basil

16 ¾-inch cubes Mozzarella cheese

2 tablespoons olive oil

1. Press "Pre-Heat", set the temperature at 400°F (204°C).

2. In a medium bowl, combine the rice, eggs, ½ cup of the bread crumbs, Parmesan cheese, and basil. Form this mixture into 16 1½-inch balls.

3. Poke a hole in each of the balls with your finger and insert a Mozzarella cube. Form the rice mixture firmly around the cheese.

4. On a shallow plate, combine the remaining 1 cup of the bread crumbs with the olive oil and mix well. Roll the rice balls in the bread crumbs to coat.

5. Air fry the arancini in batches for 8 to 11 minutes or until golden brown.

6. Serve hot.

351

MUSHROOM AND SPINACH CALZONES

Prep time: 15 minutes | **Cook time:** 26 to 27 minutes | **Serves** 4

2 tablespoons olive oil
1 onion, chopped
2 garlic cloves, minced
¼ cup chopped mushrooms
1 pound (454 g) spinach, chopped
1 tablespoon Italian seasoning
½ teaspoon oregano
Salt and black pepper, to taste
1½ cups marinara sauce
1 cup ricotta cheese, crumbled
1 (13-ounce / 369-g) pizza crust
Cooking spray

Make the Filling:

1. Heat the olive oil in a pan over medium heat until shimmering.

2. Add the onion, garlic, and mushrooms and sauté for 4 minutes, or until softened.

3. Stir in the spinach and sauté for 2 to 3 minutes, or until the

spinach is wilted. Sprinkle with the Italian seasoning, oregano, salt, and pepper and mix well.

4. Add the marinara sauce and cook for about 5 minutes, stirring occasionally, or until the sauce is thickened.

5. Remove the pan from the heat and stir in the ricotta cheese. Set aside.

Make the Calzones:

6. Press "Pre-Heat", set the temperature at 375°F (191°C). Spritz the air fryer basket with cooking spray.

7. Roll the pizza crust out with a rolling pin on a lightly floured work surface, then cut it into 4 rectangles.

8. Spoon ¼ of the filling into each rectangle and fold in half. Crimp the edges with a fork to seal. Mist them with cooking spray.

9. Place the calzones in the air fryer basket and air fry for 15 minutes, flipping once, or until the calzones are golden brown and crisp.

10. Transfer the calzones to a paper towel-lined plate and serve.

352

OLD BAY CHICKEN WINGS

Prep time: 10 minutes | **Cook time:** 12 to 15 minutes | **Serves** 4

2 tablespoons Old Bay seasoning

2 teaspoons baking powder

2 teaspoons salt

2 pounds (907 g) chicken wings, patted dry

Cooking spray

1. Press "Pre-Heat", set the temperature at 400°F (204°C). Lightly spray the air fryer basket with cooking spray.

2. Combine the Old Bay seasoning, baking powder, and salt in a large zip-top plastic bag. Add the chicken wings, seal, and shake until the wings are thoroughly coated in the seasoning mixture.

3. Lay the chicken wings in the air fryer basket in a single layer and lightly mist with cooking spray. You may need to work in batches to avoid overcrowding.

4. Air fry for 12 to 15 minutes, flipping the wings halfway through, or until the wings are lightly browned and the internal temperature reaches at least 165°F (74°C) on a meat thermometer.

5.Remove from the basket to a plate and repeat with the remaining chicken wings.

6.Serve hot.

353

PEPPERY CHICKEN MEATBALLS

Prep time: 5 minutes | **Cook time:** 13 to 20 minutes | Makes 16 meatballs

2 teaspoons olive oil
¼ cup minced onion
¼ cup minced red bell pepper
2 vanilla wafers, crushed
1 egg white
½ teaspoon dried thyme
½ pound (227 g) ground chicken breast

1. Press "Pre-Heat", set the temperature at 370°F (188°C).
2. In a baking pan, mix the olive oil, onion, and red bell pepper. Put the pan in the air fryer. Air fry for 3 to 5 minutes, or until the vegetables are tender.
3. In a medium bowl, mix the cooked vegetables, crushed wafers, egg white, and thyme until well combined
4. Mix in the chicken, gently but thoroughly, until everything is combined.
5. Form the mixture into 16 meatballs and place them in the air fryer basket. Air fry for 10 to 15 minutes, or until the meatballs

reach an internal temperature of 165°F (74°C) on a meat thermometer.

6. Serve immediately.

354

ROASTED MIXED NUTS

Prep time: 5 minutes | **Cook time:** 20 minutes | **Serves** 6

2 cups mixed nuts (walnuts, pecans, and almonds)
2 tablespoons egg white
2 tablespoons sugar
1 teaspoon paprika
1 teaspoon ground cinnamon
Cooking spray

1. Press "Pre-Heat", set the temperature at 300°F (149°C). Spray the air fryer basket with cooking spray.
2. Stir together the mixed nuts, egg white, sugar, paprika, and cinnamon in a small bowl until the nuts are fully coated.
3. Put the nuts in the air fryer basket and roast for 20 minutes. Shake the basket halfway through the cooking time for even cooking.
4. Transfer the nuts to a bowl and serve warm.

355

ROSEMARY-GARLIC SHOESTRING FRIES

Prep time: 5 minutes | **Cook time:** 18 minutes | **Serves** 2

1 large russet potato (about 12 ounces / 340 g), scrubbed clean, and julienned

1 tablespoon vegetable oil

Leaves from 1 sprig fresh rosemary

Kosher salt and freshly ground black pepper, to taste

1 garlic clove, thinly sliced

Flaky sea salt, for serving

1. Press "Pre-Heat", set the temperature at 400°F (204°C).

2. Place the julienned potatoes in a large colander and rinse under cold running water until the water runs clear. Spread the potatoes out on a double-thick layer of paper towels and pat dry.

3. In a large bowl, combine the potatoes, oil, and rosemary. Season with kosher salt and pepper and toss to coat evenly. Place the potatoes in the air fryer and air fry for 18 minutes, shaking the basket every 5 minutes and adding the garlic in the last 5 minutes of cooking, or until the fries are golden brown and crisp.

4. Transfer the fries to a plate and sprinkle with flaky sea salt while they're hot. Serve immediately.

356

SAUSAGE AND MUSHROOM EMPANADAS

Prep time: 5 minutes | **Cook time:** 12 minutes | **Serves** 4

½ pound (227 g) Kielbasa smoked sausage, chopped
4 chopped canned mushrooms
2 tablespoons chopped onion
½ teaspoon ground cumin
¼ teaspoon paprika
Salt and black pepper, to taste
½ package puff pastry dough, at room temperature
1 egg, beaten
Cooking spray

1. Preheat air fryer to 360°F (182°C). Spritz the air fryer basket with cooking spray.
2. Combine the sausage, mushrooms, onion, cumin, paprika, salt, and pepper in a bowl and stir to mix well.
3. Make the empanadas: Place the puff pastry dough on a lightly floured surface. Cut circles into the dough with a glass. Place 1 tablespoon of the sausage mixture into the center of each pastry circle. Fold each in half and pinch the edges to seal. Using a fork, crimp the edges. Brush them with the beaten egg and mist with cooking spray.

4.Place the empanadas in the air fryer basket and air fry for 12 minutes until golden brown. Flip the empanadas halfway through the cooking time.

5.Allow them to cool for 5 minutes and serve hot.

357

SHISHITO PEPPERS WITH HERB DRESSING

Prep time: 10 minutes | **Cook time:** 6 minutes | **Serves** 2 to 4

6 ounces (170 g) shishito peppers
1 tablespoon vegetable oil
Kosher salt and freshly ground black pepper, to taste
½ cup mayonnaise
2 tablespoons finely chopped fresh basil leaves
2 tablespoons finely chopped fresh flat-leaf parsley
1 tablespoon finely chopped fresh tarragon
1 tablespoon finely chopped fresh chives
Finely grated zest of ½ lemon
1 tablespoon fresh lemon juice
Flaky sea salt, for serving

1. Press "Pre-Heat", set the temperature at 400°F (204°C).

2. In a bowl, toss together the shishitos and oil to evenly coat and season with kosher salt and black pepper. Transfer to the air fryer and air fry for 6 minutes, shaking the basket halfway through, or until the shishitos are blistered and lightly charred.

3. Meanwhile, in a small bowl, whisk together the mayonnaise, basil, parsley, tarragon, chives, lemon zest, and lemon juice.

4. Pile the peppers on a plate, sprinkle with flaky sea salt, and serve hot with the dressing.

358

SPICED MIXED NUTS

Prep time: 5 minutes | **Cook time:** 6 minutes | Makes 2 cups

- ½ cup raw cashews
- ½ cup raw pecan halves
- ½ cup raw walnut halves
- ½ cup raw whole almonds
- 2 tablespoons olive oil
- 1 tablespoon light brown sugar
- 1 teaspoon chopped fresh rosemary leaves
- 1 teaspoon chopped fresh thyme leaves
- 1 teaspoon kosher salt
- ½ teaspoon ground coriander
- ¼ teaspoon onion powder
- ¼ teaspoon freshly ground black pepper
- ⅛ teaspoon garlic powder

1. Press "Pre-Heat", set the temperature at 350°F (177°C).
2. In a large bowl, combine all the ingredients and toss until the nuts are evenly coated in the herbs, spices, and sugar.
3. Scrape the nuts and seasonings into the air fryer and air fry for 6 minutes, or until golden brown and fragrant, shaking the basket halfway through.

4. Transfer the nuts to a bowl and serve warm.

359

SPICED SWEET POTATO FRIES

Prep time: 10 minutes | **Cook time:** 15 minutes | **Serves** 2

2 tablespoons olive oil

1½ teaspoons smoked paprika

1½ teaspoons kosher salt, plus more as needed

1 teaspoon chili powder

½ teaspoon ground cumin

½ teaspoon ground turmeric

½ teaspoon mustard powder

¼ teaspoon cayenne pepper

2 medium sweet potatoes (about 10 ounces / 284 g each), cut into wedges, ½ inch thick and 3 inches long

Freshly ground black pepper, to taste

⅔ cup sour cream

1 garlic clove, grated

1. Press "Pre-Heat", set the temperature at 400°F (204°C).

2. In a large bowl, combine the olive oil, paprika, salt, chili powder, cumin, turmeric, mustard powder, and cayenne. Add the sweet potatoes, season with black pepper, and toss to evenly coat.

3. Transfer the sweet potatoes to the air fryer (save the bowl with the leftover oil and spices) and air fry for 15 minutes, shaking

the basket halfway through, or until golden brown and crisp. Return the potato wedges to the reserved bowl and toss again while they are hot.

4.Meanwhile, in a small bowl, stir together the sour cream and garlic. Season with salt and black pepper and transfer to a serving dish.

5.Serve the potato wedges hot with the garlic sour cream.

360

SPICY CHICKEN WINGS

Prep time: 5 minutes | **Cook time:** 20 minutes | **Serves** 2 to 4

1¼ pounds (567 g) chicken wings, separated into flats and drumettes
1 teaspoon baking powder
1 teaspoon cayenne pepper
¼ teaspoon garlic powder
Kosher salt and freshly ground black pepper, to taste
1 tablespoon unsalted butter, melted
For serving:
Blue cheese dressing
Celery
Carrot sticks

1. Place the chicken wings on a large plate, then sprinkle evenly with the baking powder, cayenne, and garlic powder. Toss the wings with your hands, making sure the baking powder and seasonings fully coat them, until evenly incorporated. Let the wings stand in the refrigerator for 1 hour or up to overnight.
2. Press "Pre-Heat", set the temperature at 400°F (204°C).
3. Season the wings with salt and black pepper, then transfer to

the air fryer, standing them up on end against the air fryer basket wall and each other. Air fry for 20 minutes, or until the wings are cooked through and crisp and golden brown. Transfer the wings to a bowl and toss with the butter while they're hot.

4.Arrange the wings on a platter and serve warm with the blue cheese dressing, celery and carrot sticks.

361

SWEET BACON TATER TOTS

Prep time: 5 minutes | **Cook time:** 7 minutes | **Serves** 4

24 frozen tater tots

6 slices cooked bacon

2 tablespoons maple syrup

1 cup shredded Cheddar cheese

1. Press "Pre-Heat", set the temperature at 400°F (204°C).

2. Put the tater tots in the air fryer basket. Air fry for 10 minutes, shaking the basket halfway through the cooking time.

3. Meanwhile, cut the bacon into 1-inch pieces.

4. Remove the tater tots from the air fryer basket and put into a baking pan. Top with the bacon and drizzle with the maple syrup. Air fry for 5 minutes, or until the tots and bacon are crisp.

5. Top with the cheese and air fry for 2 minutes, or until the cheese is melted.

6. Serve hot.

362

TORTELLINI WITH SPICY DIPPING SAUCE

Prep time: 5 minutes | **Cook time:** 20 minutes | **Serves** 4

¾ cup mayonnaise

2 tablespoons mustard

1 egg

½ cup flour

½ teaspoon dried oregano

1½ cups bread crumbs

2 tablespoons olive oil

2 cups frozen cheese tortellini

1. Press "Pre-Heat", set the temperature at 380°F (193°C).

2. In a small bowl, combine the mayonnaise and mustard and mix well. Set aside.

3. In a shallow bowl, beat the egg. In a separate bowl, combine the flour and oregano. In another bowl, combine the bread crumbs and olive oil, and mix well.

4. Drop the tortellini, a few at a time, into the egg, then into the flour, then into the egg again, and then into the bread crumbs to coat. Put into the air fryer basket, cooking in batches.

5. Air fry for about 10 minutes, shaking halfway through the

cooking time, or until the tortellini are crisp and golden brown on the outside. Serve with the mayonnaise mixture.

363

TURKEY BACON-WRAPPED DATES

Prep time: 10 minutes | **Cook time:** 5 to 7 minutes | Makes 16 appetizers

16 whole dates, pitted
16 whole almonds
6 to 8 strips turkey bacon, cut in half
Special Equipment:
16 toothpicks, soaked in water for at least 30 minutes

1. Press "Pre-Heat", set the temperature at 390°F (199°C).
2. On a flat work surface, stuff each pitted date with a whole almond.
3. Wrap half slice of bacon around each date and secure it with a toothpick.
4. Place the bacon-wrapped dates in the air fryer basket and air fry for 5 to 7 minutes, or until the bacon is cooked to your desired crispiness.
5. Transfer the dates to a paper towel-lined plate to drain. Serve hot.

364

VEGGIE SALMON NACHOS

Prep time: 10 minutes | **Cook time:** 9 to 12 minutes | **Serves** 6

2 ounces (57 g) baked no-salt corn tortilla chips

1 (5-ounce / 142-g) baked salmon fillet, flaked

½ cup canned low-sodium black beans, rinsed and drained

1 red bell pepper, chopped

½ cup grated carrot

1 jalapeño pepper, minced

⅓ cup shredded low-sodium low-fat Swiss cheese

1 tomato, chopped

1. Press "Pre-Heat", set the temperature at 360°F (182°C).

2. In a baking pan, layer the tortilla chips. Top with the salmon, black beans, red bell pepper, carrot, jalapeño, and Swiss cheese.

3. Bake in the air fryer for 9 to 12 minutes, or until the cheese is melted and starts to brown.

4. Top with the tomato and serve.

365

VEGGIE SHRIMP TOAST

Prep time: 15 minutes | **Cook time:** 3 to 6 minutes | **Serves** 4

- 8 large raw shrimp, peeled and finely chopped
- 1 egg white
- 2 garlic cloves, minced
- 3 tablespoons minced red bell pepper
- 1 medium celery stalk, minced
- 2 tablespoons cornstarch
- ¼ teaspoon Chinese five-spice powder
- 3 slices firm thin-sliced no-sodium whole-wheat bread

1. Press "Pre-Heat", set the temperature at 350°F (177°C).

2. In a small bowl, stir together the shrimp, egg white, garlic, red bell pepper, celery, cornstarch, and five-spice powder. Top each slice of bread with one-third of the shrimp mixture, spreading it evenly to the edges. With a sharp knife, cut each slice of bread into 4 strips.

3. Place the shrimp toasts in the air fryer basket in a single layer. You may need to cook them in batches. Air fry for 3 to 6 minutes, until crisp and golden brown.

4. Serve hot.

DESSERTS

366

AIR FRYER APPLE FRITTERS

Prep time: 30 minutes | **Cook time:** 7 to 8 minutes | **Serves** 6

1 cup chopped, peeled Granny Smith apple

½ cup granulated sugar

1 teaspoon ground cinnamon

1 cup all-purpose flour

1 teaspoon baking powder

1 teaspoon salt

2 tablespoons milk

2 tablespoons butter, melted

1 large egg, beaten

Cooking spray

¼ cup confectioners' sugar (optional)

1. Mix together the apple, granulated sugar, and cinnamon in a small bowl. Allow to sit for 30 minutes.

2. Combine the flour, baking powder, and salt in a medium bowl. Add the milk, butter, and egg and stir to incorporate.

3. Pour the apple mixture into the bowl of flour mixture and stir with a spatula until a dough forms.

4. Make the fritters: On a clean work surface, divide the dough

into 12 equal portions and shape into 1-inch balls. Flatten them into patties with your hands.

5. Press "Pre-Heat", set the temperature at 350°F (177°C). Line the air fryer basket with parchment paper and spray it with cooking spray.

6. Transfer the apple fritters onto the parchment paper, evenly spaced but not too close together. Spray the fritters with cooking spray.

7. Bake for 7 to 8 minutes until lightly browned. Flip the fritters halfway through the cooking time.

8. Remove from the basket to a plate and serve with the confectioners' sugar sprinkled on top, if desired.

367

APPLE WEDGES WITH APRICOTS

Prep time: 5 minutes | **Cook time:** 15 to 18 minutes | **Serves** 4

4 large apples, peeled and sliced into 8 wedges
2 tablespoons olive oil
½ cup dried apricots, chopped
1 to 2 tablespoons sugar
½ teaspoon ground cinnamon

1. Press "Pre-Heat", set the temperature at 350°F (180°C).
2. Toss the apple wedges with the olive oil in a mixing bowl until well coated.
3. Place the apple wedges in the air fryer basket and air fry for 12 to 15 minutes.
4. Sprinkle with the dried apricots and air fry for another 3 minutes.
5. Meanwhile, thoroughly combine the sugar and cinnamon in a small bowl.
6. Remove the apple wedges from the basket to a plate. Serve sprinkled with the sugar mixture.

368

APPLESAUCE AND CHOCOLATE BROWNIES

Prep time: 10 minutes | **Cook time:** 15 minutes | **Serves** 8

¼ cup unsweetened cocoa powder

¼ cup all-purpose flour

¼ teaspoon kosher salt

½ teaspoons baking powder

3 tablespoons unsalted butter, melted

½ cup granulated sugar

1 large egg

3 tablespoons unsweetened applesauce

¼ cup miniature semisweet chocolate chips

Coarse sea salt, to taste

1. Press "Pre-Heat", set the temperature at 300°F (149°C).

2. In a large bowl, whisk together the cocoa powder, all-purpose flour, kosher salt, and baking powder.

3. In a separate large bowl, combine the butter, granulated sugar, egg, and applesauce, then use a spatula to fold in the cocoa powder mixture and the chocolate chips until well combined.

4. Spray a baking pan with nonstick cooking spray, then pour the mixture into the pan. Place the pan in the air fryer and bake

for 15 minutes or until a toothpick comes out clean when inserted in the middle.

5.Remove the brownies from the air fryer, sprinkle some coarse sea salt on top, and allow to cool in the pan on a wire rack for 20 minutes before cutting and serving.

369

BAKED APPLES

Prep time: 5 minutes | **Cook time:** 10 minutes | **Serves** 4

4 small apples, cored and cut in half

2 tablespoons salted butter or coconut oil, melted

2 tablespoons sugar

1 teaspoon apple pie spice

Ice cream, heavy cream, or whipped cream, for serving

1. Press "Pre-Heat", set the temperature at 350°F (177°C).

2. Put the apples in a large bowl. Drizzle with the melted butter and sprinkle with the sugar and apple pie spice. Use the hands to toss, ensuring the apples are evenly coated.

3. Put the apples in the air fryer basket and bake for 10 minutes. Pierce the apples with a fork to ensure they are tender.

4. Serve with ice cream, or top with a splash of heavy cream or a spoonful of whipped cream.

370

BERRY CRUMBLE

Prep time: 10 minutes | **Cook time:** 15 minutes | **Serves** 4

For the Filling:
2 cups mixed berries
2 tablespoons sugar
1 tablespoon cornstarch
1 tablespoon fresh lemon juice
For the Toppin g :
¼ cup all-purpose flour
¼ cup rolled oats
1 tablespoon sugar
2 tablespoons cold unsalted butter, cut into small cubes
Whipped cream or ice cream (optional)

1. Press "Pre-Heat", set the temperature at 400°F (204°C).
2. For the filling: In a round baking pan, gently mix the berries, sugar, cornstarch, and lemon juice until thoroughly combined.
3. For the topping: In a small bowl, combine the flour, oats, and sugar. Stir the butter into the flour mixture until the mixture has the consistency of bread crumbs.

4. Sprinkle the topping over the berries.

5. Put the pan in the air fryer basket and air fry for 15 minutes. Let cool for 5 minutes on a wire rack.

6. Serve topped with whipped cream or ice cream, if desired.

371

BLACK AND WHITE BROWNIES

Prep time: 10 minutes | **Cook time:** 20 minutes | Makes 1 dozen brownies

1 egg
¼ cup brown sugar
2 tablespoons white sugar
2 tablespoons safflower oil
1 teaspoon vanilla
⅓ cup all-purpose flour
¼ cup cocoa powder
¼ cup white chocolate chips
Nonstick cooking spray

1. Press "Pre-Heat", set the temperature at 340°F (171°C). Spritz a baking pan with nonstick cooking spray.

2. Whisk together the egg, brown sugar, and white sugar in a medium bowl. Mix in the safflower oil and vanilla and stir to combine.

3. Add the flour and cocoa powder and stir just until incorporated. Fold in the white chocolate chips.

4. Scrape the batter into the prepared baking pan.

5. Bake in the preheated air fryer for 20 minutes, or until the brownie springs back when touched lightly with your fingers.

6. Transfer to a wire rack and let cool for 30 minutes before slicing to serve.

372

BLACKBERRY CHOCOLATE CAKE

Prep time: 10 minutes | **Cook time:** 22 minutes | **Serves** 8

½ cup butter, at room temperature

2 ounces (57 g) Swerve

4 eggs

1 cup almond flour

1 teaspoon baking soda

⅓ teaspoon baking powder

½ cup cocoa powder

1 teaspoon orange zest

⅓ cup fresh blackberries

1. Press "Pre-Heat", set the temperature at 335°F (168°C).

2. With an electric mixer or hand mixer, beat the butter and Swerve until creamy.

3. One at a time, mix in the eggs and beat again until fluffy.

4. Add the almond flour, baking soda, baking powder, cocoa powder, orange zest and mix well. Add the butter mixture to the almond flour mixture and stir until well blended. Fold in the blackberries.

5. Scrape the batter to a baking pan and bake in the preheated

air fryer for 22 minutes. Check the cake for doneness: If a toothpick inserted into the center of the cake comes out clean, it's done.

    6.Allow the cake cool on a wire rack to room temperature. Serve immediately.

373

BOURBON BREAD PUDDING

Prep time: 10 minutes | **Cook time:** 20 minutes | **Serves** 4

3 slices whole grain bread, cubed
1 large egg
1 cup whole milk
2 tablespoons bourbon
½ teaspoons vanilla extract
¼ cup maple syrup, divided
½ teaspoons ground cinnamon
2 teaspoons sparkling sugar

1. Press "Pre-Heat", set the temperature at 270°F (132°C).
2. Spray a baking pan with nonstick cooking spray, then place the bread cubes in the pan.
3. In a medium bowl, whisk together the egg, milk, bourbon, vanilla extract, 3 tablespoons of maple syrup, and cinnamon. Pour the egg mixture over the bread and press down with a spatula to coat all the bread, then sprinkle the sparkling sugar on top and bake for 20 minutes.
4. Remove the pudding from the air fryer and allow to cool in the pan on a wire rack for 10 minutes. Drizzle the remaining 1 tablespoon of maple syrup on top. Slice and serve warm.

374

BRAZILIAN PINEAPPLE BAKE

Prep time: 5 minutes | **Cook time:** 16 minutes | **Serves** 4

½ cup brown sugar

2 teaspoons ground cinnamon

1 small pineapple, peeled, cored, and cut into spears

3 tablespoons unsalted butter, melted

1. Press "Pre-Heat", set the temperature at 400°F (204°C).

2. In a small bowl, mix the brown sugar and cinnamon until thoroughly combined.

3. Brush the pineapple spears with the melted butter. Sprinkle the cinnamon-sugar over the spears, pressing lightly to ensure it adheres well.

4. Put the spears in the air fryer basket in a single layer. (Depending on the size of the air fryer, you may have to do this in batches.) Bake for 10 minutes for the first batch (6 to 8 minutes for the next batch, as the air fryer will be preheated). Halfway through the cooking time, brush the spears with butter.

5. The pineapple spears are done when they are heated through and the sugar is bubbling. Serve hot.

375

CARDAMOM AND VANILLA CUSTARD

Prep time: 5 minutes | **Cook time:** 25 minutes | **Serves** 2

1 cup whole milk

1 large egg

2 tablespoons plus 1 teaspoon sugar

¼ teaspoon vanilla bean paste or pure vanilla extract

¼ teaspoon ground cardamom, plus more for sprinkling

1. Press "Pre-Heat", set the temperature at 350°F (177°C).

2. In a medium bowl, beat together the milk, egg, sugar, vanilla, and cardamom.

3. Put two ramekins in the air fryer basket. Divide the mixture between the ramekins. Sprinkle lightly with cardamom. Cover each ramekin tightly with aluminum foil. Bake for 25 minutes, or until a toothpick inserted in the center comes out clean.

4. Let the custards cool on a wire rack for 5 to 10 minutes.

5. Serve warm, or refrigerate until cold and serve chilled.

376

CHIA PUDDING

Prep time: 5 minutes | **Cook time:** 4 minutes | **Serves** 2

1 cup chia seeds
1 cup unsweetened coconut milk
1 teaspoon liquid stevia
1 tablespoon coconut oil
1 teaspoon butter, melted

1. Press "Pre-Heat", set the temperature at 360°F (182°C).
2. Mix together the chia seeds, coconut milk, and stevia in a large bowl. Add the coconut oil and melted butter and stir until well blended.
3. Divide the mixture evenly between the ramekins, filling only about ²/₃ of the way.
4. Bake in the preheated air fryer for 4 minutes.
5. Allow to cool for 5 minutes and serve warm.

377

CHICKPEA BROWNIES

Prep time: 10 minutes | **Cook time:** 20 minutes | **Serves** 6

Vegetable oil
1 (15-ounce / 425-g) can chickpeas, drained and rinsed
4 large eggs
1/3 cup coconut oil, melted
1/3 cup honey
3 tablespoons unsweetened cocoa powder
1 tablespoon espresso powder (optional)
1 teaspoon baking powder
1 teaspoon baking soda
1/2 cup chocolate chips

1. Press "Pre-Heat", set the temperature at 325°F (163°C).
2. Generously grease a baking pan with vegetable oil.
3. In a blender or food processor, combine the chickpeas, eggs, coconut oil, honey, cocoa powder, espresso powder (if using), baking powder, and baking soda. Blend or process until smooth. Transfer to the prepared pan and stir in the chocolate chips by hand.
4. Set the pan in the air fryer basket and bake for 20 minutes, or until a toothpick inserted into the center comes out clean.

5. Let cool in the pan on a wire rack for 30 minutes before cutting into squares.
6. Serve immediately.

378

CHOCOLATE AND COCONUT CAKE

Prep time: 5 minutes | **Cook time:** 15 minutes | **Serves** 6

½ cup unsweetened chocolate, chopped

½ stick butter, at room temperature

1 tablespoon liquid stevia

1½ cups coconut flour

2 eggs, whisked

½ teaspoon vanilla extract

A pinch of fine sea salt

Cooking spray

1. Place the chocolate, butter, and stevia in a microwave-safe bowl. Microwave for about 30 seconds until melted.

2. Let the chocolate mixture cool for 5 to 10 minutes.

3. Add the remaining ingredients to the bowl of chocolate mixture and whisk to incorporate.

4. Press "Pre-Heat", set the temperature at 330°F (166°C). Lightly spray a baking pan with cooking spray.

5. Scrape the chocolate mixture into the prepared baking pan.

6. Place the baking pan in the air fryer basket and bake for 15 minutes, or until the top springs back lightly when gently pressed with your fingers.

PAMELA KENDRICK

7.Let the cake cool for 5 minutes and serve.

379

CHOCOLATE CAKE

Prep time: 10 minutes | **Cook time:** 55 minutes | **Serves** 4

Unsalted butter, at room temperature
3 large eggs
1 cup almond flour
2/3 cup sugar
1/3 cup heavy cream
1/4 cup coconut oil, melted
1/4 cup unsweetened cocoa powder
1 teaspoon baking powder
1/4 cup chopped walnuts

1. Press "Pre-Heat", set the temperature at 400°F (204°C).

2. Generously butter a round baking pan. Line the bottom of the pan with parchment paper cut to fit.

3. In a large bowl, combine the eggs, almond flour, sugar, cream, coconut oil, cocoa powder, and baking powder. Beat with a hand mixer on medium speed until well blended and fluffy. (This will keep the cake from being too dense, as almond flour cakes can sometimes be.) Fold in the walnuts.

4. Pour the batter into the prepared pan. Cover the pan tightly with aluminum foil. Set the pan in the air fryer basket and bake

for 45 minutes. Remove the foil and bake for 10 to 15 minutes more until a knife (do not use a toothpick) inserted into the center of the cake comes out clean.

5.Let the cake cool in the pan on a wire rack for 10 minutes. Remove the cake from the pan and let cool on the rack for 20 minutes before slicing and serving.

380

CHOCOLATE CROISSANTS

Prep time: 5 minutes | **Cook time:** 24 minutes | **Serves** 8

1 sheet frozen puff pastry, thawed

⅓ cup chocolate-hazelnut spread

1 large egg, beaten

1. On a lightly floured surface, roll puff pastry into a 14-inch square. Cut pastry into quarters to form 4 squares. Cut each square diagonally to form 8 triangles.

2. Spread 2 teaspoons chocolate-hazelnut spread on each triangle; from wider end, roll up pastry. Brush egg on top of each roll.

3. Press "Pre-Heat", set the temperature at 375°F (191°C). Air fry rolls in batches, 3 or 4 at a time, 8 minutes per batch, or until pastry is golden brown.

4. Cool on a wire rack; serve while warm or at room temperature.

381

CHOCOLATE PECAN PIE

Prep time: 20 minutes | **Cook time:** 25 minutes | **Serves** 8

1 (9-inch) unbaked pie crust

Filling:

2 large eggs

1/3 cup butter, melted

1 cup sugar

1/2 cup all-purpose flour

1 cup milk chocolate chips

1 1/2 cups coarsely chopped pecans

2 tablespoons bourbon

1. Press "Pre-Heat", set the temperature at 350°F (177°C).

2. Whisk the eggs and melted butter in a large bowl until creamy.

3. Add the sugar and flour and stir to incorporate. Mix in the milk chocolate chips, pecans, and bourbon and stir until well combined.

4. Use a fork to prick holes in the bottom and sides of the pie crust. Pour the prepared filling into the pie crust. Place the pie crust in the air fryer basket.

5.Bake for 25 minutes until a toothpick inserted in the center comes out clean.

6.Allow the pie cool for 10 minutes in the basket before serving.

382

CINNAMON ALMONDS

Prep time: 5 minutes | **Cook time:** 8 minutes | **Serves** 4

1 cup whole almonds

2 tablespoons salted butter, melted

1 tablespoon sugar

½ teaspoon ground cinnamon

1. Press "Pre-Heat", set the temperature at 300°F (149°C).

2. In a medium bowl, combine the almonds, butter, sugar, and cinnamon. Mix well to ensure all the almonds are coated with the spiced butter.

3. Transfer the almonds to the air fryer basket and shake so they are in a single layer. Bake for 8 minutes, stirring the almonds halfway through the cooking time.

4. Let cool completely before serving.

383

CINNAMON CANDIED APPLES

Prep time: 15 minutes | **Cook time:** 12 minutes | **Serves** 4

1 cup packed light brown sugar

2 teaspoons ground cinnamon

2 medium Granny Smith apples, peeled and diced

1. Press "Pre-Heat", set the temperature at 350°F (177°C).
2. Thoroughly combine the brown sugar and cinnamon in a medium bowl.
3. Add the apples to the bowl and stir until well coated. Transfer the apples to a baking pan.
4. Bake in the preheated air fryer for 9 minutes. Stir the apples once and bake for an additional 3 minutes until softened.
5. Serve warm.

384

CLASSIC POUND CAKE

Prep time: 5 minutes | **Cook time:** 30 minutes | **Serves** 8

1 stick butter, at room temperature
1 cup Swerve
4 eggs
1½ cups coconut flour
½ cup buttermilk
½ teaspoon baking soda
½ teaspoon baking powder
¼ teaspoon salt
1 teaspoon vanilla essence
A pinch of ground star anise
A pinch of freshly grated nutmeg
Cooking spray

1. Press "Pre-Heat", set the temperature at 320°F (160°C). Spray a baking pan with cooking spray.

2. With an electric mixer or hand mixer, beat the butter and Swerve until creamy. One at a time, mix in the eggs and whisk until fluffy. Add the remaining ingredients and stir to combine.

3. Transfer the batter to the prepared baking pan. Bake in the

preheated air fryer for 30 minutes until the center of the cake is springy. Rotate the pan halfway through the cooking time.

4.Allow the cake to cool in the pan for 10 minutes before removing and serving.

385

COCONUT PINEAPPLE STICKS

Prep time: 10 minutes | **Cook time:** 10 minutes | **Serves** 4

½ fresh pineapple, cut into sticks

¼ cup desiccated coconut

1. Press "Pre-Heat", set the temperature at 400°F (204°C).
2. Place the desiccated coconut on a plate and roll the pineapple sticks in the coconut until well coated.
3. Lay the pineapple sticks in the air fryer basket and air fry for 10 minutes until crisp-tender.
4. Serve warm.

386

COFFEE CHOCOLATE CAKE

Prep time: 5 minutes | **Cook time:** 30 minutes | **Serves** 8

Dry Ingredients:
1½ cups almond flour
½ cup coconut meal
⅔ cup Swerve
1 teaspoon baking powder
¼ teaspoon salt

Wet Ingredients:
1 egg
1 stick butter, melted
½ cup hot strongly brewed coffee

Topping:
½ cup confectioner's Swerve
¼ cup coconut flour
3 tablespoons coconut oil
1 teaspoon ground cinnamon
½ teaspoon ground cardamom

1. Press "Pre-Heat", set the temperature at 330°F (166°C).
2. In a medium bowl, combine the almond flour, coconut meal, Swerve, baking powder, and salt.

3. In a large bowl, whisk the egg, melted butter, and coffee until smooth.

4. Add the dry mixture to the wet and stir until well incorporated. Transfer the batter to a greased baking pan.

5. Stir together all the ingredients for the topping in a small bowl. Spread the topping over the batter and smooth the top with a spatula.

6. Bake in the preheated air fryer for 30 minutes, or until the cake springs back when gently pressed with your fingers.

7. Rest for 10 minutes before serving.

387

CRISPY PINEAPPLE RINGS

Prep time: 5 minutes | **Cook time:** 6 to 8 minutes | **Serves** 6

1 cup rice milk
⅔ cup flour
½ cup water
¼ cup unsweetened flaked coconut
4 tablespoons sugar
½ teaspoon baking soda
½ teaspoon baking powder
½ teaspoon vanilla essence
½ teaspoon ground cinnamon
¼ teaspoon ground anise star
Pinch of kosher salt
1 medium pineapple, peeled and sliced

1. Press "Pre-Heat", set the temperature at 380°F (193°C).
2. In a large bowl, stir together all the ingredients except the pineapple.
3. Dip each pineapple slice into the batter until evenly coated.
4. Arrange the pineapple slices in the basket and air fry for 6 to 8 minutes until golden brown.

5. Remove from the basket to a plate and cool for 5 minutes before serving.

388

EASY ALMOND SHORTBREAD

Prep time: 5 minutes | **Cook time:** 12 minutes | **Serves** 8

½ cup (1 stick) unsalted butter
½ cup sugar
1 teaspoon pure almond extract
1 cup all-purpose flour

1. Press "Pre-Heat", set the temperature at 375°F (191°C).
2. In a bowl of a stand mixer fitted with the paddle attachment, beat the butter and sugar on medium speed until fluffy, 3 to 4 minutes. Add the almond extract and beat until combined, about 30 seconds. Turn the mixer to low. Add the flour a little at a time and beat for about 2 minutes more until well incorporated.
3. Pat the dough into an even layer in a round baking pan. Put the pan in the air fryer basket and bake for 12 minutes.
4. Carefully remove the pan from air fryer basket. While the shortbread is still warm and soft, cut it into 8 wedges.
5. Let cool in the pan on a wire rack for 5 minutes. Remove the wedges from the pan and let cool on the rack before serving.

389

EASY BLACKBERRY COBBLER

Prep time: 15 minutes | **Cook time:** 25 to 30 minutes | **Serves** 6

3 cups fresh or frozen blackberries

1¾ cups sugar, divided

1 teaspoon vanilla extract

8 tablespoons (1 stick) butter, melted

1 cup self-rising flour

Cooking spray

1. Press "Pre-Heat", set the temperature at 350°F (177°C). Spritz a baking pan with cooking spray.
2. Mix the blackberries, 1 cup of sugar, and vanilla in a medium bowl and stir to combine.
3. Stir together the melted butter, remaining sugar, and flour in a separate medium bowl.
4. Spread the blackberry mixture evenly in the prepared pan and top with the butter mixture.
5. Bake in the preheated air fryer for 20 to 25 minutes. Check for doneness and bake for another 5 minutes, if needed.
6. Remove from the air fryer and place on a wire rack to cool to room temperature. Serve immediately.

390

FUDGE PIE

Prep time: 15 minutes | **Cook time:** 25 to 30 minutes | **Serves** 8

1½ cups sugar

½ cup self-rising flour

⅓ cup unsweetened cocoa powder

3 large eggs, beaten

12 tablespoons (1½ sticks) butter, melted

1½ teaspoons vanilla extract

1 (9-inch) unbaked pie crust

¼ cup confectioners' sugar (optional)

1. Press "Pre-Heat", set the temperature at 350°F (177°C).

2. Thoroughly combine the sugar, flour, and cocoa powder in a medium bowl. Add the beaten eggs and butter and whisk to combine. Stir in the vanilla.

3. Pour the prepared filling into the pie crust and transfer to the air fryer basket.

4. Bake for 25 to 30 minutes until just set.

5. Allow the pie to cool for 5 minutes. Sprinkle with the confectioners' sugar, if desired. Serve warm.

391

HONEY-ROASTED PEARS

Prep time: 5 minutes | **Cook time:** 20 minutes | **Serves** 4

2 large Bosc pears, halved and deseeded
3 tablespoons honey
1 tablespoon unsalted butter
½ teaspoon ground cinnamon
¼ cup walnuts, chopped
¼ cup part skim low-fat ricotta cheese, divided

1. Press "Pre-Heat", set the temperature at 350°F (177°C).
2. In a baking pan, place the pears, cut side up.
3. In a small microwave-safe bowl, melt the honey, butter, and cinnamon. Brush this mixture over the cut sides of the pears.
4. Pour 3 tablespoons of water around the pears in the pan. Roast the pears for 20 minutes, or until tender when pierced with a fork and slightly crisp on the edges, basting once with the liquid in the pan.
5. Carefully remove the pears from the pan and place on a serving plate. Drizzle each with some liquid from the pan, sprinkle the walnuts on top, and serve with a spoonful of ricotta cheese.

392

JELLY DOUGHNUTS

Prep time: 5 minutes | **Cook time:** 5 minutes | **Serves** 8

1 (16.3-ounce / 462-g) package large refrigerator biscuits
Cooking spray
1¼ cups good-quality raspberry jam
Confectioners' sugar, for dusting

1. Press "Pre-Heat", set the temperature at 350°F (177°C).
2. Separate biscuits into 8 rounds. Spray both sides of rounds lightly with oil.
3. Spray the basket with oil and place 3 to 4 rounds in the basket. Air fry for 5 minutes, or until golden brown. Transfer to a wire rack; let cool. Repeat with the remaining rounds.
4. Fill a pastry bag, fitted with small plain tip, with raspberry jam; use tip to poke a small hole in the side of each doughnut, then fill the centers with the jam. Dust doughnuts with confectioners' sugar.
5. Serve immediately.

393

LEMON RICOTTA CAKE

Prep time: 5 minutes | **Cook time:** 25 minutes | **Serves** 6

17.5 ounces (496 g) ricotta cheese

5.4 ounces (153 g) sugar

3 eggs, beaten

3 tablespoons flour

1 lemon, juiced and zested

2 teaspoons vanilla extract

1. Press "Pre-Heat", set the temperature at 320°F (160°C).

2. In a large mixing bowl, stir together all the ingredients until the mixture reaches a creamy consistency.

3. Pour the mixture into a baking pan and place in the air fryer.

4. Bake for 25 minutes until a toothpick inserted in the center comes out clean.

5. Allow to cool for 10 minutes on a wire rack before serving.

394

LEMONY APPLE BUTTER

Prep time: 10 minutes | **Cook time:** 1 hour | Makes 1¼ cups

Cooking spray

2 cups unsweetened applesauce

⅔ cup packed light brown sugar

3 tablespoons fresh lemon juice

½ teaspoon kosher salt

¼ teaspoon ground cinnamon

⅛ teaspoon ground allspice

1. Press "Pre-Heat", set the temperature at 340°F (171°C).

2. Spray a metal cake pan with cooking spray. Whisk together all the ingredients in a bowl until smooth, then pour into the greased pan. Set the pan in the air fryer and bake until the apple mixture is caramelized, reduced to a thick purée, and fragrant, about 1 hour.

3. Remove the pan from the air fryer, stir to combine the caramelized bits at the edge with the rest, then let cool completely to thicken.

4. Serve immediately.

395

MIXED BERRIES WITH PECAN STREUSEL TOPPING

Prep time: 5 minutes | **Cook time:** 17 minutes | **Serves** 3

½ cup mixed berries

Cooking spray

Topping:

1 egg, beaten

3 tablespoons almonds, slivered

3 tablespoons chopped pecans

2 tablespoons chopped walnuts

3 tablespoons granulated Swerve

2 tablespoons cold salted butter, cut into pieces

½ teaspoon ground cinnamon

1. Press "Pre-Heat", set the temperature at 340°F (171°C). Lightly spray a baking dish with cooking spray.

2. Make the topping: In a medium bowl, stir together the beaten egg, nuts, Swerve, butter, and cinnamon until well blended.

3. Put the mixed berries in the bottom of the baking dish and spread the topping over the top.

4. Bake in the preheated air fryer for 17 minutes, or until the fruit is bubbly and topping is golden brown.

5. Allow to cool for 5 to 10 minutes before serving.

396

OATMEAL RAISIN BARS

Prep time: 15 minutes | **Cook time:** 15 minutes | **Serves** 8

⅓ cup all-purpose flour

¼ teaspoon kosher salt

¼ teaspoon baking powder

¼ teaspoon ground cinnamon

¼ cup light brown sugar, lightly packed

¼ cup granulated sugar

½ cup canola oil

1 large egg

1 teaspoon vanilla extract

1⅓ cups quick-cooking oats

⅓ cup raisins

1. Press "Pre-Heat", set the temperature at 360°F (182°C).
2. In a large bowl, combine the all-purpose flour, kosher salt, baking powder, ground cinnamon, light brown sugar, granulated sugar, canola oil, egg, vanilla extract, quick-cooking oats, and raisins.
3. Spray a baking pan with nonstick cooking spray, then pour

Desserts

the oat mixture into the pan and press down to evenly distribute. Place the pan in the air fryer and bake for 15 minutes or until golden brown.

4.Remove from the air fryer and allow to cool in the pan on a wire rack for 20 minutes before slicing and serving.

397

ORANGE AND ANISE CAKE

Prep time: 5 minutes | **Cook time:** 20 minutes | **Serves** 6

1 stick butter, at room temperature

5 tablespoons liquid monk fruit

2 eggs plus 1 egg yolk, beaten

1/3 cup hazelnuts, roughly chopped

3 tablespoons sugar-free orange marmalade

6 ounces (170 g) unbleached almond flour

1 teaspoon baking soda

1/2 teaspoon baking powder

1/2 teaspoon ground cinnamon

1/2 teaspoon ground allspice

1/2 ground anise seed

Cooking spray

1. Press "Pre-Heat", set the temperature at 310°F (154°C). Lightly spritz a baking pan with cooking spray.

2. In a mixing bowl, whisk the butter and liquid monk fruit until the mixture is pale and smooth. Mix in the beaten eggs, hazelnuts, and marmalade and whisk again until well incorporated.

Desserts

3.Add the almond flour, baking soda, baking powder, cinnamon, allspice, anise seed and stir to mix well.

4.Scrape the batter into the prepared baking pan. Bake in the preheated air fryer for about 20 minutes, or until the top of the cake springs back when gently pressed with your fingers.

5.Transfer to a wire rack and let the cake cool to room temperature. Serve immediately.

398

ORANGE COCONUT CAKE

Prep time: 5 minutes | **Cook time:** 17 minutes | **Serves** 6

1 stick butter, melted
¾ cup granulated Swerve
2 eggs, beaten
¾ cup coconut flour
¼ teaspoon salt
⅓ teaspoon grated nutmeg
⅓ cup coconut milk
1¼ cups almond flour
½ teaspoon baking powder
2 tablespoons unsweetened orange jam
Cooking spray

1. Press "Pre-Heat", set the temperature at 355°F (179°C). Coat a baking pan with cooking spray. Set aside.

2. In a large mixing bowl, whisk together the melted butter and granulated Swerve until fluffy.

3. Mix in the beaten eggs and whisk again until smooth. Stir in the coconut flour, salt, and nutmeg and gradually pour in the coconut milk. Add the remaining ingredients and stir until well incorporated.

4.Scrape the batter into the baking pan.

5.Bake in the preheated air fryer for 17 minutes until the top of the cake springs back when gently pressed with your fingers.

6.Remove from the air fryer to a wire rack to cool. Serve chilled.

399

PEANUT BUTTER-CHOCOLATE BREAD PUDDING

Prep time: 10 minutes | **Cook time:** 10 to 12 minutes | **Serves** 8

1 egg
1 egg yolk
¾ cup chocolate milk
3 tablespoons brown sugar
3 tablespoons peanut butter
2 tablespoons cocoa powder
1 teaspoon vanilla
5 slices firm white bread, cubed
Nonstick cooking spray

1. Press "Pre-Heat", set the temperature at 330°F (166°C). Spritz a baking pan with nonstick cooking spray.

2. Whisk together the egg, egg yolk, chocolate milk, brown sugar, peanut butter, cocoa powder, and vanilla until well combined.

3. Fold in the bread cubes and stir to mix well. Allow the bread soak for 10 minutes.

4. When ready, transfer the egg mixture to the prepared baking pan.

5. Bake in the preheated air fryer for 10 to 12 minutes, or until the pudding is just firm to the touch.

6. Serve at room temperature.

400

PECAN AND CHERRY STUFFED APPLES

Prep time: 10 minutes | **Cook time:** 20 minutes | **Serves** 4

4 apples (about 1¼ pounds / 567 g)
¼ cup chopped pecans
⅓ cup dried tart cherries
1 tablespoon melted butter
3 tablespoons brown sugar
¼ teaspoon allspice
Pinch salt
Ice cream, for serving

1. Cut off top ½ inch from each apple; reserve tops. With a melon baller, core through stem ends without breaking through the bottom. (Do not trim bases.)

2. Press "Pre-Heat", set the temperature at 350°F (177°C). Combine pecans, cherries, butter, brown sugar, allspice, and a pinch of salt. Stuff mixture into the hollow centers of the apples. Cover with apple tops. Put in the air fryer basket, using tongs. Air fry for 20 to 25 minutes, or just until tender.

3. Serve warm with ice cream.

401

PINEAPPLE GALETTE

Prep time: 10 minutes | **Cook time:** 40 minutes | **Serves** 2

¼ medium-size pineapple, peeled, cored, and cut crosswise into ¼-inch-thick slices

2 tablespoons dark rum

1 teaspoon vanilla extract

½ teaspoon kosher salt

Finely grated zest of ½ lime

1 store-bought sheet puff pastry, cut into an 8-inch round

3 tablespoons granulated sugar

2 tablespoons unsalted butter, cubed and chilled

Coconut ice cream, for serving

1. Press "Pre-Heat", set the temperature at 310°F (154°C).

2. In a small bowl, combine the pineapple slices, rum, vanilla, salt, and lime zest and let stand for at least 10 minutes to allow the pineapple to soak in the rum.

3. Meanwhile, press the puff pastry round into the bottom and up the sides of a round metal cake pan and use the tines of a fork to dock the bottom and sides.

4. Arrange the pineapple slices on the bottom of the pastry in more or less a single layer, then sprinkle with the sugar and dot

with the butter. Drizzle with the leftover juices from the bowl. Put the pan in the air fryer and bake until the pastry is puffed and golden brown and the pineapple is lightly caramelized on top, about 40 minutes.

5. Transfer the pan to a wire rack to cool for 15 minutes. Unmold the galette from the pan and serve warm with coconut ice cream.

402

RICOTTA LEMON POPPY SEED CAKE

Prep time: 15 minutes | **Cook time:** 55 minutes | **Serves** 4

Unsalted butter, at room temperature
1 cup almond flour
½ cup sugar
3 large eggs
¼ cup heavy cream
¼ cup full-fat ricotta cheese
¼ cup coconut oil, melted
2 tablespoons poppy seeds
1 teaspoon baking powder
1 teaspoon pure lemon extract
Grated zest and juice of 1 lemon, plus more zest for garnish

1. Press "Pre-Heat", set the temperature at 325°F (163°C).
2. Generously butter a round baking pan. Line the bottom of the pan with parchment paper cut to fit.
3. In a large bowl, combine the almond flour, sugar, eggs, cream, ricotta, coconut oil, poppy seeds, baking powder, lemon extract, lemon zest, and lemon juice. Beat with a hand mixer on medium speed until well blended and fluffy.
4. Pour the batter into the prepared pan. Cover the pan tightly

with aluminum foil. Set the pan in the air fryer basket and bake for 45 minutes. Remove the foil and bake for 10 to 15 minutes more until a knife (do not use a toothpick) inserted into the center of the cake comes out clean.

5. Let the cake cool in the pan on a wire rack for 10 minutes. Remove the cake from pan and let it cool on the rack for 15 minutes before slicing.

6. Top with additional lemon zest, slice and serve.

403

SIMPLE APPLE TURNOVERS

Prep time: 10 minutes | **Cook time:** 10 minutes | **Serves** 4

1 apple, peeled, quartered, and thinly sliced

½ teaspoons pumpkin pie spice

Juice of ½ lemon

1 tablespoon granulated sugar

Pinch of kosher salt

6 sheets phyllo dough

1. Press "Pre-Heat", set the temperature at 330°F (166°C).

2. In a medium bowl, combine the apple, pumpkin pie spice, lemon juice, granulated sugar, and kosher salt.

3. Cut the phyllo dough sheets into 4 equal pieces and place individual tablespoons of apple filling in the center of each piece, then fold in both sides and roll from front to back.

4. Spray the air fryer basket with nonstick cooking spray, then place the turnovers in the basket and bake for 10 minutes or until golden brown.

5. Remove the turnovers from the air fryer and allow to cool on a wire rack for 10 minutes before serving.

404

SPICE COOKIES

Prep time: 15 minutes | **Cook time:** 12 minutes | **Serves** 4

4 tablespoons (½ stick) unsalted butter, at room temperature
2 tablespoons agave nectar
1 large egg
2 tablespoons water
2½ cups almond flour
½ cup sugar
2 teaspoons ground ginger
1 teaspoon ground cinnamon
½ teaspoon freshly grated nutmeg
1 teaspoon baking soda
¼ teaspoon kosher salt

1. Press "Pre-Heat", set the temperature at 325°F (163°C).

2. Line the bottom of the air fryer basket with parchment paper cut to fit.

3. In a large bowl using a hand mixer, beat together the butter, agave, egg, and water on medium speed until fluffy.

4. Add the almond flour, sugar, ginger, cinnamon, nutmeg, baking soda, and salt. Beat on low speed until well combined.

5. Roll the dough into 2-tablespoon balls and arrange them on

Desserts

the parchment paper in the basket. (They don't really spread too much, but try to leave a little room between them.) Bake for 12 minutes, or until the tops of cookies are lightly browned.

6. Transfer to a wire rack and let cool completely.

7. Serve immediately

405

ULTIMATE COCONUT CHOCOLATE CAKE

Prep time: 5 minutes | **Cook time:** 15 minutes | **Serves** 10

1¼ cups unsweetened bakers' chocolate

1 stick butter

1 teaspoon liquid stevia

⅓ cup shredded coconut

2 tablespoons coconut milk

2 eggs, beaten

Cooking spray

1. Press "Pre-Heat", set the temperature at 330°F (166°C). Lightly spritz a baking pan with cooking spray.

2. Place the chocolate, butter, and stevia in a microwave-safe bowl. Microwave for about 30 seconds until melted. Let the chocolate mixture cool to room temperature.

3. Add the remaining ingredients to the chocolate mixture and stir until well incorporated. Pour the batter into the prepared baking pan.

4. Bake in the preheated air fryer until a toothpick inserted in the center comes out clean, 15 minutes.

5. Remove from the pan and allow to cool for about 10 minutes before serving.

HOLIDAY SPECIALS

406

EGGNOG BREAD

Prep time: 10 minutes | **Cook time:** 18 minutes | **Serves** 6 to 8

1 cup flour, plus more for dusting

¼ cup sugar

1 teaspoon baking powder

¼ teaspoon salt

¼ teaspoon nutmeg

½ cup eggnog

1 egg yolk

1 tablespoon plus 1 teaspoon butter, melted

¼ cup pecans

¼ cup chopped candied fruit (cherries, pineapple, or mixed fruits)

Cooking spray

1. Press "Pre-Heat", set the temperature at 360°F (182°C).
2. In a medium bowl, stir together the flour, sugar, baking powder, salt, and nutmeg.
3. Add eggnog, egg yolk, and butter. Mix well but do not beat.
4. Stir in nuts and fruit.

5. Spray a baking pan with cooking spray and dust with flour.

6. Spread batter into prepared pan and bake for 18 minutes or until top is dark golden brown and bread starts to pull away from sides of pan.

7. Serve immediately.

407

GARLICKY OLIVE STROMBOLI

Prep time: 25 minutes | **Cook time:** 25 minutes | **Serves** 8

4 large cloves garlic, unpeeled
3 tablespoons grated Parmesan cheese
½ cup packed fresh basil leaves
½ cup marinated, pitted green and black olives
¼ teaspoon crushed red pepper
½ pound (227 g) pizza dough, at room temperature
4 ounces (113 g) sliced provolone cheese (about 8 slices)
Cooking spray

1. Press "Pre-Heat", set the temperature at 370°F (188°C). Spritz the air fryer basket with cooking spray.
2. Put the unpeeled garlic in the air fryer basket.
3. Air fry for 10 minutes or until the garlic is softened completely. Remove them from the air fryer and allow to cool until you can handle.
4. Peel the garlic and place into a food processor with 2 tablespoons of Parmesan, basil, olives, and crushed red pepper. Pulse to mix well. Set aside.
5. Arrange the pizza dough on a clean work surface, then roll it out with a rolling pin into a rectangle. Cut the rectangle in half.

6. Sprinkle half of the garlic mixture over each rectangle half, and leave ½-inch edges uncover. Top them with the provolone cheese.

7. Brush one long side of each rectangle half with water, then roll them up. Spritz the air fryer basket with cooking spray. Transfer the rolls in the preheated air fryer. Spritz with cooking spray and scatter with remaining Parmesan.

8. Air fry the rolls for 15 minutes or until golden brown. Flip the rolls halfway through.

9. Remove the rolls from the air fryer and allow to cool for a few minutes before serving.

408

GOLDEN NUGGETS

Prep time: 15 minutes | **Cook time:** 4 minutes per batch | Makes 20 nuggets

1 cup all-purpose flour, plus more for dusting

1 teaspoon baking powder

½ teaspoon butter, at room temperature, plus more for brushing

¼ teaspoon salt

¼ cup water

⅛ teaspoon onion powder

¼ teaspoon garlic powder

⅛ teaspoon seasoning salt

Cooking spray

1. Press "Pre-Heat", set the temperature at 370°F (188°C). Line the air fryer basket with parchment paper.

2. Mix the flour, baking powder, butter, and salt in a large bowl. Stir to mix well. Gradually whisk in the water until a sanity dough forms.

3. Put the dough on a lightly floured work surface, then roll it out into a ½-inch thick rectangle with a rolling pin.

4. Cut the dough into about twenty 1- or 2-inch squares, then

arrange the squares in a single layer in the preheated air fryer. Spritz with cooking spray. You need to work in batches to avoid overcrowding.

5. Combine onion powder, garlic powder, and seasoning salt in a small bowl. Stir to mix well, then sprinkle the squares with the powder mixture.

6. Air fry the dough squares for 4 minutes or until golden brown. Flip the squares halfway through the cooking time.

7. Remove the golden nuggets from the air fryer and brush with more butter immediately. Serve warm.

409

HOLIDAY SPICY BEEF ROAST

Prep time: 10 minutes | **Cook time:** 45 minutes | **Serves** 8

2 pounds (907 g) roast beef, at room temperature

2 tablespoons extra-virgin olive oil

1 teaspoon sea salt flakes

1 teaspoon black pepper, preferably freshly ground

1 teaspoon smoked paprika

A few dashes of liquid smoke

2 jalapeño peppers, thinly sliced

1. Press "Pre-Heat", set the temperature at 330°F (166°C).

2. Pat the roast dry using kitchen towels. Rub with extra-virgin olive oil and all seasonings along with liquid smoke.

3. Roast for 30 minutes in the preheated air fryer. Turn the roast over and roast for additional 15 minutes.

4. Check for doneness using a meat thermometer and serve sprinkled with sliced jalapeños. Bon appétit!

410

JEWISH BLINTZES

Prep time: 5 minutes | **Cook time:** 10 minutes | Makes 8 blintzes

2 (7½-ounce / 213-g) packages farmer cheese, mashed

¼ cup cream cheese

¼ teaspoon vanilla extract

¼ cup granulated white sugar

8 egg roll wrappers

4 tablespoons butter, melted

1. Press "Pre-Heat", set the temperature at 375°F (191°C).

2. Combine the farmer cheese, cream cheese, vanilla extract, and sugar in a bowl. Stir to mix well.

3. Unfold the egg roll wrappers on a clean work surface, spread ¼ cup of the filling at the edge of each wrapper and leave a ½-inch edge uncovering.

4. Wet the edges of the wrappers with water and fold the uncovered edge over the filling. Fold the left and right sides in the center, then tuck the edge under the filling and fold to wrap the filling.

5. Brush the wrappers with melted butter, then arrange the

wrappers in a single layer in the preheated air fryer, seam side down. Leave a little space between each two wrappers. Work in batches to avoid overcrowding.

6. Air fry for 10 minutes or until golden brown.

7. Serve immediately.

411

KALE SALAD SUSHI ROLLS WITH SRIRACHA MAYONNAISE

Prep time: 10 minutes | **Cook time:** 10 minutes | **Serves** 12

Kale Salad:
1½ cups chopped kale
1 tablespoon sesame seeds
¾ teaspoon soy sauce
¾ teaspoon toasted sesame oil
½ teaspoon rice vinegar
¼ teaspoon ginger
⅛ teaspoon garlic powder

Sushi Rolls:
3 sheets sushi nori
1 batch cauliflower rice
½ avocado, sliced

Sriracha Mayonnaise:
¼ cup Sriracha sauce
¼ cup vegan mayonnaise

Coating:
½ cup panko breadcrumbs

1. Press "Pre-Heat", set the temperature at 390°F (199°C).

2. In a medium bowl, toss all the ingredients for the salad together until well coated and set aside.

3. Place a sheet of nori on a clean work surface and spread the cauliflower rice in an even layer on the nori. Scoop 2 to 3 tablespoon of kale salad on the rice and spread over. Place 1 or 2 avocado slices on top. Roll up the sushi, pressing gently to get a nice, tight roll. Repeat to make the remaining 2 rolls.

4. In a bowl, stir together the Sriracha sauce and mayonnaise until smooth. Add breadcrumbs to a separate bowl.

5. Dredge the sushi rolls in Sriracha Mayonnaise, then roll in breadcrumbs till well coated.

6. Place the coated sushi rolls in the air fryer basket and air fry for 10 minutes, or until golden brown and crispy. Flip the sushi rolls gently halfway through to ensure even cooking..

7. Transfer to a platter and rest for 5 minutes before slicing each roll into 8 pieces. Serve warm.

412

LUSH SNACK MIX

Prep time: 10 minutes | **Cook time:** 10 minutes | **Serves** 10

½ cup honey
3 tablespoons butter, melted
1 teaspoon salt
2 cups sesame sticks
2 cup pumpkin seeds
2 cups granola
1 cup cashews
2 cups crispy corn puff cereal
2 cup mini pretzel crisps

1. In a bowl, combine the honey, butter, and salt.
2. In another bowl, mix the sesame sticks, pumpkin seeds, granola, cashews, corn puff cereal, and pretzel crisps.
3. Combine the contents of the two bowls.
4. Press "Pre-Heat", set the temperature at 370°F (188°C).
5. Put the mixture in the air fryer basket and air fry for 10 to 12 minutes to toast the snack mixture, shaking the basket frequently. Do this in two batches.
6. Put the snack mix on a cookie sheet and allow it to cool fully.

7. Serve immediately.

413

MILKY PECAN TART

Prep time: 2 hours 25 minutes | **Cook time:** 30 minutes | **Serves** 8

Tart Crust:
1/4 cup firmly packed brown sugar
1/3 cup butter, softened
1 cup all-purpose flour
1/4 teaspoon kosher salt
Filling:
1/4 cup whole milk
4 tablespoons butter, diced
1/2 cup packed brown sugar
1/4 cup pure maple syrup
1 1/2 cups finely chopped pecans
1/4 teaspoon pure vanilla extract
1/4 teaspoon sea salt

1. Press "Pre-Heat", set the temperature at 350°F (177°C). Line a baking pan with aluminum foil, then spritz the pan with cooking spray.

2. Stir the brown sugar and butter in a bowl with a hand mixer until puffed, then add the flour and salt and stir until crumbled.

3. Pour the mixture in the prepared baking pan and tilt the pan to coat the bottom evenly.

4. Arrange the pan in the preheated air fryer. Bake for 13 minutes or until the crust is golden brown.

5. Meanwhile, pour the milk, butter, sugar, and maple syrup in a saucepan. Stir to mix well. Bring to a simmer, then cook for 1 more minute. Stir constantly.

6. Turn off the heat and mix the pecans and vanilla into the filling mixture.

7. Pour the filling mixture over the golden crust and spread with a spatula to coat the crust evenly.

8. Bake in the air fryer for an additional 12 minutes or until the filling mixture is set and frothy.

9. Remove the baking pan from the air fryer and sprinkle with salt. Allow to sit for 10 minutes or until cooled.

10. Transfer the pan to the refrigerator to chill for at least 2 hours, then remove the aluminum foil and slice to serve.

414

PÃO DE QUEIJO

Prep time: 37 minutes | **Cook time:** 24 minutes | Makes 12 balls

2 tablespoons butter, plus more for greasing

½ cup milk

1 ½ cups tapioca flour

½ teaspoon salt

1 large egg

⅔ cup finely grated aged Asiago cheese

1. Put the butter in a saucepan and pour in the milk, heat over medium heat until the liquid boils. Keep stirring.

2. Turn off the heat and mix in the tapioca flour and salt to form a soft dough. Transfer the dough in a large bowl, then wrap the bowl in plastic and let sit for 15 minutes.

3. Break the egg in the bowl of dough and whisk with a hand mixer for 2 minutes or until a sanity dough forms. Fold the cheese in the dough. Cover the bowl in plastic again and let sit for 10 more minutes.

4. Press "Pre-Heat", set the temperature at 375°F (191°C). Grease a cake pan with butter.

5. Scoop 2 tablespoons of the dough into the cake pan. Repeat

with the remaining dough to make dough 12 balls. Keep a little distance between each two balls. You may need to work in batches to avoid overcrowding.

6. Place the cake pan in the preheated air fryer.

7. Bake for 12 minutes or until the balls are golden brown and fluffy. Flip the balls halfway through the cooking time.

8. Remove the balls from the air fryer and allow to cool for 5 minutes before serving.

415

PIGS IN A BLANKET

Prep time: 10 minutes | **Cook time:** 8 minutes per batch | Makes 16 rolls

1 can refrigerated crescent roll dough

1 small package mini smoked sausages, patted dry

2 tablespoons melted butter

2 teaspoons sesame seeds

1 teaspoon onion powder

1. Press "Pre-Heat", set the temperature at 330°F (166°C).

2. Place the crescent roll dough on a clean work surface and separate into 8 pieces. Cut each piece in half and you will have 16 triangles.

3. Make the pigs in the blanket: Arrange each sausage on each dough triangle, then roll the sausages up.

4. Brush the pigs with melted butter and place half of the pigs in the blanket in the preheated air fryer. Sprinkle with sesame seeds and onion powder.

5. Bake for 8 minutes or until the pigs are fluffy and golden brown. Flip the pigs halfway through.

6. Serve immediately.

416

SHRIMP WITH SRIRACHA AND WORCESTERSHIRE SAUCE

Prep time: 15 minutes | **Cook time:** 10 minutes per batch | **Serves** 4

1 tablespoon Sriracha sauce

1 teaspoon Worcestershire sauce

2 tablespoons sweet chili sauce

¾ cup mayonnaise

1 egg, beaten

1 cup panko breadcrumbs

1 pound (454 g) raw shrimp, shelled and deveined, rinsed and drained

Lime wedges, for serving

Cooking spray

1. Press "Pre-Heat", set the temperature at 360°F (182°C). Spritz the air fryer basket with cooking spray.

2. Combine the Sriracha sauce, Worcestershire sauce, chili sauce, and mayo in a bowl. Stir to mix well. Reserve ⅓ cup of the mixture as the dipping sauce.

3. Combine the remaining sauce mixture with the beaten egg. Stir to mix well. Put the panko in a separate bowl.

4. Dredge the shrimp in the sauce mixture first, then into the panko. Roll the shrimp to coat well. Shake the excess off.

5. Place the shrimp in the preheated air fryer, then spritz with cooking spray. You may need to work in batches to avoid overcrowding.

6. Air fry the shrimp for 10 minutes or until opaque. Flip the shrimp halfway through the cooking time.

7. Remove the shrimp from the air fryer and serve with reserve sauce mixture and squeeze the lime wedges over.

417

SIMPLE BUTTER CAKE

Prep time: 25 minutes | **Cook time:** 20 minutes | **Serves** 8

1 cup all-purpose flour

1¼ teaspoons baking powder

¼ teaspoon salt

½ cup plus 1½ tablespoons granulated white sugar

9½ tablespoons butter, at room temperature

2 large eggs

1 large egg yolk

2½ tablespoons milk

1 teaspoon vanilla extract

Cooking spray

1. Press "Pre-Heat", set the temperature at 325°F (163°C). Spritz a cake pan with cooking spray.

2. Combine the flour, baking powder, and salt in a large bowl. Stir to mix well.

3. Whip the sugar and butter in a separate bowl with a hand mixer on medium speed for 3 minutes.

4. Whip the eggs, egg yolk, milk, and vanilla extract into the sugar and butter mix with a hand mixer.

5. Pour in the flour mixture and whip with hand mixer until sanity and smooth.

6. Scrape the batter into the cake pan and level the batter with a spatula.

7. Place the cake pan in the preheated air fryer.

8. Bake for 20 minutes or until a toothpick inserted in the center comes out clean. Check the doneness during the last 5 minutes of the baking.

9. Invert the cake on a cooling rack and allow to cool for 15 minutes before slicing to serve.

418

SUPPLÌ AL TELEFONO (RISOTTO CROQUETTES)

Prep time: 1 hour 40 minutes | **Cook time:** 1 hour | **Serves** 6

Risotto Croquettes:
4 tablespoons unsalted butter
1 small yellow onion, minced
1 cup Arborio rice
3½ cups chicken stock
½ cup dry white wine
3 eggs
Zest of 1 lemon
½ cup grated Parmesan cheese
2 ounces (57 g) fresh Mozzarella cheese
¼ cup peas
2 tablespoons water
½ cup all-purpose flour
1½ cups panko breadcrumbs
Kosher salt and ground black pepper, to taste
Cooking spray
Tomato Sauce:
2 tablespoons extra-virgin olive oil
4 cloves garlic, minced

¼ teaspoon red pepper flakes

1 (28-ounce / 794-g) can crushed tomatoes

2 teaspoons granulated sugar

Kosher salt and ground black pepper, to taste

1. Melt the butter in a pot over medium heat, then add the onion and salt to taste. Sauté for 5 minutes or until the onion in translucent.

2. Add the rice and stir to coat well. Cook for 3 minutes or until the rice is lightly browned. Pour in the chicken stock and wine.

3. Bring to a boil. Then cook for 20 minutes or until the rice is tender and liquid is almost absorbed.

4. Make the risotto: When the rice is cooked, break the egg into the pot. Add the lemon zest and Parmesan cheese. Sprinkle with salt and ground black pepper. Stir to mix well.

5. Pour the risotto in a baking sheet, then level with a spatula to spread the risotto evenly. Wrap the baking sheet in plastic and refrigerate for 1 hour.

6. Meanwhile, heat the olive oil in a saucepan over medium heat until shimmering.

7. Add the garlic and sprinkle with red pepper flakes. Sauté for a minute or until fragrant.

8. Add the crushed tomatoes and sprinkle with sugar. Stir to mix well. Bring to a boil. Reduce the heat to low and simmer for 15 minutes or until lightly thickened. Sprinkle with salt and pepper to taste. Set aside until ready to serve.

9. Remove the risotto from the refrigerator. Scoop the risotto into twelve 2-inch balls, then flatten the balls with your hands.

10. Arrange a about ½-inch piece of Mozzarella and 5 peas in the center of each flattened ball, then wrap them back into balls.

11. Transfer the balls in a baking sheet lined with parchment paper, then refrigerate for 15 minutes or until firm.

12. Press "Pre-Heat", set the temperature at 400°F (204°C).

13. Whisk the remaining 2 eggs with 2 tablespoons of water in a bowl. Pour the flour in a second bowl and pour the panko in a third bowl.

14. Dredge the risotto balls in the bowl of flour first, then into the eggs, and then into the panko. Shake the excess off.
15. Transfer the balls in the preheated air fryer and spritz with cooking spray. You may need to work in batches to avoid overcrowding.
16. Bake for 10 minutes or until golden brown. Flip the balls halfway through.
17. Serve the risotto balls with the tomato sauce.

419

TERIYAKI SHRIMP SKEWERS

Prep time: 10 minutes | **Cook time:** 6 minutes | Makes 12 skewered shrimp

1½ tablespoons mirin

1½ teaspoons ginger juice

1½ tablespoons soy sauce

12 large shrimp (about 20 shrimps per pound), peeled and deveined

1 large egg

¾ cup panko breadcrumbs

Cooking spray

1. Combine the mirin, ginger juice, and soy sauce in a large bowl. Stir to mix well.

2. Dunk the shrimp in the bowl of mirin mixture, then wrap the bowl in plastic and refrigerate for 1 hour to marinate.

3. Press "Pre-Heat", set the temperature at 400°F (204°C). Spritz the air fryer basket with cooking spray.

4. Run twelve 4-inch skewers through each shrimp.

5. Whisk the egg in the bowl of marinade to combine well. Pour the breadcrumbs on a plate.

6.Dredge the shrimp skewers in the egg mixture, then shake the excess off and roll over the breadcrumbs to coat well.

7.Arrange the shrimp skewers in the preheated air fryer and spritz with cooking spray. You need to work in batches to avoid overcrowding.

8.Air fry for 6 minutes or until the shrimp are opaque and firm. Flip the shrimp skewers halfway through.

9.Serve immediately.

420

WHOLE CHICKEN ROAST

Prep time: 10 minutes | **Cook time:** 1 hour | **Serves** 6

1 teaspoon salt
1 teaspoon Italian seasoning
½ teaspoon freshly ground black pepper
½ teaspoon paprika
½ teaspoon garlic powder
½ teaspoon onion powder
2 tablespoons olive oil, plus more as needed
1 (4-pound / 1.8-kg) fryer chicken

1. Press "Pre-Heat", set the temperature at 360°F (182°C).
2. Grease the air fryer basket lightly with olive oil.
3. In a small bowl, mix the salt, Italian seasoning, pepper, paprika, garlic powder, and onion powder.
4. Remove any giblets from the chicken. Pat the chicken dry thoroughly with paper towels, including the cavity.
5. Brush the chicken all over with the olive oil and rub it with the seasoning mixture.
6. Truss the chicken or tie the legs with butcher's twine. This will make it easier to flip the chicken during cooking.
7. Put the chicken in the air fryer basket, breast-side down. Air

fry for 30 minutes. Flip the chicken over and baste it with any drippings collected in the bottom drawer of the air fryer. Lightly brush the chicken with olive oil.

8. Air fry for 20 minutes. Flip the chicken over one last time and air fry until a thermometer inserted into the thickest part of the thigh reaches at least 165°F (74°C) and it's crispy and golden, 10 more minutes. Continue to cook, checking every 5 minutes until the chicken reaches the correct internal temperature.

9. Let the chicken rest for 10 minutes before carving and serving.

FAST AND EASY
EVERYDAY FAVORITES

421

AIR FRIED BROCCOLI

Prep time: 5 minutes | **Cook time:** 6 minutes | **Serves** 1

4 egg yolks
¼ cup butter, melted
2 cups coconut flower
Salt and pepper, to taste
2 cups broccoli florets

1. Press "Pre-Heat", set the temperature at 400°F (204°C).

2. In a bowl, whisk the egg yolks and melted butter together. Throw in the coconut flour, salt and pepper, then stir again to combine well.

3. Dip each broccoli floret into the mixture and place in the air fryer basket. Air fry for 6 minutes in batches if necessary. Take care when removing them from the air fryer and serve immediately.

422

CARROT AND CELERY CROQUETTES

Prep time: 10 minutes | **Cook time:** 6 minutes | **Serves** 4

2 medium-sized carrots, trimmed and grated
2 medium-sized celery stalks, trimmed and grated
½ cup finely chopped leek
1 tablespoon garlic paste
¼ teaspoon freshly cracked black pepper
1 teaspoon fine sea salt
1 tablespoon finely chopped fresh dill
1 egg, lightly whisked
¼ cup flour
¼ teaspoon baking powder
½ cup bread crumbs
Cooking spray
Chive mayo, for serving

1. Press "Pre-Heat", set the temperature at 360°F (182°C).
2. Drain any excess liquid from the carrots and celery by placing them on a paper towel.
3. Stir together the vegetables with all of the other ingredients, save for the bread crumbs and chive mayo.
4. Use your hands to mold 1 tablespoon of the vegetable

mixture into a ball and repeat until all of the mixture has been used up. Press down on each ball with your hand or a palette knife. Cover completely with bread crumbs. Spritz the croquettes with cooking spray.

5. Arrange the croquettes in a single layer in the air fryer basket and air fry for 6 minutes.

6. Serve warm with the chive mayo on the side.

423

CHEESY POTATO PATTIES

Prep time: 5 minutes | **Cook time:** 10 minutes | **Serves** 8

2 pounds (907 g) white potatoes

½ cup finely chopped scallions

½ teaspoon freshly ground black pepper, or more to taste

1 tablespoon fine sea salt

½ teaspoon hot paprika

2 cups shredded Colby cheese

¼ cup canola oil

1 cup crushed crackers

1. Press "Pre-Heat", set the temperature at 360°F (182°C).

2. Boil the potatoes until soft. Dry them off and peel them before mashing thoroughly, leaving no lumps.

3. Combine the mashed potatoes with scallions, pepper, salt, paprika, and cheese.

4. Mold the mixture into balls with your hands and press with your palm to flatten them into patties.

5. In a shallow dish, combine the canola oil and crushed crackers. Coat the patties in the crumb mixture.

6. Bake the patties for about 10 minutes, in multiple batches if necessary.

7. Serve hot.

424

SIMPLE AND EASY CROUTONS

Prep time: 5 minutes | **Cook time:** 8 minutes | **Serves** 4

2 slices friendly bread
1 tablespoon olive oil
Hot soup, for serving

1. Press "Pre-Heat", set the temperature at 390°F (199°C).
2. Cut the slices of bread into medium-size chunks.
3. Brush the air fryer basket with the oil.
4. Place the chunks inside and air fry for at least 8 minutes.
5. Serve with hot soup.

425

SWEET CORN AND CARROT FRITTERS

Prep time: 10 minutes | **Cook time:** 8 to 11 minutes | **Serves** 4

1 medium-sized carrot, grated

1 yellow onion, finely chopped

4 ounces (113 g) canned sweet corn kernels, drained

1 teaspoon sea salt flakes

1 tablespoon chopped fresh cilantro

1 medium-sized egg, whisked

2 tablespoons plain milk

1 cup grated Parmesan cheese

¼ cup flour

⅓ teaspoon baking powder

⅓ teaspoon sugar

Cooking spray

1. Press "Pre-Heat", set the temperature at 350°F (177°C).

2. Place the grated carrot in a colander and press down to squeeze out any excess moisture. Dry it with a paper towel.

3. Combine the carrots with the remaining ingredients.

4. Mold 1 tablespoon of the mixture into a ball and press it

down with your hand or a spoon to flatten it. Repeat until the rest of the mixture is used up.

5. Spritz the balls with cooking spray.

6. Arrange in the air fryer basket, taking care not to overlap any balls. Bake for 8 to 11 minutes, or until they're firm.

7. Serve warm.

426

BISTRO POTATO WEDGES

Prep time: 10 minutes | **Cook time:** 13 minutes | **Serves** 4

1 pound (454 g) fingerling potatoes, cut into wedges
1 teaspoon extra-virgin olive oil
½ teaspoon garlic powder
Salt and pepper, to taste
½ cup raw cashews, soaked in water overnight
½ teaspoon ground turmeric
½ teaspoon paprika
1 tablespoon nutritional yeast
1 teaspoon fresh lemon juice
2 tablespoons to ¼ cup water

1. Press "Pre-Heat", set the temperature at 400°F (204°C).
2. In a bowl, toss together the potato wedges, olive oil, garlic powder, and salt and pepper, making sure to coat the potatoes well.
3. Transfer the potatoes to the air fryer basket and air fry for 10 minutes.
4. In the meantime, prepare the cheese sauce. Pulse the cashews, turmeric, paprika, nutritional yeast, lemon juice, and

water together in a food processor. Add more water to achieve your desired consistency.

5. When the potatoes are finished cooking, transfer to a bowl and add the cheese sauce on top. Air fry for an additional 3 minutes.

6. Serve hot.

427

SPINACH AND CARROT BALLS

Prep time: 10 minutes | **Cook time:** 10 minutes | **Serves** 4

2 slices toasted bread
1 carrot, peeled and grated
1 package fresh spinach, blanched and chopped
½ onion, chopped
1 egg, beaten
½ teaspoon garlic powder
1 teaspoon minced garlic
1 teaspoon salt
½ teaspoon black pepper
1 tablespoon nutritional yeast
1 tablespoon flour

1. Press "Pre-Heat", set the temperature at 390°F (199°C).
2. In a food processor, pulse the toasted bread to form bread crumbs. Transfer into a shallow dish or bowl.
3. In a bowl, mix together all the other ingredients.
4. Use your hands to shape the mixture into small-sized balls. Roll the balls in the bread crumbs, ensuring to cover them well.
5. Put in the air fryer basket and air fry for 10 minutes.
6. Serve immediately.

428

SIMPLE PEA DELIGHT

Prep time: 5 minutes | **Cook time:** 15 minutes | **Serves** 2 to 4

1 cup flour
1 teaspoon baking powder
3 eggs
1 cup coconut milk
1 cup cream cheese
3 tablespoons pea protein
½ cup chicken or turkey strips
Pinch of sea salt
1 cup Mozzarella cheese

1. Press "Pre-Heat", set the temperature at 390°F (199°C).
2. In a large bowl, mix all ingredients together using a large wooden spoon.
3. Spoon equal amounts of the mixture into muffin cups and bake for 15 minutes.
4. Serve immediately.

429

CHEESY SAUSAGE BALLS

Prep time: 5 minutes | **Cook time:** 15 minutes | **Serves** 6

12 ounces (340 g) Jimmy Dean's Sausage
6 ounces (170 g) shredded Cheddar cheese
10 Cheddar cubes

1. Press "Pre-Heat", set the temperature at 375°F (191°C).
2. Mix the shredded cheese and sausage.
3. Divide the mixture into 12 equal parts to be stuffed.
4. Add a cube of cheese to the center of the sausage and roll into balls.
5. Air fry for 15 minutes, or until crisp.
6. Serve immediately.

430

BACON-WRAPPED BEEF HOT DOG

Prep time: 5 minutes | **Cook time:** 10 minutes | **Serves** 4

4 slices sugar-free bacon

4 beef hot dogs

1. Press "Pre-Heat", set the temperature at 370°F (188°C).
2. Take a slice of bacon and wrap it around the hot dog, securing it with a toothpick. Repeat with the other pieces of bacon and hot dogs, placing each wrapped dog in the air fryer basket.
3. Bake for 10 minutes, turning halfway through.
4. Once hot and crispy, the hot dogs are ready to serve.

431

BEEF BRATWURSTS

Prep time: 5 minutes | **Cook time:** 15 minutes | **Serves** 4

4 (3-ounce / 85-g) beef bratwursts

1. Press "Pre-Heat", set the temperature at 375°F (191°C).
2. Place the beef bratwursts in the air fryer basket and air fry for 15 minutes, turning once halfway through.
3. Serve hot.

432

EASY ROASTED ASPARAGUS

Prep time: 5 minutes | **Cook time:** 6 minutes | **Serves** 4

1 pound (454 g) asparagus, trimmed and halved crosswise

1 teaspoon extra-virgin olive oil

Salt and pepper, to taste

Lemon wedges, for serving

1. Press "Pre-Heat", set the temperature at 400°F (204°C).

2. Toss the asparagus with the oil, 1/8 teaspoon salt, and 1/8 teaspoon pepper in bowl. Transfer to air fryer basket.

3. Place the basket in air fryer and roast for 6 to 8 minutes, or until tender and bright green, tossing halfway through cooking.

4. Season with salt and pepper and serve with lemon wedges.

433

BAKED CHORIZO SCOTCH EGGS

Prep time: 5 minutes | **Cook time:** 15 to 20 minutes | Makes 4 eggs

1 pound (454 g) Mexican chorizo or other seasoned sausage meat

4 soft-boiled eggs plus 1 raw egg

1 tablespoon water

½ cup all-purpose flour

1 cup panko bread crumbs

Cooking spray

1. Divide the chorizo into 4 equal portions. Flatten each portion into a disc. Place a soft-boiled egg in the center of each disc. Wrap the chorizo around the egg, encasing it completely. Place the encased eggs on a plate and chill for at least 30 minutes.

2. Press "Pre-Heat", set the temperature at 360°F (182°C).

3. Beat the raw egg with 1 tablespoon of water. Place the flour on a small plate and the panko on a second plate. Working with 1 egg at a time, roll the encased egg in the flour, then dip it in the egg mixture. Dredge the egg in the panko and place on a plate. Repeat with the remaining eggs.

4.Spray the eggs with oil and place in the air fryer basket. Bake for 10 minutes. Turn and bake for an additional 5 to 10 minutes, or until browned and crisp on all sides.

5.Serve immediately.

434

ROSEMARY AND ORANGE ROASTED CHICKPEAS

Prep time: 5 minutes | **Cook time:** 10 to 12 minutes | Makes 4 cups

- 4 cups cooked chickpeas
- 2 tablespoons vegetable oil
- 1 teaspoon kosher salt
- 1 teaspoon cumin
- 1 teaspoon paprika
- Zest of 1 orange
- 1 tablespoon chopped fresh rosemary

1. Press "Pre-Heat", set the temperature at 400°F (204°C).
2. Make sure the chickpeas are completely dry prior to roasting. In a medium bowl, toss the chickpeas with oil, salt, cumin, and paprika.
3. Working in batches, spread the chickpeas in a single layer in the air fryer basket. Air fry for 10 to 12 minutes until crisp, shaking once halfway through.
4. Return the warm chickpeas to the bowl and toss with the orange zest and rosemary. Allow to cool completely.
5. Serve.

435

POMEGRANATE AVOCADO FRIES

Prep time: 5 minutes | **Cook time:** 7 to 8 minutes | **Serves** 4

1 cup panko bread crumbs

1 teaspoon kosher salt, plus more for sprinkling

1 teaspoon garlic powder

½ teaspoon cayenne pepper

2 ripe but firm avocados

1 egg, beaten with 1 tablespoon water

Cooking spray

Pomegranate molasses, for serving

1. Press "Pre-Heat", set the temperature at 375°F (191°C).

2. Whisk together the panko, salt, and spices on a plate. Cut each avocado in half and remove the pit. Cut each avocado half into 4 slices and scoop the slices out with a large spoon, taking care to keep the slices intact.

3. Dip each avocado slice in the egg wash and then dredge it in the panko. Place the breaded avocado slices on a plate.

4. Working in 2 batches, arrange half of the avocado slices in a single layer in the air fryer basket. Spray lightly with oil. Bake the slices for 7 to 8 minutes, turning once halfway through. Remove

the cooked slices to a platter and repeat with the remaining avocado slices.

5. Sprinkle the warm avocado slices with salt and drizzle with pomegranate molasses. Serve immediately.

436

CRUNCHY FRIED OKRA

Prep time: 5 minutes | **Cook time:** 8 to 10 minutes | **Serves** 4

1 cup self-rising yellow cornmeal
1 teaspoon Italian-style seasoning
1 teaspoon paprika
1 teaspoon salt
½ teaspoon freshly ground black pepper
2 large eggs, beaten
2 cups okra slices
Cooking spray

1. Press "Pre-Heat", set the temperature at 400°F (204°C). Line the air fryer basket with parchment paper.
2. In a shallow bowl, whisk the cornmeal, Italian-style seasoning, paprika, salt, and pepper until blended. Place the beaten eggs in a second shallow bowl.
3. Add the okra to the beaten egg and stir to coat. Add the egg and okra mixture to the cornmeal mixture and stir until coated.
4. Place the okra on the parchment and spritz it with oil.
5. Air fry for 4 minutes. Shake the basket, spritz the okra with

oil, and air fry for 4 to 6 minutes more until lightly browned and crispy.

6. Serve immediately.

437

BUTTERY SWEET POTATOES

Prep time: 5 minutes | **Cook time:** 10 minutes | **Serves** 4

2 tablespoons butter, melted

1 tablespoon light brown sugar

2 sweet potatoes, peeled and cut into ½-inch cubes

Cooking spray

1. Press "Pre-Heat", set the temperature at 400°F (204°C). Line the air fryer basket with parchment paper.

2. In a medium bowl, stir together the melted butter and brown sugar until blended. Toss the sweet potatoes in the butter mixture until coated.

3. Place the sweet potatoes on the parchment and spritz with oil.

4. Air fry for 5 minutes. Shake the basket, spritz the sweet potatoes with oil, and air fry for 5 minutes more until they're soft enough to cut with a fork.

5. Serve immediately.

438

CORN FRITTERS

Prep time: 15 minutes | **Cook time:** 8 minutes | **Serves** 6

1 cup self-rising flour
1 tablespoon sugar
1 teaspoon salt
1 large egg, lightly beaten
¼ cup buttermilk
¾ cup corn kernels
¼ cup minced onion
Cooking spray

1. Press "Pre-Heat", set the temperature at 350°F (177°C). Line the air fryer basket with parchment paper.
2. In a medium bowl, whisk the flour, sugar, and salt until blended. Stir in the egg and buttermilk. Add the corn and minced onion. Mix well. Shape the corn fritter batter into 12 balls.
3. Place the fritters on the parchment and spritz with oil. Bake for 4 minutes. Flip the fritters, spritz them with oil, and bake for 4 minutes more until firm and lightly browned.
4. Serve immediately.

439

BACON AND GREEN BEANS

Prep time: 15 minutes | **Cook time:** 8 to 10 minutes | **Serves** 4

2 (14.5-ounce / 411-g) cans cut green beans, drained
4 bacon slices, air-fried and diced
¼ cup minced onion
1 tablespoon distilled white vinegar
1 teaspoon freshly squeezed lemon juice
½ teaspoon salt
½ teaspoon freshly ground black pepper
Cooking spray

1. Press "Pre-Heat", set the temperature at 370°F (188°C).
2. Spritz a baking pan with oil. In the prepared pan, stir together the green beans, bacon, onion, vinegar, lemon juice, salt, and pepper until blended.
3. Place the pan on the air fryer basket.
4. Air fry for 4 minutes. Stir the green beans and air fry for 4 to 6 minutes more until soft.
5. Serve immediately.

440

FRICO

Prep time: 5 minutes | **Cook time:** 5 minutes | **Serves** 2

1 cup shredded aged Manchego cheese

1 teaspoon all-purpose flour

½ teaspoon cumin seeds

¼ teaspoon cracked black pepper

1. Press "Pre-Heat", set the temperature at 375°F (191°C). Line the air fryer basket with parchment paper.

2. Combine the cheese and flour in a bowl. Stir to mix well. Spread the mixture in the basket into a 4-inch round.

3. Combine the cumin and black pepper in a small bowl. Stir to mix well. Sprinkle the cumin mixture over the cheese round.

4. Air fry 5 minutes or until the cheese is lightly browned and frothy.

5. Use tongs to transfer the cheese wafer onto a plate and slice to serve.

441

GARLICKY BAKED CHERRY TOMATOES

Prep time: 5 minutes | **Cook time:** 4 to 6 minutes | **Serves** 2

2 cups cherry tomatoes
1 clove garlic, thinly sliced
1 teaspoon olive oil
⅛ teaspoon kosher salt
1 tablespoon freshly chopped basil, for topping
Cooking spray

1. Press "Pre-Heat", set the temperature at 360°F (182°C). Spritz the air fryer baking pan with cooking spray and set aside.
2. In a large bowl, toss together the cherry tomatoes, sliced garlic, olive oil, and kosher salt. Spread the mixture in an even layer in the prepared pan.
3. Bake in the preheated air fryer for 4 to 6 minutes, or until the tomatoes become soft and wilted.
4. Transfer to a bowl and rest for 5 minutes. Top with the chopped basil and serve warm.

442

GARLICKY KNOTS WITH PARSLEY

Prep time: 10 minutes | **Cook time:** 10 minutes | Makes 8 knots

1 teaspoon dried parsley

¼ cup melted butter

2 teaspoons garlic powder

1 (11-ounce / 312-g) tube refrigerated French bread dough, cut into 8 slices

1. Press "Pre-Heat", set the temperature at 350°F (177°C).

2. Combine the parsley, butter, and garlic powder in a bowl. Stir to mix well.

3. Place the French bread dough slices on a clean work surface, then roll each slice into a 6-inch long rope. Tie the ropes into knots and arrange them on a plate. Brush the knots with butter mixture.

4. Transfer the knots into the air fryer. You need to work in batches to avoid overcrowding.

5. Air fry for 5 minutes or until the knots are golden brown. Flip the knots halfway through the cooking time.

6. Serve immediately.

443

GARLICKY ZOODLES

Prep time: 10 minutes | **Cook time:** 10 minutes | **Serves** 4

2 large zucchini, peeled and spiralized
2 large yellow summer squash, peeled and spiralized
1 tablespoon olive oil, divided
½ teaspoon kosher salt
1 garlic clove, whole
2 tablespoons fresh basil, chopped
Cooking spray

1. Press "Pre-Heat", set the temperature at 360°F (182°C). Spritz the air fryer basket with cooking spray.
2. Combine the zucchini and summer squash with 1 teaspoon olive oil and salt in a large bowl. Toss to coat well.
3. Transfer the zucchini and summer squash in the preheated air fryer and add the garlic.
4. Air fry for 10 minutes or until tender and fragrant. Toss the spiralized zucchini and summer squash halfway through the cooking time.
5. Transfer the cooked zucchini and summer squash onto a plate and set aside.

6.Remove the garlic from the air fryer and allow to cool for a few minutes. Mince the garlic and combine with remaining olive oil in a small bowl. Stir to mix well.

7.Drizzle the spiralized zucchini and summer squash with garlic oil and sprinkle with basil. Toss to serve.

444

HEARTY APPLE FRITTERS

Prep time: 5 minutes | **Cook time:** 25 minutes | Makes 15 fritters

Apple Fritters:
2 firm apples, peeled, cored, and diced
½ teaspoon cinnamon
Juice of 1 lemon
1 cup all-purpose flour
1½ teaspoons baking powder
½ teaspoon kosher salt
2 eggs
¼ cup milk
2 tablespoons unsalted butter, melted
2 tablespoons granulated sugar
Cooking spray
Glaze:
½ teaspoon vanilla extract
1¼ cups powdered sugar, sifted
¼ cup water

1. Press "Pre-Heat", set the temperature at 360°F (182°C). Line the air fryer basket with parchment paper.

2. Combine the apples with cinnamon and lemon juice in a small bowl. Toss to coat well.

3. Combine the flour, baking powder, and salt in a large bowl. Stir to mix well.

4. Whisk the egg, milk, butter, and sugar in a medium bowl. Stir to mix well.

5. Make a well in the center of the flour mixture, then pour the egg mixture into the well and stir to mix well. Mix in the apple until a dough forms.

6. Use an ice cream scoop to scoop 5 balls from the dough into the air fryer. Spritz with cooking spray.

7. Air fry for 8 minutes or until golden brown. Flip them halfway through. Remove the fritters from the air fryer and repeat with the remaining dough.

8. Meanwhile, combine the ingredients for the glaze in a separate small bowl. Stir to mix well.

9. Serve the fritters with the glaze on top or use the glaze for dipping.

445

HONEY BARTLETT PEARS WITH LEMONY RICOTTA

Prep time: 10 minutes | **Cook time:** 8 minutes | **Serves** 4

2 large Bartlett pears, peeled, cut in half, cored
3 tablespoons melted butter
½ teaspoon ground ginger
¼ teaspoon ground cardamom
3 tablespoons brown sugar
½ cup whole-milk ricotta cheese
1 teaspoon pure lemon extract
1 teaspoon pure almond extract
1 tablespoon honey, plus additional for drizzling

1. Press "Pre-Heat", set the temperature at 375°F (191°C).

2. Toss the pears with butter, ginger, cardamom, and sugar in a large bowl. Toss to coat well.

3. Arrange the pears in the preheated air fryer, cut side down. Air fry for 5 minutes, then flip the pears and air fry for 3 more minutes or until the pears are soft and browned.

4. In the meantime, combine the remaining ingredients in a separate bowl. Whip for 1 minute with a hand mixer until the mixture is puffed.

5. Divide the mixture into four bowls, then put the pears over the mixture and drizzle with more honey to serve.

446

HOT WINGS

Prep time: 5 minutes | **Cook time:** 30 minutes | Makes 16 wings

16 chicken wings

3 tablespoons hot sauce

Cooking spray

1. Press "Pre-Heat", set the temperature at 360°F (182°C). Spritz the air fryer basket with cooking spray.

2. Arrange the chicken wings in the preheated air fryer. You need to work in batches to avoid overcrowding.

3. Cook for 15 minutes or until well browned. Shake the basket at lease three times during the cooking.

4. Transfer the air fried wings on a plate and serve with hot sauce.

447

GOLDEN SALMON AND CARROT CROQUETTES

Prep time: 15 minutes | **Cook time:** 10 minutes | **Serves** 6

2 egg whites
1 cup almond flour
1 cup panko breadcrumbs
1 pound (454 g) chopped salmon fillet
2/3 cup grated carrots
2 tablespoons minced garlic cloves
1/2 cup chopped onion
2 tablespoons chopped chives
Cooking spray

1. Press "Pre-Heat", set the temperature at 350°F (177°C). Spritz the air fryer basket with cooking spray.

2. Whisk the egg whites in a bowl. Put the flour in a second bowl. Pour the breadcrumbs in a third bowl. Set aside.

3. Combine the salmon, carrots, garlic, onion, and chives in a large bowl. Stir to mix well.

4. Form the mixture into balls with your hands. Dredge the balls into the flour, then egg, and then breadcrumbs to coat well.

5. Arrange the salmon balls in the preheated air fryer and spritz with cooking spray.

6.Air fry for 10 minutes or until crispy and browned. Shake the basket halfway through.

7.Serve immediately.

448

LEMONY AND GARLICKY ASPARAGUS

Prep time: 5 minutes | **Cook time:** 10 minutes | Makes 10 spears

10 spears asparagus (about ½ pound / 227 g in total), snap the ends off

1 tablespoon lemon juice

2 teaspoons minced garlic

½ teaspoon salt

¼ teaspoon ground black pepper

Cooking spray

1. Press "Pre-Heat", set the temperature at 400°F (204°C). Line a parchment paper in the air fryer basket.

2. Put the asparagus spears in a large bowl. Drizzle with lemon juice and sprinkle with minced garlic, salt, and ground black pepper. Toss to coat well.

3. Transfer the asparagus in the preheated air fryer and spritz with cooking spray. Air fryer for 10 minutes or until wilted and soft. Flip the asparagus halfway through.

4. Serve immediately.

449

PARSNIP FRIES WITH GARLIC-YOGURT DIP

Prep time: 10 minutes | **Cook time:** 10 minutes | **Serves** 4

3 medium parsnips, peeled, cut into sticks
¼ teaspoon kosher salt
1 teaspoon olive oil
1 garlic clove, unpeeled
Cooking spray
Dip:
¼ cup plain Greek yogurt
⅛ teaspoon garlic powder
1 tablespoon sour cream
¼ teaspoon kosher salt
Freshly ground black pepper, to taste

1. Press "Pre-Heat", set the temperature at 360°F (182°C). Spritz the air fryer basket with cooking spray.
2. Put the parsnip sticks in a large bowl, then sprinkle with salt and drizzle with olive oil.
3. Transfer the parsnip into the preheated air fryer and add the garlic.
4. Air fry for 5 minutes, then remove the garlic from the air

fryer and shake the basket. Air fry for 5 more minutes or until the parsnip sticks are crisp.

5.Meanwhile, peel the garlic and crush it. Combine the crushed garlic with the ingredients for the dip. Stir to mix well.

6.When the frying is complete, remove the parsnip fries from the air fryer and serve with the dipping sauce.

450

ROASTED CARROT CHIPS

Prep time: 5 minutes | **Cook time:** 15 minutes | Makes 3 cups

3 large carrots, peeled and sliced into long and thick chips diagonally

1 tablespoon granulated garlic

1 teaspoon salt

¼ teaspoon ground black pepper

1 tablespoon olive oil

1 tablespoon finely chopped fresh parsley

1. Press "Pre-Heat", set the temperature at 360°F (182°C).

2. Toss the carrots with garlic, salt, ground black pepper, and olive oil in a large bowl to coat well.

3. Place the carrots in the preheated air fryer. Roast for 15 minutes or until the carrot chips are soft. Shake the basket halfway through.

4. Serve the carrot chips with parsley on top.

451

SIMPLE AIR FRIED CRISPY BRUSSELS SPROUTS

Prep time: 5 minutes | **Cook time:** 20 minutes | **Serves** 4

¼ teaspoon salt

⅛ teaspoon ground black pepper

1 tablespoon extra-virgin olive oil

1 pound (454 g) Brussels sprouts, trimmed and halved

Lemon wedges, for garnish

1. Press "Pre-Heat", set the temperature at 350°F (177°C).

2. Combine the salt, black pepper, and olive oil in a large bowl. Stir to mix well.

3. Add the Brussels sprouts to the bowl of mixture and toss to coat well.

4. Arrange the Brussels sprouts in the preheated air fryer. Air fry for 20 minutes or until lightly browned and wilted. Shake the basket two times during the air frying.

5. Transfer the cooked Brussels sprouts to a large plate and squeeze the lemon wedges on top to serve.

452

SIMPLE AIR FRIED OKRA CHIPS

Prep time: 5 minutes | **Cook time:** 16 minutes | **Serves** 6

2 pounds (907 g) fresh okra pods, cut into 1-inch pieces

2 tablespoons canola oil

1 teaspoon coarse sea salt

1. Press "Pre-Heat", set the temperature at 400°F (204°C).
2. Stir the oil and salt in a bowl to mix well. Add the okra and toss to coat well.
3. Place the okra in the preheated air fryer. Air fry for 16 minutes or until lightly browned. Shake the basket at least three times during the cooking time.
4. Serve immediately.

453

SIMPLE BAKED GREEN BEANS

Prep time: 5 minutes | **Cook time:** 10 minutes | Makes 2 cups

½ teaspoon lemon pepper
2 teaspoons granulated garlic
½ teaspoon salt
1 tablespoon olive oil
2 cups fresh green beans, trimmed and snapped in half

1. Press "Pre-Heat", set the temperature at 370°F (188°C).
2. Combine the lemon pepper, garlic, salt, and olive oil in a bowl. Stir to mix well.
3. Add the green beans to the bowl of mixture and toss to coat well.
4. Arrange the green beans in the preheated air fryer. Bake for 10 minutes or until tender and crispy. Shake the basket halfway through to make sure the green beans are cooked evenly.
5. Serve immediately.

454

SIMPLE CHEESY SHRIMPS

Prep time: 10 minutes | **Cook time:** 16 minutes | **Serves** 4 to 6

2/3 cup grated Parmesan cheese
4 minced garlic cloves
1 teaspoon onion powder
½ teaspoon oregano
1 teaspoon basil
1 teaspoon ground black pepper
2 tablespoons olive oil
2 pounds (907 g) cooked large shrimps, peeled and deveined
Lemon wedges, for topping
Cooking spray

1. Press "Pre-Heat", set the temperature at 350°F (177°C). Spritz the air fryer basket with cooking spray.
2. Combine all the ingredients, except for the shrimps, in a large bowl. Stir to mix well.
3. Dunk the shrimps in the mixture and toss to coat well. Shake the excess off.
4. Arrange the shrimps in the preheated air fryer. Air fry for 8

minutes or until opaque. Flip the shrimps halfway through. You may need to work in batches to avoid overcrowding.

5. Transfer the cooked shrimps on a large plate and squeeze the lemon wedges over before serving.

455

SPANAKOPITA

Prep time: 5 minutes | **Cook time:** 25 minutes | **Serves** 6

½ (10-ounce / 284-g) package frozen spinach, thawed and squeezed dry

1 egg, lightly beaten

¼ cup pine nuts, toasted

¼ cup grated Parmesan cheese

¾ cup crumbled feta cheese

⅛ teaspoon ground nutmeg

½ teaspoon salt

Freshly ground black pepper, to taste

6 sheets phyllo dough

½ cup butter, melted

1. Combine all the ingredients, except for the phyllo dough and butter, in a large bowl. Whisk to combine well. Set aside.

2. Place a sheet of phyllo dough on a clean work surface. Brush with butter then top with another layer sheet of phyllo. Brush with butter, then cut the layered sheets into six 3-inch-wide strips.

3. Top each strip with 1 tablespoon of the spinach mixture, then fold the bottom left corner over the mixture towards the

right strip edge to make a triangle. Keep folding triangles until each strip is folded over.

4.Brush the triangles with butter and repeat with remaining strips and phyllo dough.

5.Press "Pre-Heat", set the temperature at 350°F (177°C).

6.Place six triangles in the preheated air fryer. Air fry for 8 minutes or until golden brown. Flip the triangles halfway through. Repeat with the remaining triangles.

7.Serve immediately.

456

SPICY AIR FRIED OLD BAY SHRIMP

Prep time: 7 minutes | **Cook time:** 10 minutes | Makes 2 cups

½ teaspoon Old Bay Seasoning

1 teaspoon ground cayenne pepper

½ teaspoon paprika

1 tablespoon olive oil

⅛ teaspoon salt

½ pound (227 g) shrimps, peeled and deveined

Juice of half a lemon

1. Press "Pre-Heat", set the temperature at 390°F (199°C).

2. Combine the Old Bay Seasoning, cayenne pepper, paprika, olive oil, and salt in a large bowl, then add the shrimps and toss to coat well.

3. Put the shrimps in the preheated air fryer. Air fry for 10 minutes or until opaque. Flip the shrimps halfway through.

4. Serve the shrimps with lemon juice on top.

457

SOUTH CAROLINA SHRIMP AND CORN BAKE

Prep time: 10 minutes | **Cook time:** 18 minutes | **Serves** 2

1 ear corn, husk and silk removed, cut into 2-inch rounds

8 ounces (227 g) red potatoes, unpeeled, cut into 1-inch pieces

2 teaspoons Old Bay Seasoning, divided

2 teaspoons vegetable oil, divided

¼ teaspoon ground black pepper

8 ounces (227 g) large shrimps (about 12 shrimps), deveined

6 ounces (170 g) andouille or chorizo sausage, cut into 1-inch pieces

2 garlic cloves, minced

1 tablespoon chopped fresh parsley

1. Press "Pre-Heat", set the temperature at 400°F (204°C).

2. Put the corn rounds and potatoes in a large bowl. Sprinkle with 1 teaspoon of Old Bay seasoning and drizzle with vegetable oil. Toss to coat well.

3. Transfer the corn rounds and potatoes on a baking sheet, then put in the preheated air fryer.

4. Bake for 12 minutes or until soft and browned. Shake the basket halfway through the cooking time.

5. Meanwhile, cut slits into the shrimps but be careful not to

cut them through. Combine the shrimps, sausage, remaining Old Bay seasoning, and remaining vegetable oil in the large bowl. Toss to coat well.

6. When the baking of the potatoes and corn rounds is complete, add the shrimps and sausage and bake for 6 more minutes or until the shrimps are opaque. Shake the basket halfway through the cooking time.

7. When the baking is finished, serve them on a plate and spread with parsley before serving.

458

SOUTHWEST CORN AND BELL PEPPER ROAST

Prep time: 10 minutes | **Cook time:** 10 minutes | **Serves** 4

For the Corn:
1½ cups thawed frozen corn kernels
1 cup mixed diced bell peppers
1 jalapeño, diced
1 cup diced yellow onion
½ teaspoon ancho chile powder
1 tablespoon fresh lemon juice
1 teaspoon ground cumin
½ teaspoon kosher salt
Cooking spray

For Serving:
¼ cup feta cheese
¼ cup chopped fresh cilantro
1 tablespoon fresh lemon juice

1. Press "Pre-Heat", set the temperature at 375°F (191°C). Spritz the air fryer with cooking spray.

2. Combine the ingredients for the corn in a large bowl. Stir to mix well.

3. Pout the mixture into the air fryer. Air fry for 10 minutes or until the corn and bell peppers are soft. Shake the basket halfway through the cooking time.

4. Transfer them onto a large plate, then spread with feta cheese and cilantro. Drizzle with lemon juice and serve.

459

SWEET AND SOUR PEANUTS

Prep time: 5 minutes | **Cook time:** 5 minutes | **Serves** 9

3 cups shelled raw peanuts

1 tablespoon hot red pepper sauce

3 tablespoons granulated white sugar

1. Press "Pre-Heat", set the temperature at 400°F (204°C).

2. Put the peanuts in a large bowl, then drizzle with hot red pepper sauce and sprinkle with sugar. Toss to coat well.

3. Pour the peanuts in the preheated air fryer. Air fry for 5 minutes or until the peanuts are crispy and browned. Shake the basket halfway through.

4. Serve immediately.

CASSEROLES, FRITTATAS AND QUICHES

460

BROCCOLI, CARROT, AND TOMATO QUICHE

Prep time: 6 minutes | **Cook time:** 14 minutes | **Serves** 4

4 eggs
1 teaspoon dried thyme
1 cup whole milk
1 steamed carrots, diced
2 cups steamed broccoli florets
2 medium tomatoes, diced
¼ cup crumbled feta cheese
1 cup grated Cheddar cheese
1 teaspoon chopped parsley
Salt and ground black pepper, to taste
Cooking spray

1. Press "Pre-Heat", set the temperature at 350°F (177°C). Spritz a baking pan with cooking spray.

2. Whisk together the eggs, thyme, salt, and ground black pepper in a bowl and fold in the milk while mixing.

3. Put the carrots, broccoli, and tomatoes in the prepared baking pan, then spread with feta cheese and ½ cup Cheddar cheese. Pour the egg mixture over, then scatter with remaining Cheddar on top.

4.Put the pan in the preheated air fryer. Bake for 14 minutes or until the eggs are set and the quiche is puffed.

5.Remove the quiche from the air fryer and top with chopped parsley, then slice to serve.

461

CHEESY BACON QUICHE

Prep time: 15 minutes | **Cook time:** 20 minutes | **Serves** 4

1 tablespoon olive oil
1 shortcrust pastry
3 tablespoons Greek yogurt
½ cup grated Cheddar cheese
3 ounces (85 g) chopped bacon
4 eggs, beaten
¼ teaspoon garlic powder
Pinch of black pepper
¼ teaspoon onion powder
¼ teaspoon sea salt
Flour, for sprinkling

1. Press "Pre-Heat", set the temperature at 330°F (166°C).
2. Take 8 ramekins and grease with olive oil. Coat with a sprinkling of flour, tapping to remove any excess.
3. Cut the shortcrust pastry in 8 and place each piece at the bottom of each ramekin.
4. Put all the other ingredients in a bowl and combine well. Spoon equal amounts of the filling into each piece of pastry.

5. Bake the ramekins in the air fryer for 20 minutes.
6. Serve warm.

CHICKEN AND MUSHROOM CASSEROLE

Prep time: 15 minutes | **Cook time:** 20 minutes | **Serves** 4

4 chicken breasts
1 tablespoon curry powder
1 cup coconut milk
Salt, to taste
1 broccoli, cut into florets
1 cup mushrooms
½ cup shredded Parmesan cheese
Cooking spray

1. Press "Pre-Heat", set the temperature at 350°F (177°C). Spritz a casserole dish with cooking spray.
2. Cube the chicken breasts and combine with curry powder and coconut milk in a bowl. Season with salt.
3. Add the broccoli and mushroom and mix well.
4. Pour the mixture into the casserole dish. Top with the cheese.
5. Transfer to the air fryer and bake for about 20 minutes.
6. Serve warm.

463

CHICKEN DIVAN

Prep time: 5 minutes | **Cook time:** 24 minutes | **Serves** 4

4 chicken breasts
Salt and ground black pepper, to taste
1 head broccoli, cut into florets
½ cup cream of mushroom soup
1 cup shredded Cheddar cheese
½ cup croutons
Cooking spray

1. Press "Pre-Heat", set the temperature at 390°F (199°C). Spritz the air fryer basket with cooking spray.

2. Put the chicken breasts in the preheated air fryer and sprinkle with salt and ground black pepper.

3. Air fry for 14 minutes or until well browned and tender. Flip the breasts halfway through the cooking time.

4. Remove the breasts from the air fryer and allow to cool for a few minutes on a plate, then cut the breasts into bite-size pieces.

5. Combine the chicken, broccoli, mushroom soup, and Cheddar cheese in a large bowl. Stir to mix well.

6. Spritz a baking pan with cooking spray. Pour the chicken mixture into the pan. Spread the croutons over the mixture.

7. Place the baking pan in the preheated air fryer. Bake for 10 minutes or until the croutons are lightly browned and the mixture is set.

8. Remove the baking pan from the air fryer and serve immediately.

464

CHORIZO, CORN, AND POTATO FRITTATA

Prep time: 8 minutes | **Cook time:** 12 minutes | **Serves** 4

2 tablespoons olive oil

1 chorizo, sliced

4 eggs

½ cup corn

1 large potato, boiled and cubed

1 tablespoon chopped parsley

½ cup feta cheese, crumbled

Salt and ground black pepper, to taste

1. Press "Pre-Heat", set the temperature at 330°F (166°C).

2. Heat the olive oil in a nonstick skillet over medium heat until shimmering.

3. Add the chorizo and cook for 4 minutes or until golden brown.

4. Whisk the eggs in a bowl, then sprinkle with salt and ground black pepper.

5. Mix the remaining ingredients in the egg mixture, then pour the chorizo and its fat into a baking pan. Pour in the egg mixture.

6. Place the pan in the preheated air fryer. Bake for 8 minutes or until the eggs are set.

7. Serve immediately.

465

CREAMY PORK GRATIN

Prep time: 15 minutes | **Cook time:** 21 minutes | **Serves** 4

2 tablespoons olive oil
2 pounds (907 g) pork tenderloin, cut into serving-size pieces
1 teaspoon dried marjoram
¼ teaspoon chili powder
1 teaspoon coarse sea salt
½ teaspoon freshly ground black pepper
1 cup Ricotta cheese
1½ cups chicken broth
1 tablespoon mustard
Cooking spray

1. Press "Pre-Heat", set the temperature at 350°F (177°C). Spritz a baking pan with cooking spray.

2. Heat the olive oil in a nonstick skillet over medium-high heat until shimmering.

3. Add the pork and sauté for 6 minutes or until lightly browned.

4. Transfer the pork to the prepared baking pan and sprinkle with marjoram, chili powder, salt, and ground black pepper.

5.Combine the remaining ingredients in a large bowl. Stir to mix well. Pour the mixture over the pork in the pan.

6.Arrange the pan in the preheated air fryer and bake for 15 minutes or until frothy and the cheese melts. Stir the mixture halfway through.

7.Serve immediately.

466

CREAMY TOMATO CASSEROLE

Prep time: 5 minutes | **Cook time:** 30 minutes | **Serves** 4

5 eggs

2 tablespoons heavy cream

3 tablespoons chunky tomato sauce

2 tablespoons grated Parmesan cheese, plus more for topping

1. Press "Pre-Heat", set the temperature at 350°F (177°C).

2. Combine the eggs and cream in a bowl.

3. Mix in the tomato sauce and add the cheese.

4. Spread into a glass baking dish and bake in the preheated air fryer for 30 minutes.

5. Top with extra cheese and serve.

467

GOAT CHEESE AND ASPARAGUS FRITTATA

Prep time: 5 minutes | **Cook time:** 25 minutes | **Serves** 2 to 4

1 cup asparagus spears, cut into 1-inch pieces

1 teaspoon vegetable oil

1 tablespoon milk

6 eggs, beaten

2 ounces (57 g) goat cheese, crumbled

1 tablespoon minced chives, optional

Kosher salt and pepper, to taste

1. Press "Pre-Heat", set the temperature at 400°F (204°C).

2. Add the asparagus spears to a small bowl and drizzle with the vegetable oil. Toss until well coated and transfer to a cake pan.

3. Place the pan in the air fryer. Bake for 5 minutes, or until the asparagus become tender and slightly wilted. Remove then pan from the air fryer.

4. Stir together the milk and eggs in a medium bowl. Pour the mixture over the asparagus in the pan. Sprinkle with the goat cheese and the chives (if using) over the eggs. Season with a pinch of salt and pepper.

5. Place the pan back to the air fryer and bake at 320°F (160°C) for 20 minutes or until the top is lightly golden and the eggs are set.

6. Transfer to a serving dish. Slice and serve.

468

GREEK FRITTATA

Prep time: 7 minutes | **Cook time:** 8 minutes | **Serves** 2

1 cup chopped mushrooms

2 cups spinach, chopped

4 eggs, lightly beaten

3 ounces (85 g) feta cheese, crumbled

2 tablespoons heavy cream

A handful of fresh parsley, chopped

Salt and ground black pepper, to taste

Cooking spray

1. Press "Pre-Heat", set the temperature at 350°F (177°C). Spritz a baking pan with cooking spray.

2. Whisk together all the ingredients in a large bowl. Stir to mix well.

3. Pour the mixture in the prepared baking pan and place the pan in the preheated air fryer.

4. Bake for 8 minutes or until the eggs are set.

5. Serve immediately.

469

HERBED CHEDDAR FRITTATA

Prep time: 10 minutes | **Cook time:** 20 minutes | **Serves** 4

½ cup shredded Cheddar cheese
½ cup half-and-half
4 large eggs
2 tablespoons chopped scallion greens
2 tablespoons chopped fresh parsley
½ teaspoon kosher salt
½ teaspoon ground black pepper
Cooking spray

1. Press "Pre-Heat", set the temperature at 300°F (149°C). Spritz a baking pan with cooking spray.

2. Whisk together all the ingredients in a large bowl, then pour the mixture into the prepared baking pan.

3. Set the pan in the preheated air fryer and bake for 20 minutes or until set.

4. Serve immediately.

470

KALE FRITTATA

Prep time: 5 minutes | **Cook time:** 11 minutes | **Serves** 2

1 cup kale, chopped
1 teaspoon olive oil
4 large eggs, beaten
Kosher salt, to taste
2 tablespoons water
3 tablespoons crumbled feta
Cooking spray

1. Press "Pre-Heat", set the temperature at 360°F (182°C). Spritz an air fryer baking pan with cooking spray.

2. Add the kale to the baking pan and drizzle with olive oil. Arrange the pan in the preheated air fryer. Broil for 3 minutes.

3. Meanwhile, combine the eggs with salt and water in a large bowl. Stir to mix well.

4. Make the frittata: When the broiling time is complete, pour the eggs into the baking pan and spread with feta cheese. Reduce the temperature to 300°F (149°C).

5. Bake for 8 minutes or until the eggs are set and the cheese melts.

6.Remove the baking pan from the air fryer and serve the frittata immediately.

KETO CHEESE QUICHE

Prep time: 20 minutes | **Cook time:** 1 hour | **Serves** 8

Crust:
1¼ cups blanched almond flour
1 large egg, beaten
1¼ cups grated Parmesan cheese
¼ teaspoon fine sea salt

Filling:
4 ounces (113 g) cream cheese
1 cup shredded Swiss cheese
⅓ cup minced leeks
4 large eggs, beaten
½ cup chicken broth
⅛ teaspoon cayenne pepper
¾ teaspoon fine sea salt
1 tablespoon unsalted butter, melted
Chopped green onions, for garnish
Cooking spray

1. Press "Pre-Heat", set the temperature at 325°F (163°C). Spritz a pie pan basket with cooking spray.

2. Combine the flour, egg, Parmesan, and salt in a large bowl. Stir to mix until a satiny and firm dough forms.

3. Arrange the dough between two grease parchment papers, then roll the dough into a $1/16$-inch thick circle.

4. Make the crust: Transfer the dough into the prepared pie pan and press to coat the bottom, then arrange the pie pan in the preheated air fryer.

5. Bake for 12 minutes or until the edges of the crust are lightly browned.

6. Meanwhile, combine the ingredient for the filling, except for the green onions in a large bowl.

7. Pour the filling over the cooked crust and cover the edges of the crust with aluminum foil. Bake for 15 more minutes, then reduce the heat to 300°F (149°C) and bake for another 30 minutes or until a toothpick inserted in the center comes out clean.

8. Remove the pie pan from the air fryer and allow to cool for 10 minutes before serving.

472

MEDITERRANEAN QUICHE

Prep time: 10 minutes | **Cook time:** 30 minutes | **Serves** 4

4 eggs
¼ cup chopped Kalamata olives
½ cup chopped tomatoes
¼ cup chopped onion
½ cup milk
1 cup crumbled feta cheese
½ tablespoon chopped oregano
½ tablespoon chopped basil
Salt and ground black pepper, to taste
Cooking spray

1. Preheat air fryer to 340°F (171°C). Spritz a baking pan with cooking spray.
2. Whisk the eggs with remaining ingredients in a large bowl. Stir to mix well.
3. Pour the mixture into the prepared baking pan, then place the pan in the preheated air fryer.
4. Bake for 30 minutes or until the eggs are set and a toothpick inserted in the center comes out clean. Check the doneness of the quiche during the last 10 minutes of baking.

PAMELA KENDRICK

5. Serve immediately.

473

SHRIMP QUICHE

Prep time: 15 minutes | **Cook time:** 20 minutes | **Serves** 2

2 teaspoons vegetable oil

4 large eggs

½ cup half-and-half

4 ounces (113 g) raw shrimp, chopped

1 cup shredded Parmesan or Swiss cheese

¼ cup chopped scallions

1 teaspoon sweet smoked paprika

1 teaspoon herbes de Provence

1 teaspoon black pepper

½ to 1 teaspoon kosher salt

1. Press "Pre-Heat", set the temperature at 300°F (149°C). Generously grease a round baking pan with 4-inch sides with vegetable oil.

2. In a large bowl, beat together the eggs and half-and-half. Add the shrimp, ¾ cup of the cheese, the scallions, paprika, herbes de Provence, pepper, and salt. Stir with a fork to thoroughly combine. Pour the egg mixture into the prepared pan.

3. Put the pan in the air fryer basket and bake for 20 minutes.

After 17 minutes, sprinkle the remaining ¼ cup cheese on top and bake for the remaining 3 minutes, or until the cheese has melted, the eggs are set, and a toothpick inserted into the center comes out clean.

4. Serve the quiche warm.

474

SHRIMP SPINACH FRITTATA

Prep time: 6 minutes | **Cook time:** 14 minutes | **Serves** 4

4 whole eggs
1 teaspoon dried basil
½ cup shrimp, cooked and chopped
½ cup baby spinach
½ cup rice, cooked
½ cup Monterey Jack cheese, grated
Salt, to taste
Cooking spray

1. Press "Pre-Heat", set the temperature at 360°F (182°C). Spritz a baking pan with cooking spray.
2. Whisk the eggs with basil and salt in a large bowl until bubbly, then mix in the shrimp, spinach, rice, and cheese.
3. Pour the mixture into the baking pan, then place the pan in the preheated air fryer.
4. Bake for 14 minutes or until the eggs are set and the frittata is golden brown.
5. Slice to serve.

475

SMOKED TROUT AND CRÈME FRAICHE FRITTATA

Prep time: 8 minutes | **Cook time:** 17 minutes | **Serves** 4

2 tablespoons olive oil

1 onion, sliced

1 egg, beaten

½ tablespoon horseradish sauce

6 tablespoons crème fraiche

1 cup diced smoked trout

2 tablespoons chopped fresh dill

Cooking spray

1. Press "Pre-Heat", set the temperature at 350°F (177°C). Spritz a baking pan with cooking spray.

2. Heat the olive oil in a nonstick skillet over medium heat until shimmering.

3. Add the onion and sauté for 3 minutes or until translucent.

4. Combine the egg, horseradish sauce, and crème fraiche in a large bowl. Stir to mix well, then mix in the sautéed onion, smoked trout, and dill.

5. Pour the mixture in the prepared baking pan, then set the pan in the preheated air fryer.

6. Bake for 14 minutes or until the egg is set and the edges are lightly browned.

7. Serve immediately.

476

SPINACH CASSEROLE

Prep time: 10 minutes | **Cook time:** 20 minutes | **Serves** 4

1 (13.5-ounce / 383-g) can spinach, drained and squeezed
1 cup cottage cheese
2 large eggs, beaten
¼ cup crumbled feta cheese
2 tablespoons all-purpose flour
2 tablespoons butter, melted
1 clove garlic, minced, or more to taste
1 ½ teaspoons onion powder
⅛ teaspoon ground nutmeg
Cooking spray

1. Press "Pre-Heat", set the temperature at 375°F (191°C). Grease an 8-inch pie pan with cooking spray and set aside.
2. Combine spinach, cottage cheese, eggs, feta cheese, flour, butter, garlic, onion powder, and nutmeg in a bowl. Stir until all ingredients are well incorporated. Pour into the prepared pie pan.
3. Air fry until the center is set, 18 to 20 minutes.
4. Serve warm.

477

SUMPTUOUS BEEF AND BEAN CHILI CASSEROLE

Prep time: 15 minutes | **Cook time:** 31 minutes | **Serves** 4

1 tablespoon olive oil
½ cup finely chopped bell pepper
½ cup chopped celery
1 onion, chopped
2 garlic cloves, minced
1 pound (454 g) ground beef
1 can diced tomatoes
½ teaspoon parsley
½ tablespoon chili powder
1 teaspoon chopped cilantro
1½ cups vegetable broth
1 (8-ounce / 227-g) can cannellini beans
Salt and ground black pepper, to taste

1. Press "Pre-Heat", set the temperature at 350°F (177°C).
2. Heat the olive oil in a nonstick skillet over medium heat until shimmering.
3. Add the bell pepper, celery, onion, and garlic to the skillet and sauté for 5 minutes or until the onion is translucent.

4. Add the ground beef and sauté for an additional 6 minutes or until lightly browned.

5. Mix in the tomatoes, parsley, chili powder, cilantro and vegetable broth, then cook for 10 more minutes. Stir constantly.

6. Pour them in a baking pan, then mix in the beans and sprinkle with salt and ground black pepper.

7. Transfer the pan in the preheated air fryer. Bake for 10 minutes or until the vegetables are tender and the beef is well browned.

8. Remove the baking pan from the air fryer and serve immediately.

478

SUMPTUOUS VEGETABLE FRITTATA

Prep time: 15 minutes | **Cook time:** 20 minutes | **Serves** 2

4 eggs
$1/3$ cup milk
2 teaspoons olive oil
1 large zucchini, sliced
2 asparagus, sliced thinly
$1/3$ cup sliced mushrooms
1 cup baby spinach
1 small red onion, sliced
$1/3$ cup crumbled feta cheese
$1/3$ cup grated Cheddar cheese
$1/4$ cup chopped chives
Salt and ground black pepper, to taste

1. Press "Pre-Heat", set the temperature at 380°F (193°C). Line a baking pan basket with parchment paper.

2. Whisk together the eggs, milk, salt, and ground black pepper in a large bowl. Set aside.

3. Heat the olive oil in a nonstick skillet over medium heat until shimmering.

4. Add the zucchini, asparagus, mushrooms, spinach, and onion to the skillet and sauté for 5 minutes or until tender.

5. Pour the sautéed vegetables into the prepared baking pan, then spread the egg mixture over and scatter with cheeses.

6. Place the baking pan in the preheated air fryer. Bake for 15 minutes or until the eggs are set the edges are lightly browned.

7. Remove the frittata from the air fryer and sprinkle with chives before serving.

479

TACO BEEF AND CHILE CASSEROLE

Prep time: 10 minutes | **Cook time:** 15 minutes | **Serves** 4

1 pound (454 g) 85% lean ground beef
1 tablespoon taco seasoning
1 (7-ounce / 198-g) can diced mild green chiles
½ cup milk
2 large eggs
1 cup shredded Mexican cheese blend
2 tablespoons all-purpose flour
½ teaspoon kosher salt
Cooking spray

1. Press "Pre-Heat", set the temperature at 350°F (177°C). Spritz a baking pan with cooking spray.
2. Toss the ground beef with taco seasoning in a large bowl to mix well. Pour the seasoned ground beef in the prepared baking pan.
3. Combing the remaining ingredients in a medium bowl. Whisk to mix well, then pour the mixture over the ground beef.
4. Arrange the pan in the air fryer. Bake for 15 minutes or until a toothpick inserted in the center comes out clean.

5. Remove the casserole from the air fryer and allow to cool for 5 minutes, then slice to serve.

APPENDIX 1: MEASUREMENT CONVERSION CHART

VOLUME EQUIVALENTS (DRY)

US STANDARD	METRIC (APPROXIMATE)
1/8 teaspoon	0.5 mL
1/4 teaspoon	1 mL
1/2 teaspoon	2 mL
3/4 teaspoon	4 mL
1 teaspoon	5 mL
1 tablespoon	15 mL
1/4 cup	59 mL
1/2 cup	118 mL
3/4 cup	177 mL
1 cup	235 mL
2 cups	475 mL
3 cups	700 mL
4 cups	1 L

VOLUME EQUIVALENTS (LIQUID)

US STANDARD	US STANDARD (OUNCES)	METRIC (APPROXIMATE)
2 tablespoons	1 fl.oz.	30 mL
1/4 cup	2 fl.oz.	60 mL
1/2 cup	4 fl.oz.	120 mL
1 cup	8 fl.oz.	240 mL
1 1/2 cup	12 fl.oz.	355 mL
2 cups or 1 pint	16 fl.oz.	475 mL
4 cups or 1 quart	32 fl.oz.	1 L
1 gallon	128 fl.oz.	4 L

WEIGHT EQUIVALENTS

US STANDARD	METRIC (APPROXIMATE)
1 ounce	28 g
2 ounces	57 g
5 ounces	142 g
10 ounces	284 g
15 ounces	425 g
16 ounces (1 pound)	455 g
1.5 pounds	680 g
2 pounds	907 g

TEMPERATURES EQUIVALENTS

FAHRENHEIT (F)	CELSIUS (C) (APPROXIMATE)
225 °F	107 °C
250 °F	120 °C
275 °F	135 °C
300 °F	150 °C
325 °F	160 °C
350 °F	180 °C
375 °F	190 °C
400 °F	205 °C
425 °F	220 °C
450 °F	235 °C
475 °F	245 °C
500 °F	260 °C

APPENDIX 2: AIR FRYER COOKING TIMETABLE

Beef

Item	Temp (°F)	Time (mins)	Item	Temp (°F)	Time (mins)
Beef Eye Round Roast (4 lbs.)	400 °F	45 to 55	Meatballs (1-inch)	370 °F	7
Burger Patty (4 oz.)	370 °F	16 to 20	Meatballs (3-inch)	380 °F	10
Filet Mignon (8 oz.)	400 °F	18	Ribeye, bone-in (1-inch, 8 oz)	400 °F	10 to 15
Flank Steak (1.5 lbs.)	400 °F	12	Sirloin steak (1-inch, 12 oz)	400 °F	9 to 14
Flank Steak (2 lbs.)	400 °F	20 to 28			

Chicken

Item	Temp (°F)	Time (mins)	Item	Temp (°F)	Time (mins)
Breasts, bone-in (1 ¼ lb.)	370 °F	25	Legs, bone-in (1 ¾ lb.)	380 °F	30
Breasts, boneless (4 oz)	380 °F	12	Thighs, boneless (1 ½ lb.)	380 °F	18 to 20
Drumsticks (2 ½ lb.)	370 °F	20	Wings (2 lb.)	400 °F	12
Game Hen (halved 2 lb.)	390 °F	20	Whole Chicken	360 °F	75
Thighs, bone-in (2 lb.)	380 °F	22	Tenders	360 °F	8 to 10

Pork & Lamb

Item	Temp (°F)	Time (mins)	Item	Temp (°F)	Time (mins)
Bacon (regular)	400 °F	5 to 7	Pork Tenderloin	370 °F	15
Bacon (thick cut)	400 °F	6 to 10	Sausages	380 °F	15
Pork Loin (2 lb.)	360 °F	55	Lamb Loin Chops (1-inch thick)	400 °F	8 to 12
Pork Chops, bone in (1-inch, 6.5 oz)	400 °F	12	Rack of Lamb (1.5 – 2 lb.)	380 °F	22

Fish & Seafood

Item	Temp (°F)	Time (mins)	Item	Temp (°F)	Time (mins)
Calamari (8 oz)	400 °F	4	Tuna Steak	400 °F	7 to 10
Fish Fillet (1-inch, 8 oz)	400 °F	10	Scallops	400 °F	5 to 7
Salmon, fillet (6 oz)	380 °F	12	Shrimp	400 °F	5
Swordfish steak	400 °F	10			

Appendix 2: Air Fryer Cooking Timetable

Vegetables

INGREDIENT	AMOUNT	PREPARATION	OIL	TEMP	COOK TIME
Asparagus	2 bunches	Cut in half, trim stems	2 Tbsp	420°F	12-15 mins
Beets	1½ lbs	Peel, cut in ½-inch cubes	1 Tbsp	390°F	28-30 mins
Bell peppers (for roasting)	4 peppers	Cut in quarters, remove seeds	1 Tbsp	400°F	15-20 mins
Broccoli	1 large head	Cut in 1-2-inch florets	1 Tbsp	400°F	15-20 mins
Brussels sprouts	1 lb	Cut in half, remove stems	1 Tbsp	425°F	15-20 mins
Carrots	1 lb	Peel, cut in ½-inch rounds	1 Tbsp	425°F	10-15 mins
Cauliflower	1 head	Cut in 1-2-inch florets	2 Tbsp	400°F	20-22 mins
Corn on the cob	7 ears	Whole ears, remove husks	1 Tbsp	400°F	14-17 mins
Green beans	1 bag (12 oz)	Trim	1 Tbsp	420°F	18-20 mins
Kale (for chips)	4 oz	Tear into pieces, remove stems	None	325°F	5-8 mins
Mushrooms	16 oz	Rinse, slice thinly	1 Tbsp	390°F	25-30 mins
Potatoes, russet	1½ lbs	Cut in 1-inch wedges	1 Tbps	390°F	25-30 mins
Potatoes, russet	1 lb	Hand-cut fries, soak 30 mins in cold water, then pat dry	½-3 Tbps	400°F	25-28 mins
Potatoes, sweet	1 lb	Hand-cut fries, soak 30 mins in cold water, then pat dry	1 Tbps	400°F	25-28 mins
Zucchini	1 lb	Cut in eighths lengthwise, then cut in half	1 Tbps	400°F	15-20 mins

www.ingramcontent.com/pod-product-compliance
Lightning Source LLC
Chambersburg PA
CBHW071551080526
44588CB00010B/871